# FROME *unzipped*

*Sun Inn, Catherine Street*

# FROME
## *unzipped*

from Prehistory to Post-Punk

CRYSSE MORRISON

First published in the United Kingdom in 2018

by The Hobnob Press,
8 Lock Warehouse, Severn Road, Gloucester GL1 2GA
www.hobnobpress.co.uk

British Library Cataloguing in Publication Data
A catalogue record for this book is available from the British Library

ISBN 978-1-906978-55-6

Typeset in Chaparral Pro.
Typesetting and origination by John Chandler

Printed by Lightning Source

*Front cover picture:*
The Great Ascent of Cheap Street by SATCO (Sunday Afternoon Theatre Company), Frome Festival 2012 (Author)
*Back cover picture:*
Graffito on a post in Gentle Street (Author)

# DISCLAIMER

FROME IS AN EXTRAORDINARY TOWN, and extraordinarily aware of that fact too. Frome people have written books to examine, extol, analyse, summarise and celebrate it; there are societies dedicated to research it and online sites devoted to illustrate it – you'll find the ones I know about in the references – and there's a very good museum too, with a massive archive.

I join this phalanx with temerity, more as flâneur than historian. Instead of trying to précis existing works I talked to people about the town they grew up in or came to live in, and this book is dedicated to everyone I met or heard about, and those I didn't, with huge appreciation to everyone who has shared with me their memories, opinions, books and cuttings: Aaron Bradley, Alan Campbell, Amy McFadyen, Andrew Shackleton, Andrew Ziminski, Andy Wrintmore & Charlie Jones-West, Annabelle Macfadyen, Ant Head & Pete Prochazka, Boann Lambert, Badger, Bob Ashford, Brian Marshall, Chris Bailey, Chris Bowden, Chris Stringer, Ciara Nolan, Claudia Pepler, Cliff Howard, Colin Alsbury, David Lassman, Dave Moss, Des Harris, Di Cole, Ed Green, Fay Goodridge, Gavin Eddy, Gill Harry, Hannah Morden, Helen Langford, Helen Rowlinson, Hilary Daniels, Howard Vause, Jake XJX Hight, James Bartholomew, Jean Lowe, Jill Miller, Jim Parsons, John Baxter, John Birkett-Smith, John Hedges, John Payne, John Plaxton, Jon Evans, Jude Kelly, Julian Hight, Karin Campagna, Katy Duke, Lark Porter, Laura, Laurie Parnell, Luke Manning, Mahesh Sharma Kommu, Marian Bruce, Mark Bruce, Martin Dimery, Mick & Val Ridgard, Mike Witt, Neil Howlett, Nick Hersey, Nick Ray, Nick Wilton, Nigel Shoosmith, Nikki Lloyd, Patrick Otoid, Paul Boswell, Peter Clark, Peter Clink, Peter Macfadyen, Phil Moakes, Ralph Michard, Richard Churchyard, Rob Gill, Robin Cowley, Robin Lambert, Rog & Becky Lee, Sally-Anne Fraser, Sheila Gore, Sheila Hedges, Simon Carpenter, Simon Lewis, Sioux How, Steph & Elliott, Steve Poole, Steve Small, Sue Crisfield, Sue Watts, Terry Pinto, Tony Bennett, Tony May, Vaughn Jublees, Wendy Miller Williams, Will Angeloro, Also big thanks to John Chandler for his suggestion and encouragement, and to David Goodman for his support throughout my obsessive immersion in the life and times of my adoptive home, Frome.

**Crysse Morrison** has written short fiction, articles, education books (pub. Macdonald Educational), two novels (pub. Hodder & Stoughton), plays (produced Theatre West and Stepping Out Theatre Company) and poetry (pub. Burning Eye). She currently writes mainly about events in and around Frome in her arts blog http://crysse.blogspot.co.uk, and reviews for *Plays International*. You can see upcoming events on her facebook page and archive on her website: www.crysse.com

# INTRODUCTION

*rough and tough, religious, rebellious, or apathetic: will the real Frome please stand up*

WHEN I ARRIVED in 1987 I was informed at a Social Services meeting in Taunton that Frome was not in Somerset. I told one of the other delegates and she laughed. 'Well you're not Somerset really, are you? The Peoples Republic of Frome, that's what you lot think you are.'

'Frome, near Bath,' I'd say, wherever in the world I was asked where we lived. Because nobody had heard of it back then. But the main road from Bath makes no mention of Frome on signs and you need to follow the route to Warminster, in Wiltshire, until you reach the village of Woolverton. Only then does the A36 signage acknowledge the town is a mere five miles further on. The next direction is to Frome Market and if you follow that you'll miss the town entirely and end up in Standerwick.

Martin Dimery, Frome's Green Party County Councillor, agrees that Frome's geography, as well as its strident individualism, does present a problem to the rest of the county.

'It's very easy to get forgotten' he admits, 'when you're on the north-eastern corner of an enormously big geographical county in which the hub is a town an hour and a half's drive away. You have to beat at the door, every time'.

Frome's very name arouses uncertainty, and there's a huge huff over whether we who live here are Fromers or Fromites or Froomies so I'll avoid antagonising anyone by not calling us anything. It's the river that gives the town its name, of course, from an ancient Celtic word meaning 'fair and brisk', but that's confusing too: there are four river Fromes in the south-west. Ours rises in Witham Friary and joins the Avon at Freshford, in a brisk flow that nurtured the wool trade with clean power as well as regularly flooding the town streets.

With wool came wealth, with decline came trouble. By the end of the 20th Century, Frome was struggling and unknown, yet like some transmogrifying phoenix it has soared to cult status, frequented by stars and featured in every newspaper's Top-10 Places in the UK. The 'on-trend' listings cite quaint cobbled streets, 'retro' shopping opportunities and 'in' places for celeb-spotting, with the more serious articles focusing on Frome's pioneering politics, sustainability developments and cultural scene. 'The artsy-foodie-music vibe is worthy of Hackney' trilled one article in 2016, attributing the proximity of Babington House (a hotel-cum-club six miles away) for enticing 'the cool crowd' while in the same article reporting T-shirts printed 'Independent State of Frome.' FYI, *Sunday Times*, you can now buy a cap with the legend 'Make Frome Shit Again', which seems an appropriate aim for Frome's dissident population. From Mechanisation to Gentrification, this is the town that likes to say No.

So with so much now published about Frome, why this book? Partly it's the proselytising passion of anyone discovering late in life what it feels like to find a sense of 'home', and partly to collect and share memories perhaps not previously chronicled together. A friend said to me recently that someone told him Frome had 64 pubs serving in living memory and now there were only fourteen. At the time we were passing the now-abandoned *Ring o' Bells*, where twenty years before the landlady told me her cellar was haunted by a poltergeist who turned off the fridges each night, and I wondered how many other stories are slowly fading as gentrification spreads like a sparkling-yet-scouring cleaning agent over the ancient patina of the town.[1] And it's not just old pubs – every inch of Frome has secret imprints. My hope is that this exploration will encourage others to recall and collect their own tales before they fade from our collective memory.

So this is not a linear narration, it's more of a zigzag through time and times to create an overlapping image – Frome as Francis Bacon might paint it, you could say. If there's a dominant colour in that portrait, it would be a deep defiant red, the madder-root dye used from ancient days: the rebel's choice – the colour of dissent.

---

1   There's always online search of course, but you have to know what to google. In this particular case it's *Public Houses, Inns & Taverns of Frome,* where the *Ring o' Bells* is still shown as active – though there's no mention of the naughty ghost on the Paranormal Database of the southwest. Nor is it in the excellent study of *Historic Inns of Frome* which is crammed with lurid tales in comparison with which Eastenders' Vic seems quite demure.

This dissenting trait isn't the passive negativity of small-town resentment to development, it's almost an energy that flows through the place itself. Frome seems to both breed and attract people who refuse to see themselves as a peg in a hole, whether round or square. With a history of resistant nonconformity, Frome is now at the forefront of political innovation as the first town in the UK to vote in a council entirely composed of councillors unaffiliated to any national party; as I write this, a Multicultural Day here is celebrating the fact that our community is home to people of forty different nationalities, while an exhibition of *Frome in Palestine* demonstrates and supports commitment beyond our borders too. There are active groups working to stop wars, encourage subsistence, promote fair trade, provide food, find housing, save wildlife, improve environment, promote creativity... if it's a positive step for a better life, Frome's place is in the struggle. In a country that sings God Save The Monarch, the hymn-sheet for Frome seems to read instead, We Save the Others.

Interestingly, the townsfolk's apparent indifference to national hierarchical changes has been characterised by historians as 'apathetic' but where rulings and decrees touch on ordinary life, Frome shows its true colour. Never more clearly is that evidenced than in 1832 when for the first time Frome was granted its own MP by the Great Reform Act. The whole town celebrated, even though most of the working men and all the women were still barred from voting. The actual elections aroused so much frustration in the disenfranchised townspeople that after three days of rioting the Dragoons were sent in. These were not apathetic people. The fact that records show Mr Sheppard, the contentiously elected MP, kept his seat again by only four votes at a cost of £10,000 in bribes in 1837 gives some idea of the frustrations faced by the working people considered by the wealthy as merely 'the mob'.[2] Riots continued integral to the election process until 1856 when a Working Men's

---

2   As an interesting as-we-go-to-press footnote, a petition with 6,000 Frome signatories was submitted last week to Mendip District Council pleading for them not to undermine Frome's vital Sunday trading, and its big weekend events at the Cheese & Grain, by hefty parking charges. Both these aspects are vital to the town's economy as well as its thriving image. The document was dismissed by the Chair of the Council as an attempt at 'mob rule.' Plus ça change...

Association was formed in Frome to press for an extension of franchise irrespective of wealth or property status. This was eight years before the International Working Men's Association started in London.

So we have to look beyond the doings of the landed gentry and the policies of kings to find the story of Frome.[3] There's no castle or palace here, no garrison or fort. The Romans never built a settlement, probably because it was too awkward and impractical for their logical routes. Yet from the ice-age, people have crossed this river and walked these hills. Frome's history is not about unseen kings and absentee bishops, it is about ordinary people, and we miss the point of the story if we focus only on men who wore crowns or mitres. The history of Frome is more alluvial, and more interesting.

There is, of course, no denying that wherever you go in Frome, you are never far from a church. After the 1662 'Great Ejection'[4] religion become a useful philosophical litmus: 18th-century Tories were Anglican and Liberals were Methodist. The significance of religion in nurturing dissent as Frome's defining characteristic probably can't be overestimated – as evidenced in the long satirical poem by Samuel Bowden[5]

---

3   In 934 a royal charter granting a land holding to the priests of Winchester was signed in Frome, witnessed by Athelstan, King of Wessex, the archbishops of Canterbury and York and assorted bishops and ministers, near the current church of St John. This might have been a palace of some sort or the original church Aldhelm built in 685, also in that area. However significant it may have been to these absentee owners, a treaty that firmed up allegiances within church and monarchy is unlikely to have meant much to the townspeople of Frome. The fact that Henry I at some point in the early 12th Century gave the entire hundred of Frome to 'a certain Roger de Curtellis, to hold freely of himself and his heirs' – and nobody knew till an inspection of 1445 – gives some indication of how little royal decisions impacted life.

4   A mass expulsion of clergy who refused to conform to the Book of Common Prayer imposed by the Act of Uniformity. Several thousand dissenting clerics were expelled, and the Church of England never fully recovered. There will be more about this in section 4.

5   He was a Frome resident and friend of Elizabeth Singer Rowe, also himself a poet and a member of Rook Lane congregational church. It's not clear whether he was applauding such fervour or intended this to be a parody of working class uppityness.

Say, brother fanatics, what led you to Frome
Where weavers expound as they sit at the loom;
Where mechanics inspired, the Gospel explain
And weave at a text as well as a chain?
Here tinkers and tailors deep doctrines can handle
By the light of the Spirit – or the light of the candle.

In many accounts, Frome 'began' with the first church: its significant buildings are churches, and its most quoted townsfolk are usually churchmen, or at least defined by their sect. Nonconformism spread swiftly throughout England, and Frome was a self-confident artisan town with largely-literate population who would have been well able to read tracts and follow debates, so it's not surprising that 'dissent' in this religious definition became a defining characteristic. Another view might be that dissent itself was the defining characteristic, and religion became a very useful way of expressing it.

While 'the Church' played a big role in community support, attendance was never an essential part of life for the working people. Church services were more a thing for the wealthy:

Many places of worship had a clearly defined hierarchy, with rented seats at the front and free seats in galleries or behind pillars. Going to church could thus be a humiliating rather than uplifting experience for the poor... For many working-class women, non-involvement in the church was not so much a deliberate choice as an inevitable part of a way of life that was overwhelmingly concentrated on home and kitchen.' [6]

Another principle strand in this account, if an unzipping is allowed strands, is that Frome was not only a woollen town that lost its trade, it was also an agricultural town that lost its cattle market. The farmers and their families who came from miles around each week brought and exchanged not only animals and produce, but news and gossip. Such trade was energising as well as useful: it kept the pubs and ale-houses

6    summarised by historian-blogger Richard Brown here: http://richardjohnbr. blogspot.co.uk/2011/11/why-was-state-of-working-class-religion.html

thriving and supported every kind of local craftsfolk and shop owners. The cattle market itself has survived and thrived in nearby Standerwick, but without it – and with the last mills closed – Frome town began the 21st century depleted of both the key roles of its identity: neither an important player in the cloth trade nor a hub for the farming community. No wonder something close to identity-crisis happened. Older people I spoke to still mourn the move to Standerwick like a bereavement, even in the same breath as acknowledging that it had to go.

Frome had to re-invent itself and, grabbing what it had around – a backdrop of old streets and a cast of enterprising people – has put on a show which turned the gaze of the world from indifference to adulatory hyperbole. Using a combination of cafe-and-bar culture plus imaginative creativity, you could almost say Frome invented a new business: the Renaissance Industry. Many of those involved are still active, and this book will name some of them, but it's a huge, understandably resented, misunderstanding to think that Frome had no creative culture until the beginning of this century. And this goes way back. The spread of the printing industry led to a confetti-storm of pamphlets, the popularity of which shows that most working people were literate beyond the level of many in these days of deliberate dumbing down vocabularies by the media – in fact, more literate than earlier historians assumed.[7] You only have to look at the complex recipe books of the dye-houses at Wallbridge and Welshmill[8] to see the level of complexity involved in calculating and transcribing these complex equations – bearing in mind any error by writer or reader would have resulted in considerable financial loss if the buyer refused the cloth.

---

7   Social historian Adam Fox has shown that the distinction between the 'literate' and 'illiterate' accepted by historians is largely mistaken since in early modern England, 'illiteracy' referred to the inability to read Latin. Vernacular literature had been established since 1362 and most people would understand vernacular language in print, whether or not they ever needed to write a letter. This misunderstanding has led to a wide assumption of cultural ignorance among the lower orders – especially women.

8   WOAD TO THIS has beautiful examples of the pages of these books – and there must have been many more writings now lost to us. Paper is one of the most destructible commodities on the planet: the mill records were solidly bound but ordinary correspondence and diaries would not be: just because journals and letters have not survived doesn't mean they weren't written.

Frome was always a town of artisans, adept at making and trading, ready to argue the toss with anyone, and the industries that arrived to fill the gaps left by the cloth trade brought new creative vibrance to the community. Their social clubs put on variety shows, plays and concerts, created carnival floats and organised sporting events and trips for their workers, in some cases even after the factories' closure. History is written by those with leisure to write it, though, which is why much of Frome's story has been shaped around men with wealth like Thomas Bunn, whose ambition to outdo the sweeping crescents of Bath is evidenced in the two Grecian columns which stand, like Ozymandias' trunkless legs of stone, on Christchurch street while those who worked for them were judged 'rough, tough and much given to lawlessness and riot.'[9] And the history now seems all about Frome's emergence from a long dull past of inertia into a glorious technicolour of recent outsider-initiated activity. There's a danger in that, too.

Frome is a paradox, a town of roller-coaster fortunes and striking contrasts. One of the last areas of England to accept the notion of official policing, resisting innovations in the textile industry that would have stopped its wealth from dribbling away, allowing development to scythe architectural treasure in the 1960s – yet it has been home for innovators and campaigners and is now quoted around Europe as a symbol of political initiative. Søren Kierkegaard said 'Life can only be understood backwards but it must be lived forwards': understanding however is mostly a matter of opinion and even the notion of 'forwards' suggests a linear journey. Life is chaotic, a kaleidoscope of episodic fragments confined in space and time but forever rearranging into a different perception. This book is not chronological, its structure is fragmentary and spiral, its opinions inconsistent and its omissions incomprehensible. In these respects I hope you will feel it's just like life.

> 'We are surrounded by the greatest of free shows. Places. Most of them made by man, remade by man... Everything is fantastical, if you stare at it for long enough, everything is interesting. There is no such thing as a boring place.'
> – Jonathan Meades, *Museums without walls*.

---

9   *The Book of Frome* by Michael McGarvie. He credits the strong, stale, beer.

*Cheap Street leat*

# 1   PEOPLE

*– who comes here? activists – entrepreneurial women –
constructive dissent – the lens of history and the illusion of
change – the IfF story and precedents –
– the tale of three festivals – the market, a story of revivals –
– things people do – tomorrow's world –*

'*Places are made special by the people who live in them*'
— Jacqueline Peverley, chairperson,
The Mount Community Association

'*It's a strange and special mix – I've never lived anywhere like it*'
— Dave Clark, musician

'*As an American coming here to live, I've found there's only one degree of
separation. Everyone you speak to knows someone you know.*'
— James Bartholomew, photographer

THIS SECTION GIVES VOICE to some of the people who have
given Frome its present identity. At a time when Britain has chosen
to redefine itself in isolationist and xenophobic terms, it feels good
to be part of a community with different priorities altogether. There's
been much written about notables of previous eras – idealists and
visionaries, industrialists and philanthropists – but the story currently
is Frome's Renaissance, a cultural phenomenon as unprecedented as it
is extraordinary,[1] the story of a dismal town that time forgot suddenly
blooming like a desert rose.

---

1   Even as I was writing, the usually reliable George Monbiot, commending yet
    another excellent Frome initiative, found it necessary to enhance his praise
    with the fact that thirty years ago the town was a 'buttoned-down, dreary
    place.'

It didn't, of course. Frome has always had fans and detractors – it still does. But the resilience, independence, initiative, and other qualities, are engrained in the fabric of the town. Frome has no major focus of cultural identity – no stadium, no cathedral, no university – no imposed symbolic status of any sort, only those places where its community meets to trade, work, walk, revere, relax and party. The town I'm writing about now has been created by the vision of a great many amazing people.

Back at the start of the era when Envy-TV[2] began there was a series called *Through the Keyhole*. Each show opened with a location shot and a voice oozing 'Who lives in a house like this?' It was a banal concept but a good catchphrase: the 'tells' of conversation and body-language dwindle to insignificance compared to the evidence of the place where we live. A town is not just its terrain and structures, though it is that too: it's the rich, colourful, complex ant-hill of everyone who has ever lived in it. So, who'd live in a place like Frome?

Most accounts begin in 685 when the abbot of Malmesbury, whose imagined features now adorn the railings in the town centre, felt this part of Selwood forest was getting a bit wild and could do with a settlement. The theme of uncontrolled behaviour recurs often among chroniclers who report rowdiness in the town and poaching in the big estates beyond it.[3] The journals of Isaac Gregory, an early Constable of Frome, evoke a townscape of men and women mostly sozzled and 'Idle Fellows about Gambling' and from the histories of the hundred-plus inns of the town it appears few landlords avoided court appearances for allowing drunkenness, debauchery, and lewd carousing. Right up to the start of the 21st Century, Frome had a reputation for rough behaviour and fights – apart of course from the dignitaries – the churchmen and

---

2   A term for the deliberate and cynical trivialising of media to dumb-down culture and prioritise consumerist values.

3   'Drunkenness, with its concomitant vices, raged fearfully. The habits of the poorer classes especially were profligate and disgusting in the extreme' – Wesleyan Steven Tuck in 1837, writing about an earlier, pre-Wesleyan, era so there may be some partisan exaggeration here. Frome's spicy reputation survived into the postcard era, with placid town views adorned by the legend 'Frome, a town dating from very early times, was surrounded by Selwood Forest which afforded shelter to a body of bandits who were the terror of the neighbourhood.'

leaders of industry, the worthy and the wealthy.[4] But if we take away the lens of class hierarchies and their perspectives of moral values, there's an alternative history of Frome: not as a town polarised between worthies and layabouts, but peopled by workers and traders who were both politically literate. This section aims to do a kind of Grayson Perry tapestry thing, showing the context and a few of the many individuals who are part of that fabric.

And since history has traditionally been dominated by the exploits of men, I'll start with some of Frome's influential women. Alice Seeley, Emma Shepherd and Jill Miller all were pioneers and agents for social change, and in different ways epitomise the stubborn spirit of Frome: it was, after all, noted by Chartist pioneer Henry Vincent that 'The ladies of Frome are excellent Radicals.'[5]

Alice Seeley was born in Frome in 1870 and married the missionary John Hobbis Harris when she was twenty-eight, travelling with him to Africa to convert the Congolese. At that time the Christian mission was a key part of Victorian Imperialism[6], with 'civilising' an important step towards future trading rather than stemming from desire to save souls for Jesus. King Leopold II of Belgium, after failing to persuade his government to support his colonising policy, had in 1885 mustered enough international support to allow him to acquire his own personal colony in Africa. He called it, euphemistically, Congo Free State.

---

4   It was not until the 1970s that this kind of automatic class distinction was significantly questioned, after E P Thompson in his 1966 essay *History from Below* urged a different perspective: 'I am seeking to rescue the poor stockinger, the Luddite cropper, the "obsolete" hand-loom weaver, the "Utopian" artisan .. from the enormous condescension of posterity. Their crafts and traditions may have been dying. Their hostility to the new industrialism may have been backward-looking. Their insurrectionary conspiracies may have been foolhardy. But they lived through these times of acute social disturbance, and we did not. Their aspirations were valid in terms of their own experience; and, if they were casualties of history, they remain, condemned in their own lives, as casualties.'
5   *Life and Rambles* – Henry Vincent 1838-39
6   The Christian Mission and Victorian Imperialism: schools-history.com https://kenbaker.wordpress.com/2009/01/06/christian-mission-and-victorian-imperialism/

Here, Alice arrived with her husband in the 1890s to teach English to the natives. They were both totally shocked at the abuse and cruelty they saw all around them in plantations which Leopold regarded not as a land with its own indigenous people but as his own private rubber plantation, existing to supplement his wealth now that the developing car industry was making this trade immensely lucrative. Communities were allocated quotas for sap collection, and any default by the men was punished by whippings, severing of hands and arms, slaughter of their wives and children. Thousands suffered slavery, mutilations, rape, and murder.

Alice began to photograph the atrocities she saw. If you look at the Liverpool Museum Archives online[7] you can see an example of her photographs, but as the site warns, they are distressing. One of the most famous is described here:

> In 1904 two men arrived at their mission from a village attacked by 'sentries' of the Anglo-Belgian India Rubber Company (ABIR) after failing to provide the required rubber quota. One of the men, Nsala, was holding a small bundle of leaves which when opened revealed the severed hand and foot of a child. Sentries had killed and mutilated Nsala's wife and daughter. Appalled, Alice persuaded Nsala to pose with his child's remains on the veranda of her home for a picture that would be one of the most shocking in the Seeley Harris' collection.

It's hard, in these days of graphic imagery in the palms of our hands at touch, to imagine the impact of Alice Seeley's photographs. American writer Mark Twain in 1905 could. His satiric pamphlet *King Leopold's Soliloquy*[8] envisaged the Belgian monarch fuming:

> The kodak has been a sore calamity indeed ...in the early days we had no trouble in getting the press to 'expose' these tales as inventions of busybody missionaries and we got Christian nations everywhere to turn an irritated and unbelieving ear. Then all of a sudden – crash! The incorruptible kodak, and all harmony went to hell! That trivial

---

7   http://www.liverpoolmuseums.org.uk/ism/exhibitions/brutal-exposure/alice-seeley-harris.aspx

8   available to download: http://diglib1.amnh.org/articles/kls/twain.pdf

little kodak[9] that a child can carry in its pocket, gets up, uttering
never a word – the only witness I couldn't bribe.

Alice's photographs raised public awareness of the hypocrisy
of King Leopold II's promised colonial benevolence, and caused a
worldwide outcry. With her husband she toured Europe and the US
with the *Harris Lantern Slide Show*, effectively the first photo-journalist
campaign for Human Rights. Alerted by John's initial reports, the UK
had commissioned the Casement report and, with this graphic evidence,
in 1908 Leopold was compelled by his own parliament to cede rights
to the Congo. The International Slavery Museum has an image of the
campaigner with a group of naked Congolese children posing proudly
around her, many with arms folded, perhaps not all having hands. Lady
Alice stands demurely in the centre in a long white frock and broad-
brimmed sunhat, looking every inch the Merchant Ivory heroine. And
heroine she was – there's an interview on the Unsung Hero Project
website, made by BBC Radio 4 in 1970 when she was 100 years old.
Alice's husband, Sir John Hobbis Harris, was knighted in 1933 for the
couples' work for the Anti-Slavery and Aborigines Protection Society,
and is buried in Frome Dissenters Cemetery with the words 'CHAMPION
OF THE OPPRESSED' engraved on his tomb. So much did his reputation
overshadow his wife's that it wasn't until 2017 that, after an appeal from
her Canadian biographer,[10] a plaque was installed on Merchant's Barton
to Alice Seeley Harris, known around the world as 'the Mother of Human
Rights'.

HALF A CENTURY before Alice publicised her humanitarian
concerns, another Frome woman had been working to improve the
quality of life for social victims closer to home: Emma Sheppard, wife of
George, from the manufacturing family dominating the cloth industry

---

9   In fact, although the Box Brownie has entered folklore as Alice's choice,
    according to the 'Unsung Hero Project' in Kansas where her work and
    achievements are celebrated, Alice took pictures of the Congolese with her
    Goerz-Anschutz Folding Camera (manufactured 1896 to 1926), given to her
    by Harry Guinness, who worked with the Congo Balolo Mission.
10  Judy Pollard Smith, *Don't Call Me Lady: The Journey of Lady Alice Seeley Harris*
    (Abbott Press 2014)

at that time. Wives of affluent figures were expected to visit the parish
workhouse to comfort or admonish the inmates, and Frome's Union
Workhouse was built in Weymouth Road in 1837 to accommodate 350
impoverished townsfolk.[11] What was slightly different about Emma
was that she not only decided that the 'fallen' women of the workhouse
should be helped rather than censured, she felt strongly enough to write
a 'little pamphlet' to urge other women to share her view.

 *Sunshine in the Workhouse, the Experiences of a Workhouse Visitor*
was published in 1857 and reprinted two years later: it's clearly the
expression of an evangelising spirit as well as a compassionate educated
woman, and although to modern minds it may seem merely typical of her
patronising era, in fact Emma's reforming concept carries the seeds of
views later expressed by early feminist writers like Mary Wollstonecraft.
At that time the prevailing concept of weak womanhood can be seen
as summarised by William Hogarth's work *The Harlot's Progress* which,
although engraved a hundred years earlier, expresses a paternalistic
morality still thriving. The series shows a woman seduced and thus
unable to prevent herself from falling passively into self-destructive
vice.[12] This story reflected the sentimental and sanctimonious mood of
the age, and the theme was immensely popular.[13]

 Meanwhile Emma was steadfastly visiting these 'fallen' women
in the workhouse, improving their lives in practical ways (as well as

---

11 This was built to the design of Sampson Kempthorne who seems to have
   specialised in workhouses and used a hexagonal plan with entrance in the
   main building, administration block at the side, and accommodation in three
   blocks at the rear, with exercise yards, for 'various classes of inmates. It later
   became Selwood Hospital till 1988 and is was then converted to modern flats
   as Ecos Court. The school block became Whitewell Childrens' Home around
   1913.
12 Hogarth also envisaged *The Rake's Progress* but that narrative was about the
   wanton self-indulgence of a reprobate, whereas the female version depicted
   a woman abused initially and consequently following an inevitable and
   hopeless pattern without stamina or mentality to recover, constitutionally
   programmed to self-destruct.
13 Between 1850 and 1860 there were no fewer than four morbid examples
   of the genre – Frederick Watts ('Found Drowned') Dante Gabriel Rossetti
   ('Found') Augustus Egg ('Misfortune, Prayer, and Despair') and Abraham
   Soloman ('Drowned! drowned!'). The phenomenon is explored in *Chastity
   and Transgression in Women's Writing 1792-1897* by R. Eberle

indulging in short bursts of bible-reading, to which they submitted as willingly as anyone would after receiving good food and clean clothes) and publishing her recommendation for

> a Reformatory Ward attached to a Workhouse where these poor creatures may be taught to earn their bread honestly, where a more liberal diet would re-establish their broken health and after a few months' probation, they might leave the Workhouse fit for service or to gain their own livelihood respectably.

Her proposition is couched primly, true, but no other terminology would have made Emma's practical point acceptable. She was not, despite her sometimes florid passages, unrealistic in her expectations, writing 'I think there is a great error in the way many penitents of this class are treated. They cannot be made religious all at once... . we expect and demand too much, and too soon.' But she believed these 'poor creatures' were perfectly capable of staying away from the streets if any other option to earn their living was available to them, and she set out to prove it.

Emma Sheppard offered herself and the workhouse of Frome as a case-study approach. She did all the things a lady of her status could do – bringing gifts, finding work for the able through her husband's contacts – and also significantly more. In *Sunshine in the Workhouse,* she describes how she insisted on visiting the 'Foul Ward' – 'for women of bad character' – bringing them kindness and gifts and supporting them

> for many weeks after they leave, and never found reason to fear they had gone back to their 'wallowing in the mire' till the very last penny was spent. Oh how I used to long for some kind of Reformatory Asylum attached to the Union Workhouse as part of its machinery, where they would not only be fed and warmed but where, when recovered, they could be taught a trade, and live decently.

And as no-one in authority apparently had any confidence in this reversal of the 'Harlot's Progress' model, she set up a scheme like that herself.

In 1859 Emma rented a house for £6, spent £20 on equipping

it, and found a woman to run it. She invited all the prostitutes in Frome for tea, and told them they could stay there free for as long as they gave up prostitution. Only four initially took up the offer but within three years there were 33 women living there, earning their living in the fabric trade the Sheppards knew so well. Emma sourced calico for them to make skirts, and demand often outstripped supply. Just as she had pleaded in her writings, she had created a community where women could show they were not beyond redemption once 'fallen', and in that sense she was in the vanguard of feminist reformers who rewrote the received rule of female mental weakness. She died in 1871, aged only 57, and is buried in Holy Trinity Church, near the blackberries. The cross on her grave has broken off, which seems a sad tribute to so devout a woman, but in 2013 the Emma Sheppard Centre for people with mild to moderate dementia was opened at Rowden House.

THE SHEPPARD NAME is still written, literally, all over Frome and we're now taking a diversion down Sheppards Barton[14] for the story of another significant woman, as from 1975 this was home to a key contributor to the Women's Movement: a feminist whose 1984 novel remained for several decades on the reading list for women's studies courses on both sides of the Atlantic and has been translated, dramatised, analysed and lionised around the world.

Jill Miller, life-long socialist and fierce campaigner for a range of causes, became later known for founding a Frome charity, but I first knew Jill as the writer of *Happy as a Dead Cat* – a frank and funny exposé of the real life of working class women which shocked, delighted, and – importantly – informed an entire generation. Jill was a feminist at a time when the word was most often used negatively by many who saw no need for a substantive shift in social values. She wrote *Dead Cat* as a critique of the male-dominated society she experienced as a working woman, and sent to her chosen publisher with a note beginning 'Dear Womens' Press, Rumour has it you support working-class writers. Here's your chance to put your money where your mouth is . . .' They did, and after its publication in 1983 *Happy as a Dead Cat* remained in print for

---

14 A barton was a kind of small-holding: origin *bere-tun,* an enclosure where barley was grown, eventually becoming just a name for an enclosure, or a short street.

two decades and was chosen by British librarians as one of a hundred books to take into the new millennium.

Jill recalls her life in Sheppards Barton as a socialist collectivist's dream: communal cooking and shared parenting characterised the life 'on the hill'. 'Us mums would be out on the streets on summer evenings,' she told me, 'It was a wonderful sociable time, exhilarating. The children had the freedom to wander to any house to be fed and watered – all of us had an open door policy. In the evening we'd hose the street down, and get our chairs out, and make plans.

> We began with communal cooking, each taking a turn in providing the evening meal for four days a week. It went down like a bag of wet cement with the men, but we were unyielding. We started to think about energy consumption and how to share appliances. I went to women's groups, women's workshops, rallies and Greenham Common, found my vagina, and got my subscription to Spare Rib. I bloody stormed the battlements at the side of my sisters. It was on the back of my anger and with the support of women friends, I wrote a book in three days, furiously scribbling on odd scraps of paper wherever I happened to be.

Jill continued to follow her fiercely pioneering flame. Diagnosed with cancer in 1993 when there was little aid and big apprehension, she turned her experience into a network of support for others. *Positive Action on Cancer* started as a telephone helpline in Jill's kitchen. 'I didn't want others to go through what I went through,' she says, 'there seemed to be nothing at that time to help them through the trauma of being told they had the illness. So I wrote a leaflet, and put it round the doctors, with my phone number on it..'  She responded to every call, and would visit wherever she could – a kind of one-woman Samaritan agency but with outreach. Once the national telephone helpline was established Jill shifted PAC's emphasis and took on a trained counsellor, Tricia Greenwood, initially a volunteer, to develop her charity into an effective counselling service. 'One of the things I'm most proud of was that it grew organically. John (her husband) and I paid for everything – I didn't know about funding at the start and I was going to do it anyway, come hell or high water. If we have no compassion, what are we doing in this world?'

Jill created a touring theatre and wrote a play based on her experiences in the treatment of her cancer: *Little Gift* aimed to change medical attitudes by showing that current treatment was damaging women's sense of self-worth not just as females but as humans. She resisted the self-concealment of 'reconstruction' and embraced her amazon body-image as positively as she has all her life experiences.[15] Attitudes have changed, and Jill is one of the people at the forefront of that shift. She chose the name of her charity to 'name the beast' and affirm positivity, though sadly this was lost in a rebranding after she stepped down from her active role, but the service she founded is still in Frome.

FINALLY IN THIS QUARTET of women pioneers, a short spotlight on Eunice Overend, whose geological study of Frome[16] is still the only significant text on this subject. Eunice seems to have known just about everything about anything that lay under or moved on land, but her real passion was badgers. She had a community of them in her home, naming each (she let them sleep in her bed and thumped them when they bit her) and she fearlessly confronted the Ministry of Agriculture Fisheries and Food over the Government's policy of badger control. Eunice was influential in ending the gassing of badgers but when MAFF changed their policy to trapping she continued her protests, going out at night to free the creatures and lift the traps. 'They call us all animal rights activists these days,' she told an *Independent* interviewer in 1993, 'but it's up to your own conscience what you do.' When she died in 2016, just three years short of her centenary, obituaries acknowledged the impact of her 40-year campaign. Eccentric but not dotty, was the conclusion of documentary film-maker Maurice Tibbles in the Anglia TV series Survival: 'She's an incredible woman, she tells the Ministry of Defence they should be conserving badger setts when they want tank tracks on Salisbury Plain. The army calls her the Badger Mother.'

---

15  Jill's view of 'illness, medicine, and what matters in the end' chimes with that of Atul Gawande whose seminal book *Being Mortal* makes a plea for human connection over medical intervention, and who wrote: *'The battle of being mortal is to maintain the integrity of one's life – to avoid becoming so diminished or dissipated or subjected that who you are becomes disconnected from who you were.'*

16  *The Geology of the Frome Area – and some of the matters arising from it.*

Constructive dissent, you could say. Another independent-minded woman who found her way to Frome. The story of Catherine Hill in a later section features among others Lyn Waller and Fay Goodridge, who moved in at a crucial time for its recovery, with credit too to Katy Duke, who as Regeneration Officer safeguarded retail on the hill by preventing outlets from changing status to housing or offices, and remains a strong voice of information and opinion.[17] And while I've no intention of indulging in feminist revisionism, there are very many impressive women around now, and women have probably always played a significant role in Frome's life and culture: their readiness to accept new ideologies, both political and theological, is a repeated theme in recorded histories, as we can know from Chartist Henry Vincent[18] and Wesleyan Stephen Tuck[19] who both especially commended the responsiveness of women. Women of course historically had no voice in the running of the town. The Church and (until 1918) Parliament barred women, and though the wool trade provided plenty of employment, this was mostly in their own homes as spinners. With the coming of light industries, women had the strength of a workforce identity behind them but before that time few had any status except as members of an owning family.[20] The hospitality business however has

---

17  Katy manages *Keep Frome Local* a facebook group to share information and opinion on projected developments, in line with the UK 'Town Centre Movement'. A 2013 government initiative *Action on Town Centres* emphasises 'local leadership and diversity. Every area needs their own plan... local authorities working with local businesses to transform their town centres."

18  Henry Vincent on his 1839 tour was impressed by the size of the Frome crowd '400 of whom were females — the majority of them very neatly clad,' recording that 'excellent' ladies of Frome 'intend shortly to form an association. Several influential individuals expressed themselves converted to the principles of Radicalism.'

19  In 1751 Sarah Seagram hosted the first indoor Wesleyan meeting, a move so pioneering that she suffered considerable abuse and 'the good women, though Methodists, thought self-defence justifiable, and in the scuffle one of the pious missionaries (ie their hostile attackers) had his shirt torn' according to Stephen Tuck's history of Methodism. Another early Wesleyan preacher after first fearing 'no immediate good' in his open-air mission, reported a breakthrough due to an attentive young woman and her friends.

20  Even much-loved Ellen Bray, who ran the stationers of that name, inherited from her father.

always needed people-skills, and now more than ever women are a visible and vocal part of Frome's identity. Helen Rowlinson, recently in charge of *The Three Swans* as one of the current swathe of entrepreneurial owners and managers, agrees.

> Frome is lucky in that there's a good band of strong women here now – there's Ellen (Porteous) at *Fat Radish* and Jude (Kelly) running *La Strada*, Sue who's run the *Blue Boar* for donkey's years – *Lamb and Fountain*, that's 'Mother' and her daughter Sue who runs it now, and Lotte who ran the café in Victoria Park, doing well in her new bar-bistro up at Badcox. I have a lot of admiration for them all, because you have to be hard sometimes in this work.

So now that Samuel Johnson's scathing dismissal of women who speak out[21] has been refuted, a wider look at the personal energies which have combined to create the distinctive personality of the town.

There's a stubborn undauntedness about the people of Frome that historians have found hard to explain, perhaps because it can present itself as indifference to matters of assumed importance. 'Nothing important ever happened in Frome, that's one of its delights,' a spokesman for the Frome Society for Local Study assured a *Somerset Life* journalist in 2010. Another[22] summarises the town as 'a gentle place, unpretentious and retiring... (whose) people are sometimes accused of apathy'. Even insightful Peter Belham[23] describes Frome as unconcerned about political events, 'passively' pro-Parliament during the Civil War, and not even 'jolted out its calm' by Monmouth's rebellion – this based on the fact that when the rebel leader arrived in Frome[24] he found no further militia available to join him. In fact a proclamation in the town centre had declared Frome's support for the Duke of Monmouth's claim on the crown as soon as the news arrived, and according to a contemporary report the people not only disobeyed the order to detain

---

21 Johnson to Boswell: "Sir, a woman's preaching is like a dog's walking on his hind legs. It is not done well; but you are surprised to find it done at all."
22 *Frome in Old Picture Postcards* (1989)
23 *The Making of Frome* (1973)
24 Monmouth Chambers, 3 Cork Street, built around 1600, is credited as the lodging house of the ill-fated Duke for three days in 1685

Monmouth as he rode around the town, they even 'called him King as confidently as if he had the crown on his head'.

It's worth looking in more detail at Frome's assumed indifference to the spasmic reign of 'King Monmouth' in 1685, because this has cast a long shadow. Ralph Mitchard, Frome musician and historian, researched the Duke's short-lived rebellion which began and died in the south-west.[25] He points out that

> Frome was unique in declaring for Monmouth before he even arrived. They gathered in the town centre with weapons, and then the Wiltshire militia came and disarmed them and took a few, one was hung, before the Duke even came. So by the time he arrived there was a lack of weapons, and they had already had their wrists slapped by the militia. [26]

This rebellion against the succession of catholic James II after the death of his brother Charles II, a pragmatic protestant, came in the final stage of England's battle to free itself from monarchy and become a republic. Commonwealth gained through civil war had lasted only nine years, and once protestants William and Mary replaced James, the struggle was abandoned. In the Southwest, however, the stain of that bloody skirmish remained. Most of the area had committed to the protestant cause, and many of its population had died for it, either killed in battle or executed by order of sadistic Judge Jeffries whose 'Bloody Assizes' hanged hundreds and transported thousands to the West Indies as slaves in the sugar plantations. Over six hundred Somerset men left in eight ships; many died on the voyage, others died on the quayside awaiting auction.[27]

---

25 *The Days of King Monmouth* – see references
26 Treatment of locals by the king's army under the sadistic General Kirke was appalling, with many complaints of assaults, rapes, and thefts – an officer on his own side wrote 'In plain English, I have seen too much violence and wickedness practised to be fond of this trade, and trust we may soon put a period to the business, for what we every day practise among these poor people cannot be supported by any man of the least morality.'
27 Slavery and trade in humans was already embedded in the life of wealthy Somerset families, who built their grand homes using profits from their plantations. These people, some of them also local philanthropists and

Four centuries later the consequences may still resonate: 'The West Country' in the 17th Century was a thriving area of important towns, while the image evoked nowadays is of rural cottages and cream teas.' Ralph Mitchard's study suggests that the commitment to rebellion, plus loss of so many able and energetic men, played a big part in this downsizing.

So in the present decade, should we be wondering why the town's personality has changed so much? Perhaps that's the wrong question. Perhaps the question should be, has Frome's personality really radically changed? Integration of incomers has undoubtedly encouraged community enterprises to thrive, but it's hardly plausible that Frome's identity took a gigantic U-turn at their arrival. History has been seen traditionally with an eye on thrones and pulpits, and contemporary accounts, while invaluable, inevitably impose their own social perspective. Perhaps Frome is not newly radical, but radical in the way it always was: unimpressed by the passions and conflicts of the ruling classes and finding its own imperatives. Instead of hierarchy and theoretic dogma, the egalitarian values that developed are rooted in community and creativity.

Hilary Daniels, a lifelong resident already in his teens during World War II and a senior legal advisor in his family firm by the time of his retirement, gave me his view of the accelerated activity in the town since demolition of the Trinity area was aborted. This, with other aspects of Frome's physical structure, is explained and more fully discussed in a later section but it's interesting that it was assault on an area where working people had lived, not the demolishing of a fine manor house, that stirred the townsfolk.

> I think people thought, why do you want to do this?... so, much to the upsetting of our town clerk, we got together and said, No we're not going to become just another place which has had its heart knocked out, we love what we've got and we want to keep it. And I think this consciousness of Frome as a good place to live in – because of its geography, and its history and its look – is what started to attract people from outside. Very few of the people I grew up with

church-goers, are also part of the story of Frome.

are still in the town. Nowadays things have happened because of newcomers – they run things, so the effect of this egress was largely beneficial, it left spaces for other people to develop interests. We don't mind, we're very happy.

Peter Clark, writer and one of the 'newcomers who runs things', agrees.

A lot of people who have come to Frome are not concerned about the values of the metropolis. It's a town which attracts outsiders with curious minds and intellectual energy[28] – independent, public-spirited, people who are unambitious and not self-seeking. There's a lot of poverty in the towns in Somerset but in Frome there are people who are doing something about it, in a totally disinterested and public-spirited way.

Support for the most needy of Frome is of course not new. There had been an almshouse for old women in town since 1461[29] and its 1721 replacement, the Blue House[30], added to this role a charity school for boys. In 1833[31] the list of Frome's charitable institutions included two churches, three schools and a Sunday school, a hospital for old men and an Asylum[32] for girls, a 'Bequest', three 'Gifts' and 'Various Benefactions'

---

28  Frome Society for Local Study has 460 members, and the Frome Writers Collective, also unique in its organisation, currently has over 100.
29  Founded by William Leversedge, one of the early ruling families of Frome. As an aside, Frome was a royal manor until the reign of Henry II when it devolved to the FitzBernard family and passed down through marriage to the Leversedges who held it for 200 years though selling off sections continuously, until the last bits went in lots in 1905. You see what I mean about the unlikelihood of Frome's working people having much reason to feel loyal connection with their overlords?
30  The boys were taught to read and write and religion 'as professed and taught in the Church of England' and given a blue uniform comprising a long coat, waistcoat, breeches, shirt, band, cap and stockings. The tassels on the charity boys' caps were white, to distinguish them from the red-tasselled paying scholars.
31  W.P. Penny, *History and Description of the Public Charities in the Town of Frome.*
32  The Asylum was not for lunatics, it was established to prepare 16 poor girls- 'natives of Frome' – for domestic service. In 1892 a new scheme allowed girls

– and the tradition of support for those in need has continued strongly. Several initiatives have come from our Independent town council; others are simply groups of individuals using their time and energy to support ideas they value. 'There's a buzz of sociability, a sense of common purpose and a creative, exciting atmosphere that make it feel quite different from many English market towns,' George Monbiot wrote in *The Guardian*[33] and the best way to appreciate the result is a look at the organisations founded and run by the people of Frome.

*Fair Frome* is the umbrella organisation for *Frome Food Bank, Frome Furniture Bank, Community Dining*, and individual campaigns on social issues. It was set up in 2013 by the newly independent Town Council to alleviate the effects of poverty, and covers a wide range of projects. The geographic hub is the food bank outside the Town Hall, a point of contact for many and meeting-place for referring agencies and campaign leaders. *Fair Frome* is not just an administrative concept, it's an attitude to community that finds expression in many other outlets. There's *Fair Housing for Frome, Active and In Touch Frome* to connect the isolated, *Hope Frome* soup kitchen, and free food for anyone from Edventure's *Community Fridge*. Looking after the environment is *Sustainable Frome,*[34] *FROGS* (Frome Recreation & Open Ground Supporters), *SOS* (Save Open Spaces) *Friends of the River Frome, Frome's Missing Links* to support SUSTRANS cycle routes, *Frome Car Share* to support electric car use and *Frome Anti-Fracking. Friends of Frome Hospital* and other volunteer groups support the local aid network, and looking outward there's *Frome Friends of Palestine,*[35] *Frome Stop War,* and *RAISE* to support refugees and

---

from other places to be received into the home and trained on payment of 7s a week. John and Richard Stevens also left a benefaction of land to endow a hospital for 10 aged men to be clothed and given a weekly allowance. The hospital and asylum together formed the single large building at Keyford.

33 https://www.theguardian.com/commentisfree/2018/feb/21/Frome

34 *Sustainable Frome* had already formed 'to create a vibrant and sustainable community… using much less energy and resources than at present' when a 2006 project started in Totnes using the term *Transition Town* caught the zeitgeist and an international network quickly spread. Since Frome already had its own thriving group, rather than re-invent itself under a different label, *Sustainable Frome* continues its active work for a greener future.

35 When in 2016 *The Freedom Theatre of Jenin*, the 'cultural resistance' group from a refugee camp in occupied Palestine, toured Europe with their

take donations to Calais. And naturally the town still has its traditional charity outlets, and societies like the Rotary Club and the Lions Club which have long been a vital and valued arm of support.[36]

This network of care doesn't discourage individual initiatives – those Sponsor-Me feats of endurance to collect donations for local people hurt in an accident or sick. A good example of this might be the campaign for survival funding in 2017 by *Routes*, our local YMCA and youth drop-in centre in Palmer Street. Hearing that this important facility was in danger of closure without a significant funding boost, local photographer Tim Gander organised an exhibition in *La Strada* cafe which featured portraits of the young people who relied on it, with thumbnail quotes from each. Donations in response to his photographs made a big contribution to the funding campaign – one café visitor promptly sent £30,000 – and *Routes* was officially safe for at least another year.

'Make the world you want to live in' seems the motto of so many people in the town. Even while I was writing this section, Frome's positive impact was hailed (in the Monbiot article mentioned above) as 'the town that's found a cure for illness' with lessons for the rest of the country. The *Compassionate Frome* project was launched in 2013 by Frome GP Helen Kingston, who was disturbed by what she saw as the 'medicalisation' of patients' lives, and the negative consequences of treating people as 'a cluster of symptoms rather than a human being who happened to have health problems.'[37]

---

production *The Siege*, there was a storm of outrage in the right-wing press and only ten UK venues agreed to host Nabil Al-Raee's controversial play. Frome was one of these. The company performed at the Merlin, with Ken Loach chairing a Q&A, to a full house with a standing ovation, a tribute to the play and to the vision (and fund-raising) of the *Frome Friends of Palestine* group. In another creative connection, Frome's best-known street artist Paris in 2017 contributed to the graffiti on the infamous Separation Wall.

36 We've also seen the birth of national and international support groups, with *Thrive* (Horticultural Therapy) and *ADD* (Action on Disability and Development) both founded here.

37 I refer you again to Atul Gawande, who in *Being Mortal* emphasised the urgent need for change in doctor/patient relationships, writing: 'All we ask is to be allowed to remain the writers of our own story – to retain the freedom to shape our lives in ways consistent with our characters and loyalties.' This

Wiltshire journalist Dan Worrow,[38] writing with faux-annoyance, extends the list of Frome's recent glories.

> I swear every news story I hear about Frome is a happy-ending-tale of civic action. Funky, freewheeling 'Fromies' with their community bank for folk to build a business, to their community fridge project reducing food waste and directly helping the struggling; I'm not jealous of their inventive and social experiments, no!
>
> From its thriving arts scene which converts a closed public loo into an art gallery with each cubicle showcasing a local artist, or hosting an explosive annual music festival, to the Library of Things share-shop and the super market, with their entrepreneurial essence – somebody stop them, throw an orthodox spanner in the works...
>
> The list of Frome's radical, extravagant social and environmental projects goes on and on; an electric/hybrid car club anyone, or a publicly owned renewable energy company perhaps, or courageous community buy-outs of rural locations prior to stop developers getting their grubby hands on them? ....Was it the voting in of an independent town council which turned this potential ghost town into the thriving municipal community it is today...and could Devizes follow by its example?

An independent town council may or may not be a transferable solution, but Peter Macfadyen, a town councillor and prime mover in the 'independent revolution' acknowledges, modestly, the wide-ranging impact of Frome's new democratic image.

> It is a thing we are well known for, especially now there's political tourism going on to a significant extent. As we speak there are two Dutch professors and a Danish film crew looking at our participation schemes. The furthest afield was South Korean civil servants, who

_____

seminal work was seen as boundary breaking in 2014, so it's all the more impressive that a doctor in a small market town was already activating a plan.

38 https://indexwiltshire.co.uk/no-surprises-living-in-devizes-frome-wasnt-built-in-a-day/

came to take ideas back to Seoul. I don't know what they thought because their film is subtitled in South Korean. But none of us is in this for ego – or power – we're only interested in getting something done for Frome.

Back in 2010 a group of us were disillusioned with the council and we felt part of the problem was political parties bickering because their ideology came from Westminster. We wanted to change that. [39]

Co-conspirator Mel Usher remembers:

We put an advert in the paper and said, Come along. All you needed was a telephone number and email address, and one side of paper saying what you wanted to do for Frome. They were then selected by an independent group of people. And they were genuinely independent. [40]

Peter again:

So we got together as a group and decided our ethos is to offer a set of values rather than a manifesto of planned actions. And that's a fairly novel approach, to knock on someone's door and to say, 'I don't know what we're doing yet, let's work it out together.' What you're saying is, 'Trust me.'

We had a meeting in the Cornerhouse and found we could put up seventeen candidates for the seventeen seats in 2011. We won ten and right from the beginning we started making changes because we refused to do anything just because 'That's the way it's always done.' A lot of time and money went on bureaucracy, so we got rid of the

---

39 Journalist John Harris, himself a local, wrote in the *Guardian* about the extraordinary success of the IfF – Independents for Frome – concept of town management: https://www.independent.co.uk/voices/comment/what-a-democratic-revolution-in-the-somerset-town-of-frome-could-teach-our-political-class-8312163.html

40 Notice here the similarity to Jill's account of the start of her charity PAC : 'I wrote a leaflet, and put it round the doctors, with my phone number on it.' Little acorns. Big oaks. Very Frome.

unnecessary protocols and effectively suspended the constitution. Some people were very upset, and there was an official complaint that I was wearing shorts, but we wanted the people to judge us on what we did. For example, in Sheppards Barton, a majorly beautiful zone, the County Council had used tarmac for repairs, so we dug it up ourselves and put paving stones in. And after initial outrage, even the County Council agreed it was much better.

We've carried on being maverick in lots of ways. And we've attracted some fantastic people because our ethos is basically to let the staff use their expertise. We have the only Resilience Officer in the UK working on creating a town more able to cope with environmental change – we aim to be carbon free in 30 years. We already have Community Cars with volunteer drivers and Car Share and we're working on other transport initiatives. And the Rangers, who have replaced the park-keepers, chat to people as part of their job – we want everyone to feel connected with what's happening in their town.'

Not surprisingly, the radical council was popular with Frome's people as well as curious Danes. Four years after they were first voted in, the IfF town council candidate surge went bionic. Once again independent candidates stood for all the seventeen seats, and as the long day of counting ward votes wore on, results were posted online for the watchers in town. *10 out of 10.... 13....15... 16...* and then a long wait. It was late afternoon before the final message: *17 out of 17, we're coming home...* The final vote had taken two recounts to convince the defeated Tory candidate, but celebrations were loud and long at the *Cornerhouse*, in a bar, where it all began,.

I reminded Peter, and he allowed himself a reminiscent smile.

It was a moment, yes. The Peoples' Republic of Frome, the *Guardian* called it. And of course it was more difficult than the first time, because we weren't selling change – it was a verdict on what we'd done. It has been different this term, but way easier since we moved into the new Town Hall – which we bought back from the County Council who got it for a quid about forty years ago and sold it back to us for a quarter of a million quid – outrageous really, but it is brilliant to have it.'[41]

Frome's independent status, unique in both concept and activation, roused so much interest that Peter wrote a do-it-yourself manual for other communities: 'Flatpack Democracy has sold over 4,000 copies and aroused interest literally around the world,' Peter says, sounding pleased but surprised: 'There are now little revolutions all over the place, because there's a zeitgeist around that party politics at local level doesn't work.'

As Peter's Flatpack journey shows, international interest continued – and so too, naturally, do the challenges. Some question whether a dominant group of likeminded independents, even though not tied to national party values, has inevitably rebranded itself as a party, and consequently lacks a vital element of scrupulous enquiry. And some people just don't like some of their decisions, like the development of the market square surrounding the Boyles Cross fountain which has removed car parking so effectively that the space now seems inadequate for a market there, the right for which Frome gained in its Royal Charter in 1239. But Frome will still forever be the first independent town council in the history of England.

Why here, and why now? Personalities and attitudes are the obvious answer, but Frome was able to achieve political independence in part because the town was already recovering stamina after the more acute stages of blight – here summarised by Bob Ashford, ex Mayor and currently deeply involved with Fair Frome:

Thirty years ago Frome was a bustling manufacturing town with factories like Cuprinol, Singers, Beswicks, and Butler and Tanner

---

41 There's a complex background which isn't widely realised: The Town Hall was owned by the Rural District Council and when Mendip was created, all the assets were shared out between the District and the County councils, leaving Frome with just two parks and an office. Over the years the town council has bought back as much as they could of what was lost – the showfields, the Dippy, Wallbridge, allotments and various other bits of land. It's been slow and costly, as there are legal fees 'so we have to pay their legal department to give us back what they took from us, which is very galling' as Peter puts it. Most people in Frome approve of the purchase – there was actually a small public protest in favour of recovery in 2016, with a little banner across the steps.

printworks. People had well paid jobs and the firms all had social
clubs providing holidays, events, social outings – they put floats
into the carnival and most people belonged to one of these. They
had a place, and most of them had worked there all their lives, their
parents had before them, and they thought they were jobs for life. So
there was a strong sense of social fabric.

And then it all started to go wrong. Factories were closing
one by one and all of a sudden from being a fairly wealthy semi-
industrial town, there was 23% unemployment. And it was grim.
The social clubs kept going some years after the industries closed
down, so there was still a strong community feeling, but the town
centre really got hit, because there was no money about. I stood for
election in the Keyford ward in 1992 and became the first Labour
councillor in Frome for decades – then first Labour Mayor, in '96
and '97, when a new Labour administration ran the council. One of
our biggest achievements was signing the lease and developing the
Cheese and Grain[42] as a music and community venue. We did it all
as economically as possible – I remember the night before it opened,
on the floor with the town clerk, Sheila Rae, painting the floor. We
redeveloped the park, and the Millennium Green, and kickstarted
the Mount Community Association. And we made consultation a key
feature of our approach to get to the heart of the community. I'm
proud of what we did, and when I finished a ten-year job in London[43]
and Fair Frome had started, I became chair of trustees. Our purpose
is to direct resources to people who are struggling, and also to give
a voice to the growing divide happening in Frome. Voices are being
ignored because maybe they're not very polite, or cultured, or 'on
message' but there are voices that need to be heard that are very
critical. It's important to get a spectrum.

I'm pressing pause there because there's more about this in
the final section. At this point I want to move to a different aspect
of community, because even before we featured in political reports,

---

42  The Cheese and Grain had been leased initially to Jon Evans in a dilapidated
    state, and he had developed it into a usable venue by a series of mini-
    festivals plus income from his 'One World' festivals – of which more later.
43  Bob had spent some years in London working with Youth Justice.

Frome was headlining the media's culture columns once we had joined
the Southwest festival scene. Not as another music festival or an Art
Fayre or a Lit Fest: the Frome Festival was a festival of everything, for
everyone. All ages, all interests, all genres. There were only a handful of
opportunities to stay in town at that time so this grand concept could
have been destined to crash and burn, but the Frome Festival has, on
a shoe-string and with massive voluntary input and local enthusiasm,
grown and thrived.

Martin Bax, from a professional theatre background,[44] conceived the
idea in 2001 and realised it by the simple expedient of gathering a group
of people from different artistic areas and asking them to suggest events,
and then to use their contacts to put them on, all together, throughout
ten days in July. Frome's writers[45] joined with groups from visual arts,
classical music, world music, and drama to put together a programme,
Butler & Tanner printed the brochure for free, and since then every
year there has been a Frome Festival with events so wide-ranging and
splendid that it really deserves a (lavishly illustrated) book all of its own.
The highlight for many is the open-air international Food Feast, and even
more important than the prestigious acts and performers consistently
attracted is the shared celebration throughout the community – the
sense of a town delighted to show off its gardens and venues, and to
open its art studios and parade its bands freely to all.

In 2008 the mantle of artistic director passed from Martin Bax to
Martin Dimery, then a director at Cheese & Grain, and Frome Festival

---

44 As an actor with the National Theatre in the 1970s, in productions like
   Equus, Martin had become friends with a casting director on her retirement
   and asked for help with the restoration of an old house near Frome.
   Martin had initially trained as an electrician and is also a self-confessed
   perfectionist, and in the ensuing long months of rewiring he had plenty
   of time to visit and fall in love with Frome. He became a councillor almost
   accidentally, thinking he was standing as a paper candidate in Frome Park
   ward for Labour but won by a landslide and immediately focussed on
   regeneration projects.
45 I heard about this from writer John Payne, meeting him for the first time
   after he left a note at the Garden Café to suggest there should be a 'literary
   strand' in Martin's venture, so we formed a subgroup and Words at the Frome
   Festival contributed a range of events including soap-box poets and writers
   in shops as well as more traditional literary lunches and talks.

is now the largest – and longest – community arts festival in the South West.[46] After a decade characterised by decline, with community options massively depleted by the loss of the social clubs, it might seem surprising that Frome was so responsive to the notion, but while its success is a credit to everyone involved, it shouldn't be forgotten – though it sometimes is – that the foundations for this glorious edifice were already in position throughout the grimy days. Throughout the '80s and '90s there was already a vast amount of creative activity in Frome, all of which fertilised the ground for Martin Bax's great idea. Just as major radical change in council had been pre-shadowed by a few dynamic councillors with genuine concern, so the way to a town festival had already been paved – twice, actually:

For one thing, there had already been a Frome Festival, organised by Jon Evans who, with Luke Piper and Scott Collingston, used his Glastonbury experience and contacts for a weekend gig in 1995 and again in 1996, in a field site beside the A361 just outside Frome. Featuring names like Ozric Tentacles, Baka Beyond, Eat Static and the Revolutionary Dub Warriors, the gathering had a mission that was more than to entertain, it was 'to rejuvenate Frome's cultural and commercial identity in a rapidly changing world – Act local, think global.'

Next year the *Frome Times*[47] reported 'Frome Festival now in its third year, will be the largest event yet to be staged by promoters One World. Attendance is likely to rise from around 5000 to 8000 people.' Sadly, the huge attendance in 1997 brought disaster to the fledgling festival. The death of Princess Diana meant the police attendance

---

46 Interestingly, the festival has never had significant Arts funding. Martin took a chance on the first year by underwriting bookings with his own money, and then it was too late for start-up eligibility and too reliant on volunteers for grants. Perhaps this failure was its strength, as the several richer festivals have been forced to contract or close when their funding is reduced or withdrawn. Friends of Frome Festival, the army of volunteer stewards, plus the enthusiasm of local performers and artists and the high profile we have now, all combine to reassure us our festival will survive and continue to thrive.

47 A small quarterly magazine put out at that time by David MacGregor, manager of the Catherine Hill Traders Association, 'to promote Frome and its various facilities, services and shops, and to focus on the town's many positive aspects.'

organised by Jon was diverted to deal with the thousands of mourners heading for her funeral that weekend, leaving the site open to a massive convoy. Portaloos had failed to arrive too so as John Killah, defending,[48] said at Jon Evan's later court appearance, through absolutely no fault of the organisers, everything that could go wrong did go wrong... And after helplessly watching a near riot all night Jon made his way in the morning to the Little Chef at Nunney where the waitress greeted him 'Did you hear about that festival in the field? Turned into complete mayhem and now the organiser's gone away, he's off to Spain with fifty thousand pounds in his pocket!'

But the *One World Frome Festival* in its aim to 'make connections... appreciating each other's ideas and perceptions' clearly left its seed, in terms of potential to enhance community consciousness. In 1999 the Mount Community Association put on its own festival as the finale of a summer project by residents, including the school and support agencies, showing once again that Frome's people were happy to engage with the idea of festival.[49] The *Made in Frome* project, which will be unpacked in a later section, also involved a group of Frome's artists working together to put on an extensive event, so this in its way was also a precursor of the Frome Festival, now so widely admired and enjoyed.

ND IF YOU DON'T FOLLOW POLITICS so you don't know about IfF and you don't like arty stuff so you've never heard of Frome Festival, there's another feather in Frome's cap you must surely know: Frome Independent, the biggest street market in the country. It's owned by

---

48  John Killah-Defending was for years so frequently seen and said as to seem almost a hyphenated name for this much respected specialist criminal defence lawyer. He also fought very strongly against the closure of the Magistrates Court in Frome – see later section.

49  One element in this project was the Mount Map, created by artists Laurie and Nell from Artspark as a personalised 'parish map' illustrated with tiny figures and delightful comments like *foxes come to be fed here* and *"The shoulder of mutton"= old field name* and many personal memories. This at that time isolated area, firmly boundaried by roads, river, and 'The Dippy' area – now a very pleasant wildlife walk – is shown in this map as a special haven, and it's not surprising that 18 positive outcomes were clearly identified at the end of the festival.

Gavin Eddy who came to Frome in 2007 – 'I just fell in love with it' – [50] and bought the old Wesleyan Church School building now converted into *Forward Space,* a shared workspace for freelancers and small businesses – with a café open to the public (which is a great work space.)

He saw the potential of Catherine Hill and invested in the fragile retail trade there by buying some of the empty shops and renovating them, with the aim of letting them to young retailers to create the ethos for regeneration.

> My background is in business so I could mentor them a bit, with strategy and advice. But Catherine Hill is a secondary retail area and even the primary areas in Frome didn't have much footfall, so the market was about creating an event that would bring a whole new audience to the hill, driving footfall to the shops that we were filling with young entrepreneurs and retailers.
>
> For us it's really key that the Frome Independent brand is strong and has certain connotations in terms of quality, and localism – other things can happen alongside it, like the Magpie market, and in summer we have the beach and donkey rides. Most importantly, the market has achieved that aim of bringing a whole new audience of people to Frome, and that was why I set it up in the first place – it was about supporting the shops – adding extra customers, not taking customers away.
>
> I didn't set out thinking, I want to change the way the town is, all I thought was, this is a lovely place, there's something special about it, what can I do that enhances what it already has, and opens it up to more people to see it. And that was really the only ambition I had, and maybe in some ways it got ahead of that ambition – I never expected this to grow to the stage it has, or become as popular as it's become, and that creates its own challenges.

50 'I came sort of by accident, I'd never heard of Frome, but there was something about the aesthetic of the way it's built in a bowl with a river at the bottom, something really lovely about all these streets that lead to the centre, some-thing about the built environment that I loved, and the fact that it had sort-of been left behind, in a way, and I think that was the best thing for it. It looked a bit forlorn but there was something lovely about it.' I've quoted Gavin's reason-for-coming in full here because I think he nails it for many of us.

'The Independent' gives Frome the opportunity to reinvent its lost market-town identity in style, revitalising on a massive scale the local traditional stall-holding products and street performances (there's a busking stage I always head for.) And once again, it may seem to have come as a bolt from the blue but as the old TV show says, *let's examine the evidence...*

The road to the Independent market was already being paved by a group of dedicated people who worked to turn around the fortunes of Catherine Hill and make it the success story it is today. From their work to recreate an artisan vibe on the hill came the first craft markets: when I came in 1987 there were medieval street fairs on the hill with stall-holders in Chaucerian-looking garb, which dwindled and disappeared, until *Craft on the Hill* inspired the *Artisan Market,* which developed into the *Sunday Supermarket* by spreading across the town to join up with an art boot-sale and the Magpie Market by the river. And then it kept on growing, into the *Frome Independent*, which swallows the whole town monthly, with scores of stewards, road closures and Park & Ride areas to cope with the thousands who come each month.

Lyn Waller was one of the early pioneers. She came to Catherine Hill in 1997 as one of a very few traders on a street that she remembers three-quarters empty and boarded up, with the Mendip regeneration officer Julie Grail having 'an extremely uphill struggle.' She and her family lived in their shop despite the street vandalism and sometimes violence at nights: they had a 'non-tolerance' policy and phoned the police when they saw fights developing, and Lynn became a central figure in both the traders' and the residents' associations for the Catherine Hill area.

> I have a bossy organisational streak, so I got involved along with Hilary Beardmore and we worked on a lot of projects together, including the Medieval Street Fair – introducing things like competitions for best costume. I joined the traders' association (adjusting its name to Catherine Hill Association of Traders, so we could refer to it as CHAT) and the Chamber of Commerce [51] and other

---

51  https://fromechamber.com/

groups to make sure the hill was seen as a valuable part of the town and not a poor relation.'

And from this ragged start – 'a bit like herding cats' – the street market, and the Catherine Hill identity that so enchants visitors now, all developed – despite opposition from people who saw an opportunity to buy derelict properties and turn them cheaply into flats to let. 'I did fight an awful lot of planning applications, so I was pretty unpopular with some people,' she says, 'but it was worth it.' Clearly it was. Nobody visits a town to walk up a residential street, and without the vision and unpopular persistence of those early traders, none of the other initiatives would have developed.

Fay Goodridge was also a key player at that time. In the early 90s she moved her framing business to Catherine Hill to take advantage of an early promotion of this declining area, but soon found herself virtually alone.

Everything around me was boarded up,' she recalls, 'It was really grotty. The building I bought was hanging, really, but it gave me an affordable place to live and work, and I wasn't there to make a fast buck, I was there for the long term.

Nobody had any pride in that street. On a Friday and Saturday night it was like the OK Corral – everybody would get tanked up at The Ship and at 11 o'clock they'd be effing and jeffing down the hill to McGuinness's night club, then the same up again half two in the morning, windows popping and fights breaking out – it was that bad.[52] But Kate (Semple) and I started renovating our properties, and we started to get other businesses in. I encouraged people to paint murals and we did this massive street-clean and pressure-wash one Sunday morning. The council helped us – we'd had a meeting, and I said, If a street's dirty and boarded up, and doesn't look like anybody

---

52  It's worth clarifying that the dereliction of Catherine Hill was not a consequence of failing industries. As early as mid 1980s, extra policing had been required and organised to deal with regular late-night violence attributed to young people on a good wage living at home so with no significant expenses, in the habit of spending their evenings in the pubs and emerging inebriated when the pubs closed at 11.

cares for it, of course it's going to get vandalised! You got to make it look better, so let's start with a street clean. Next day there wasn't even a fag-butt on the street and people started to have a bit of pride in the place.

That was the turning point, really. We had enough creatives to launch Made in Frome, and we started Craft on the Hill, which was amazing really,[53] and which was a precursor to the Artisan Market, and then Gavin Eddy came along, prepared to put some money into some market stalls and get it going.'

Any one of these initiatives would have put Frome firmly on the map. In the last twenty years we have seen three – the independent festival in 2001, the independent council in 2011, the independent market in 2013. I could say that during those dark days maybe we had only the Catherine Hill leyline to keep the flame of hope alive but actually Mendip had appointed a regeneration officer, and even more importantly there were the creative people – artisans, artists, craft workers – who either lived here already or had come here because it was cheap to get workshops, and friendly.

In the words of Alan Campbell, a film-maker who uses his professional expertise to support projects in Frome: 'People only come to Frome if they want what Frome is. It's got such a strong identity'. For that reason I have not in this section made any differentiation between those born in Frome and those choosing to live here. As well as the loyal locals who preserved precious tales of unique ancient aspects of life, much of Frome's history has been researched by people who arrived, fell in love with the town, and stayed to create a new generation of locals. Derek Gill, for example, arrived from Falmouth to teach in Milk Street school and became captivated by the town's quirky history.[54]

---

53 An open-air art exhibition-cum-craft sale about which Fay further recalls: 'We had Charlie Oldham wood-carving, potters throwing, Kate Semple chipping at stone, Martin Bax glass-blowing in a glory-hole outside my shop which had Health & Safety seen they would have shut down immediately – I remember expecting it to blow away like a giant bubble... But Sonja Klingler was there.'

54 His extensive writings were all donated after his death in 2014 to the Frome Museum where the library is named after him. Derek was a meticulous researcher, and notorious for recycling so that much of his data was written

Derek didn't just write about the town's history, he participated in it. Realising on arrival that the Trinity area was half-demolished with another assault about to come, he called in on his archeologist friend Roger Leech[55] to study the site with him.

'He couldn't understand why they were doing it, he could see it was an unusual housing area,' his son Rob, who helped him pull boards off the doomed houses to measure them for his survey, told me.

> That's when they realised it was the oldest industrial housing estate in the country. They formed the Civic Society to fight for the survival of the rest of it, and that's what they managed to do. He was just upset they didn't manage to save the first phase, but it's proved a point – the part that was rebuilt has already been demolished and rebuilt again, and the preserved bit is still going strong.

There will be more of the assault on Trinity in a later section, but it's a powerful example of the way incomers are sensitive to, and effective in supporting, the essential character of Frome.

Perhaps as a consequence of the 1990s shredding of that solid network of major employers, work ethos in Frome today seems to have little to do with conventional cradle-to-grave full-time jobs. Many opt for a patchwork portfolio of concurrent part-time employments. When our independent bookshop *Hunting Raven* changed hands in 2017, the new owner was surprised to find the business had been thriving robustly under part-time management. Previous owner John Birkett-Smith summarised: 'People outside don't realise that in Frome, workers don't want that kind of single career path because they have a different world view – they want to spend time doing different things – volunteering,

---

on the back of information relating to other events: as his son told me 'He'd never waste a piece of paper – he'd write on the back of letters too, so you'd never know which was the side he wanted to keep.'

55 That's Professor Roger H Leech, formerly Head of Archaeology in the Royal Commission on the Historical Monuments of England, before which Assistant Director of the Western Archaeological Trust in Bristol, concerned with rescue archaeology projects in Avon, Gloucestershire and Somerset. Also former President of the Bristol and Gloucestershire Archaeological Society, and council member of the Royal Archaeological Institute.

developing their own interests. It's Frome. We do things differently here.' Faces you see behind a counter will be there again behind a bar or offering ice-cream at the cinema – probably to finance a band or some other personal project – and these patchwork careers bring spin-off benefit to the community as well as to the individual: the focus of the 'work' becomes interaction, the skills are flexibility and human relationships rather than routine mechanics. And in a world where mechanics are constantly changing, this has to be a good thing. People who don't define themselves by job status will interact flexibly and humanly in every role.

ANOTHER ASPECT that interested me about Frome as a community is the vitality and cultural contribution of the young. We have no university,[56] no art college, no music academy or degree-style course for any of the arts – and these higher education courses are generally considered to bring an influx of diversity and energy to a town. It is of course a transient, often exclusive, energy, usually with no long-term commitment, but nevertheless it does bring some cross-fertilisation to the 'host' community. Do the young people miss that 'student' vibe in town?

They don't seem to. Frome's school-leavers can go anywhere to study but many choose Bath so they can maintain their social contacts here – whether that's a band or a job. It seems that in the absence of a student energy, the town's own older teens have stepped confidently into the cultural breach.

Aaron, working in his friend's men's shop *Kushi*, saw no reason to go to university and says and most of his mates don't want to either:

> It's one of those things you 'have-to' do, and in Frome we don't like doing things we 'have-to' do, we're very sort-of set on doing things we want-to do, not in a snobby arrogant way, but we'd rather do things we're interested in than be pushed. If I want to do something, I don't have to pay £40,000 to do it over three years, I'd rather set my own my thing up and end up with something that I'm proud of. The fact there's no higher education here actually helps, because everybody knows each

---

56 Not even vocational FE courses in fact, as Frome College in the 1990s for some reason allowed these to discontinue and the building in Park Road was demolished.

other, and we're not competing. Coming from Frome is a confidence boost definitely, we are definitely different from other people.

Jake, a returned student successfully making his name as a rapper and performer, agrees that Frome has always had its own individual character. 'People my age even if they move away, they come back. We're different to other towns – more alternative. And I've definitely noticed a lot more diversity in the last five years. It was always bubbly, but the Market has really changed it.'

Amy who co-runs the Rye Bakery with her partner Owen, never expected to settle in Frome after travelling and living in France,

> but the more I came back to visit, and the more vibrant it became, and the more things going on, I thought – it's quite cool here! Actually it was always quite cool, but it's also changed in the eight years I was away. There's a sense that Frome's going somewhere now, and things are going on that are bringing other young people here – things like Edventure.[57] Frome is constantly changing – it doesn't feel like it's met its plateau yet – it's going to continue.'

I'm including here also a view from Lark Porter, who with her partner Toby runs the music venue 23 *Bath Street*, because she shows where this optimistic attitude can take the imaginative young people of Frome. Both Lark and Toby worked behind the bar in this venue as teenagers, when it was *The Wheatsheaves* and the bar upstairs was 'the only alternative space you could go, as back then Frome was quite chavvy, you had the boy racers and the rave crew, hippies and people into more alternative stuff. Downstairs they'd be drinking pints and we used to put our hoods up and run through the pub and come straight up to the Loft bar,'

Lark travelled initially after leaving school, then trained to run arts

---

57 Edventure is another Frome first. Initiated in 2012 by Johannes Moeller for young people interested in social enterprise, this has evolved into ten-week courses to give hands-on learning experience within the Frome community, giving the town some of its most valued initiatives as well as providing a qualification for participants. The best known projects are the Community Fridge, 'SHARE – a Library of Things', Edspace (the tiny homes building company), Remakery Frome, and the Welsh Mill Hub community workspace.

venues in London while Toby did an apprenticeship locally in sound engineering. Fast forward a few years and they were together again, he technical manager for the Cheese & Grain, and she running the Komedia in Bath –

> which was an amazing experience but about a 70 hour week, and we were married by then with two kids and wanted to be working together in Frome. So we both quit our jobs. *The Wheatsheaves* had been empty for eight months then, and our friends kept saying, 'You should take it on!' And originally I was like, 'No Way! There's never been an alternative music venue in Frome that's survived.' But we love Frome and arts and music, and our friends kept saying 'I've got some money you can borrow,' so we came and had a look at it, and we thought, You know what? Let's just try.

One of Lark's first steps was to transform the Loft bar with wall decor by Paris, Frome's best-known graffiti artist.[58] Downstairs, there's still an informal pubby atmosphere but the professional rig, sound desk and staging – plus facilities – dressing room and back stage area – have already made 23 Bath Street a hugely popular performance venue.

One name recently leaving the music scene and still much mourned: Griff Daniels brought a special charisma and sense of open opportunity to the town. Griff supported musicians with tireless generosity, and is in a big part responsible for the immensely vibrant music scene we have in Frome today, with live music in pubs and bars throughout the town. He left his own legacy in recordings and is remembered wherever people come together to play.

You'll find other impressive people in the Humans of Frome[59] biographies collected by Ciara Nolan who herself has a strong connection with music.[60] Ciara's column in *Frome Times* introduces readers to people

---

58 Graham 'Paris' Drew, who also did the artwork for Coldplay's Mylo Xyloto album and tour.

59 https://www.facebook.com/Humansoffrome/

60 Ciara worked for EMI for 15 years in the record company and in the studios before leaving London to come to Frome in 2004. She worked with major names like Shirley Bassey, and currently manages the band *Phoria*. 'I do things very independently so I set up my own record label *X Novo*, 'Ciara says, 'I don't really believe in the traditional model of record companies any more.'

we may see around town but not fully appreciate, like busker Ron Tree: 'Ron plays guitar like a demon. When I announced on the Humans of Frome page that this amazingly humble busker is Ron Tree of Hawkwind and now Hawklords fame, half my followers were stunned and the other half delighted he was getting the recognition he so deserves.'

But now the picture is getting like the Sergeant Pepper album cover, swarming with faces who all deserve attention. Like the quest to decide Frome's favourite tree, choice is limitless and everyone reading this will know names I've omitted – colleagues, friends, neighbours, family members – who've contributed to the life of Frome and really should have been given a mention. Tell them next time you see them, and tell them why.

F ROME IS LIKE those Vector illustrations of interconnecting cogs, all on their own trajectory but cooperating wherever they engage. Sport and hobbies is the area where people of all outlooks meet, so this randomly populated section will conclude with a quick look at Frome's options: Basically there's a society for everything[61]: From hatches (Mothers Love Frome) to despatches (Befriending Death Circles) there's online support in Frome – and a welcome as you arrive, too (Frome Newbies). And there are scores of options to join live groups: sports teams, fitness clubs, or weekend amblers. There are groups for people to talk, like Elderventure (inspired by the contrast between attitudes to the old in China compared to here) and Campfire Convention (for 'creating and debating'.) There are societies for makers, performers, architects, writers, readers, food consumers and food providers, bee-keepers, butterfly-counters, otter-hunters and tree-lovers, mens' groups, women's groups and groups for the elderly, to remember together or forget together and simply sing...[62]

As well as cosy knit-&-natter sessions[63] there are high-status guilds too: the Embroiderers Guild has over sixty members, and there's

---

61 There's no definitive directory of the groups and supportive projects in the town, I was told, because it grows and changes constantly – plus the people who make things happen rarely have time spare to keep their information up to date. Movers and shakers are not always note-takers.

62 'Frome Family History Group' and 'Songs for the Memory':

63 Renowned pattern designer Mary Henderson who lives here also teaches knitting

a thriving Guild of Weavers, Spinners & Dyers, one of only two still remaining in the county.[64] We have our own 'University of the Third Age': Frome 3A like the national group is aimed at people in retirement except it's independent (of course) and includes esoteric options like discussing technical advances in robotics.

Sporting options are similarly wide-ranging: from archery to zumba, you can do just about anything[65] not barred by terrain like deep-sea fishing. Football, rugby, and cricket all have grounds in town, and websites with their historical highlights – like an 8,000 crowd at the football ground to watch Frome lose to Leyton Orient in 1954, and the forming of the ladies team in 1980 (they are currently in the SW Premier division). Older locals remember when Frome was one of the major swimming clubs in Somerset, its swimming team West of England Champions and with a polo team too. My own interest is – or was – running[66]: In the boom days of the late '80s scores of us would hit the streets – there's still a popular Half Marathon plus 10k run annually in Frome. The Sports Centre is one hub, and the Bojangles Dance Studio another, but there are classes all over town for dance, yoga, meditation – as my sports consultant for this project summed up, If you're interested in something, there'll be a club for it in Frome. Random heroic endeavours occur too, usually as money-raisers for local causes, like abseiling down the 100-foot tower of St Mary's Church[67] and the cinema-powering bicyclethons for SUSTRANS 'missing links'[68].

---

64  Frome Textile Workshop has seven floor looms, eighteen table looms, and spinning wheels to create your own yarn.

65  Frome has the only Wing Chun kung fu academy in the southwest. So far we haven't got parkour, although a 2009 issue of *Furball,* our sadly-short-lived alternative listing/arts magazine, has an interview with one young enthusiast hoping to start a club. Teddy South, I'm guessing at 24 you've given up on that but I do hope Frome's cobbles, rails, and Grade II listing don't deter the fearless and fit forever.

66  I joined the Frome Running Club when I arrived, and with their encouragement later completed the New Forest Marathon in 4hrs15m – the 12th FV home. However while I was writing this section Eilidh Doyle, who currently lives in Frome, was picking up her 15th championship medal in the Commonwealth Games, winning silver for Scotland in the 400m hurdles in 54.80 seconds. Now that IS impressive...

67  £535 was raised in October 2017 for SOS Africa

68  Just two miles outside Frome town centre lies the start of a virtually traffic free cycle route that takes cyclists and pedestrians to Radstock and then on

A ND WHAT ABOUT the people of tomorrow? Frome seethes with facilities and activities for the developing generation. Play projects, support groups both actual and online, clubs for hobbies like Lego, and every kind of team sport. There are parks, play spaces, craft sessions in shops like Millie Moon, Postscript, and Enigma's pottery studio, art events in Black Swan and drama & dance at Merlin Theatre. Children are integrated into most shared activities except pub lock-ins (dogs have the advantage on them there) including celebrations of customs from lantern-making to withy bending, and it's virtually impossible to go to any event in Frome, with the (presumable) exception of Remembrance Day, without face-painting.

'It's very special like that here, there's something vibrant about the kids, they don't look numb,' was how choreographer and director Mark Bruce put it, which chimed with the comment of a peripatetic music teacher: 'You can tell when a kid's from Frome as soon as they walk in the room – they breed them differently there.'

Young people who know they are valued are able to value themselves. In 2016, a group of Frome College school-leavers took over the Silk Mill and filled it with their paintings, drawings and installations. The 'artists statement' of the *Abnormalists* was pinned on the pillar as you entered:

> Frome does things differently. Undeniably this part of the country is very different to everywhere else in the world. There's a strong focus on Home in this region and in Frome as well. And we want this in our exhibition. Where we've been raised is unlike any other place, due to the amount of freedom there is here. Always respect your roots.
>
> This is about independence. We do things in our own way, every person is an individual. Life right now is changing for everyone, so let's stop, and come together, to praise those who are moving with us.'

---

to Bath. Plans have long been in place to continue this route alongside the existing railway line, onto the riverside footpath and into Frome.

**S**O HOW DID YOU FIND FROME? – some extracts from letters & chronicles:

**1542**   The Towne hath a metly good Market and is set on the Clefe of a Stony Hille.. there be dyvers fayre stone Howses in the Towne that standythe most by Clothinge

– John Leland, Henry VIII's antiquary.

**1724**   The town of Froom, or, as it is written in our maps, Frome Sellwood, is so prodigiously increased within these last Twenty or Thirty years, that they have built a New Church, and so many New Streets of Houses, and those houses are so full of inhabitants, that Frome is now reckoned to have more people in it, than the city of Bath, and some say, than even Salisbury itself, and if their Trade continues to increase for a few years more, as it has done for those past, it is very likely to be one of the greatest and wealthiest Inland Towns in England.

– Daniel Defoe
*Tour Through the Whole Island of Great Britain*

**1754**   Frome is a large town of about 1000 houses prettily situated on the sides of hills over the river, and consists of two or three long streets. It is a great town for the woollen trade of broad cloths .. they are also famous for malt liquor. There are a great number of Dissenters here of all sorts.

– *Travels through England of Dr Richard Pococke,*

**1757**   'It is exceeding strange that any considerable good should be done at poor, dead, quarrelsome Frome.'

– John Wesley in a letter to a fellow preacher

**1790**   This town has been a long time noted for its fine beer, which they keep to a great age, and is generally preferred by the gentry to the wines of France and Portugal. It is the chief town of this part of the country, which was anciently one great forest called Selwoodshire, and in the latter end of the last century, in those called Frome-Woodlands, there was a considerable gang of money coiners or clippers of whom many were taken and executed, and their covert laid open.

*– England's Gazetteer,*
edited Philip Luckombe,

**1801** The town of Frome is situated on the descent and at the foot of a rapid hill, and though full of streets, they are all narrow, incommodious, and irregular. Its population in the year 1798 was estimated at 7,737 who were between 15 and 60 years of age. From the opulence which the woollen trade has thrown into the place, its inhabitants have been enabled to form several generous institutions for the succour of the helpless, and the comfort of the poor; and, perhaps, no place in England, of a similar size, affords so many instances of benevolence applied in this laudable manner.

*– Rev Richard Warner*
*Excursions from Bath*

**1806** There are very few persons here in whom I feel any particular interest. ...I should nauseate the place if I had habituated to it a century. I felt an intense loathing, I hated every house, timber, stone, and brick in the town and almost the very trees, fields and flowers in the country around.

*– John Foster, essayist & reluctant minister*
at Sheppards Barton 1804-1806.

**1817** June 28 Peace proclaimed at Frome. The grandest procession that ever took place in the Town was presented to the Inhabitants. ....There was an immense number of strangers and the day was remarkably fine, and here would be a glorious ending if I could stop here, but the lower classes of people got very drunk in the evening and then began to quarrel and fight. I always find mild treatment at such times best. Some think different and tell me I am too mild.

*– Isaac Gregory,*
Constable of Frome in his *Journals*

**1822**    The situation of Frome is extremely pleasant, the surrounding countryside being agreeably diversified with hills, valleys, large enclosures and fine woods... The lower part of the town has lately gone through very great improvements; the mean and tottering buildings which surround the market place have been removed, and on their site, handsome and lofty houses erected which together with the new market-house, the assembly room, and the fine opening into Bath-street, cannot fail to interest the traveller and to reflect honour on the taste and spirit of the inhabitants...not fewer than 1500 children are educated here in sundry schools... there are also three very good inns, the George, the Crown, and a newly established house called the Wheat Sheaves which is very elegantly fitted up...

– from Pigot's *London and Provincial Directory*

**1830**    I was, I must confess, glad to find proofs of the irretrievable decay of the place....Their poor work-people cannot be worse off than they long have been.

I found the working people at Frome very intelligent; very well informed as to the cause of their misery; not at all humbugged by the canters, whether about religion or loyalty. I sent my post-chaise boy to tell one or two of the weavers to come to me at the inn. The landlord did not at first like to let such ragged fellows up stairs. I insisted, and I had a long talk with them. They had much clearer views of what is likely to happen than the pretty gentlemen of Whitehall seem to have... However, all salutary and humane law really seems to be drawing towards an end in this now miserable country, where the thousands are caused to wallow in luxury, to be surfeited with food and drink, while the millions are continually on the point of famishing ...there must be a change, there must be a complete and radical change; or England must become a country of the basest slavery that ever disgraced the earth.

– *William Cobbett*
*Rural Rides*

**1839**    I could not help observing the squalid appearance of many of the men and women: their care-worn faces bore sad evidence of toil and starvation. Surely, I thought, there must be something wrong in government and society to make hardworking people so destitute and wretched. I was shocked to hear of the misery of the people — some of them earning no more than four or five shillings per week. How they exist I cannot conceive. If a speedy stop be not put to the present system, a dreadful commotion must take place

– Henry Vincent
*Life and Rambles*

**1848**   The town is pleasantly situated on the north-east declivity of a hill, and consists of a great number of streets, for the most part irregularly built, and some of them inconveniently narrow, but tolerably clean. The buildings in general are constructed of small rough stone, and roofed with stone dug in the neighbourhood; the inhabitants are well supplied with water, and the town has a commodious market-house. Over the Frome, which abounds with excellent trout and eels, is a neat stone bridge of five arches.

Frome has long been celebrated for its woollen manufacture, of which the principal articles are broadcloths and kerseymeres of very superior quality; the manufacture of wool-cards is also carried on to a large extent, and formerly they were supplied from this place to almost every town in England. The beer brewed here is in high repute, and is usually kept to a great age.

– *A Topographical Dictionary of England*,
published by S Lewis, London

**1852**   Frome is a dull dirty looking place full of Plumbers, one could fancy the Bennet controversy must have been a godsend to it – The Inn and Town were so disagreeable that I went back presently to the station preferring to wait there. . .

– Jane Welsh Carlyle,
*letter to Thomas Carlyle*

**1894**   From Shepton Mallet I proceeded to Frome hoping, rather against hope I must confess, that I should find some subjects there of interest. But I was doomed to be disappointed.... pictorially the place is a blank.

– C R B Barrett,
*Highways Byways and Waterways*

**1919**   A visitor would not call the town beautiful; the older streets are steep, narrow, and crooked, and much of the small property has a dilapidated appearance; on the outskirts there are many well-built modern houses. If in search of beauty you need not go very far – The residence of the Marquess of Bath is admitted to be the finest Elizabethan mansion in England. It is now used for the benefit of our wounded soldiers, every possible comfort and recreation being provided.

– Rev W Brass
*The Christian Messenger*

**2016**   Frome is not a constant free festival nor hippy commune but an organised community acting upon issues, often against conformity, to create a distinctiveness and liberal attitude which makes Brighton look like North Korea. Oh, blast that funky freewheeling Frome. . .

– Darren Warrow
*No Surprises Living In Devizes*

*path to Vallis Vale*

# 2   LAND AND ORIGINS

*– geology shapes history – scratching the surface –*
*– stones, water, trees –  Green Frome – spaces & places –*
*– wild life & telling the bees – Case Study: the farmer –*

'The town is an accumulation of three parts which, in sum, are greater than
the sections. The town is the people who live there, the buildings which they
have erected, and it is the land'

*– Stephen King.*

THERE'S SOMETHING ELEMENTAL about Frome. It was never a
fortress, nor had any castle to defend with permanent armies.
There's no significant battleground, no mythical swords in our stones,
nor did marching legions encamp in the place we now call home. The first
specific settlement, as far as we know, was in Saxon times, and this was
not a military base but a mission station. Perhaps, with none of these
trace memories, the town that grew has always essentially belonged to
the 'ordinary' people who live here.

Long before the official chronicle begins, since the thawing of
the ice age, there was only one place to cross the marshes, and it was
here. Frome rests on Oolitic limestone,[1] which has created the spring
that feeds the town and also gives us the stone that built it. The hard
surrounding rocks have a gap between them only about six miles wide
suitable as a passing place from the western side to Salisbury Plain.
The 'Selwood Gap' – as this has become called – is the route prehistoric
people would have taken, fording the marshes at the natural crossing
point.

Frome's own geologist Eunice Overend has written about the cats-
cradle of streams and the coincidences of rock convergence which created
a place where six or seven tracks could later meet at a passable point, in

---

1   About 140 million years ago, this area was under shallow water where corals,
shells and other marine life left their calcium carbonate skeletal debris, over
time compressed by succeeding layers into Oolitic limestone.

the area we now call Spring Gardens. 'The present pattern of roads is a product both of geology, which provides marshes and steep slopes to be avoided, fords to use and ridges to be followed, and of human necessity,' Eunice summarises, 'Like badger-paths in the long grass, they are histograms of use. The more the traffic, the more distinct the track.[2]

Eunice's badgers, and the people who used these routes, were following 'lines of desire' – paths grooved as chosen passages over the land which inevitably shape the future. Frome grew simply as the logical crossing point for anyone travelling this marshy terrain.

Eunice's observations connect with a more contentious study so there's a small digression here: Leylines, because to those with interest and belief, Frome is riddled with them. Catherine Hill in particular has been identified frequently, sometimes by enthusiasts with divining rods, as carrying a leyline all the way from Glastonbury Tor to Cley Hill. The leyline theory is that sites of ancient importance align and are connected, but it's not clear whether by early man-made routes or by lines of invisible power which track across the countryside indifferent to human movement. According to this idea the most important of these in England is the St Michael line of traditional dragon sites which follows an intriguing trajectory from the island monastery off the coast of Cornwall to the shrine at Bury St Edmunds, taking in Burrowbridge Mump, Glastonbury, an iron hill fort, and Avebury stone circle en route. If you track the section between Burrowbridge and Avebury, you will see it goes pretty well right through Frome.[3]

So which is supposed to have come first, the magical energy or the land itself? Man-made divisions and boundaries have overlain nature, but it's often struck me that Frome is so close to Cley Hill that if it were not for the artificial concept of a county border, this powerful ancient landmark would be considered part of our town's heritage – after all,

---

2   The tracks recorded by Eunice probably connected neolithic sites at Fromefield and Murtry, and were used throughout the bronze and iron ages.

3   Ley lines were seen as 'arteries' of the earth, 'veins' of energy flow, and equivalent to chi (qi) pathways of the body used in acupuncture . Whatever your view of these mysterious, unproven, invisible lines of connection that allegedly criss-cross the countryside, the notion does still seem to have an appeal today.

Longleat claims connection through family rights.[4] Frome folk seem
to have a natural affinity with this strange mound inhabited mainly by
sheep, rabbits, and wild flowers: it's a favourite place for hand-fasting,
midsummer parties, solstice fires, New Year walks, May-day celebrations
and Druid rituals...

Back to the early land, and not before time you may say. The geology
that shaped our history can be identified in terms of layering sediments,
apart from one anomaly, and that one anomaly is massively important
worldwide. It's called the De La Beche Unconformity and it's a magnet
for geologists because this extraordinary rock formation, in Vallis Vale,
evidences a time gap in layering between the early Carboniferous and
later Jurassic which should not exist. But, this being Frome, it does
here.[5]

Centuries pass, ice ages come and and go, and eventually people
move around this land. The first tribes would have been foragers, hunter-
gatherers travelling in small bands collecting and eating mushrooms,
leaves, berries, nuts – anything in season – and small animals. Research
suggests that their intelligence was more developed and their brain size
larger than ours,[6] certainly they would have had more resilience, and
more freedom, than their descendants the rural peasants and urban
poor. They were probably animists, but archaeology can't show their
beliefs. We can be fairly sure though that much of the trade in prehistoric
times was by barter at tribal boundaries, so the wetland below the bridge
arches we regularly travel now would have been crossed since the ice age.

---

4   In 1536 the dissolution of the monasteries provided a bun-fight of a land
    grab after which the Thynne family 'owned' the entire stretch of land that is
    now preserved as the Longleat estate. Other beneficiaries were the Horners
    who got Mells (a 'plum' estate, as in the nursery rhyme), the Champneys who
    took Orchardleigh, the Hungerfords (*Time Trieth Troth* on the Frome blazon
    was their motto) and the Earls of Cork and Orrery who took the Marston
    estate.
5   It's on the far side of the river from the path, but accessible, and its
    significance was explained to me by geologist Simon Carpenter: 'The normal
    deposit pattern is in succession, oldest at the bottom, youngest on top, but
    here the carboniferous rocks have turned at an angle so there's been erosion
    and then at a much later date other rocks came, so there's a period of earth's
    history missing.' About a hundred million years, apparently.
6   *Sapiens* – Yuval Noah Harari : part 1 – 3, footnote 5

When groups begin to settle, they choose a place with fresh water, land to grow food, woods to forage, and usually some high places, for rituals and burials. While there are no stone circles near Frome, there are quite a few sarsens – blocks of quartzite of the type that built Stonehenge – which must have been dragged here over some distance for a purpose not clear.[7] Several burial mounds are allegedly visible quite close to Frome although not on Ordnance Survey maps, and there's a Long Barrow at the top of North Parade, all suggesting prehistoric settlement.

For a long time the area where our town developed was too densely wooded for habitation – even the Romans' nearest road passed on the eastern side. Early Britons called it Coit Maur' (Great Wood) and avoided it, but the Saxons who battled their way here were less deterred, presumably being more used to inhospitable forests. By the time William the Conqueror grabbed Selwood for recreational hunting, it would have been largely reduced to an area of coppice and grassland – the term 'forest' being Kingly shorthand for 'Keep off My Land'.

Very little is actually known about the first people who lived here. After the 43AD invasions, Britons became slowly culturally Romanised until around 400 years later when all troops withdrew to defend other parts of their empire, leaving Britain to the Anglo-Saxons till 1066. They established Wessex as one of four kingdoms but as historian David Craig points out 'Many who lived in Selwood and the Mendips owed no allegiance to anyone and would scarcely be aware that the Romans had arrived, let alone departed. There are some parts of the Mendips which feel that way today.' So during the early development of the town, for most people the only relevant aspect of ownership would be land they had chosen to live on.[8]

---

7   One can be seen outside the Lamb and Fountain, and another in the Dissenters' Cemetery.
8   The problems came much later, with the breakdown of the moral economy in the 18th Century when enforced enclosures took the peasants' strips from them, culminating shockingly in the 1801 General Enclosure Act allowing the landowners in any village to enclose all its land if three-quarters of them agreed – which is a bit like asking foxes if they fancied chicken for supper. Hundreds of tenants suddenly lost their common rights and many who resorted to poaching were arrested and sent to the colonies to service the new sugar-plantation industry that would bring further wealth to the merchants.

After slow clearance the land would be looking more like it does now, and the ford was first bridged in Saxon times. Additions were piecemeal but by Regency days it was the fine edifice we see today, supporting two-storey buildings, making Frome one of only three in the country (the others are Bath and Lincoln) that can still boast thriving shops and businesses on their town bridge.

And, as stone-mason and author Andrew Ziminski showed me, the amazing history of Frome's origins is free for anyone to see – if they put on long wellies, ensure the river is low, then slither down the bank along the Saxonvale side. With the Blue House ahead, slush your way down-river towards the heart of Frome. Here, as you wade past the Blue Boar, the oldest pub in town, you're walking where people have crossed for thousands of years. 'This fording point is why we're all here,' says Andrew as we shuffle in the mulch near an otter's holt (they come to hunt crayfish) – 'this was the most fordable point. It's canalised today, but in medieval days it spread out as a broad marsh from the Blue House across to where W H Smiths is, and across to Button Bridge. This is the hub where the town spawned.'

The water as we proceed becomes dark and deep. An iron railing preventing further crossing was inserted, Andrew says, a few years ago after an escaping shoplifter darted under the bridge and got stuck in a tight exit. He had to be rescued and treated for hypothermia. 'Came out like a cork from a bottle,' says Andrew cheerily.

Our underbelly exploration reveals striking timezone shifts as Georgian construction takes over from medieval, then with Victorian additions – you can even see the distinctive adzed stones of Saxon building. There are possible Roman traces too, as although there was no Roman bridge there may have been a Roman ford there.

The Domesday Book of 1086 shows a market already established, so a bridge of some sort (a wooden one of two spans was recorded in 1380) would have been in regular use for two centuries by the time self-styled 'antiquarius' John Leland visited 'Frome Celwood in Somersetshire' in 1544 and admired its five-span stone bridge.[9]

---

9   His 'Itinerary' records: 'In the botom of the towne rennithe From ryver levinge the towne on the lyfte rype, and there is a stone bridge of fyve arches, and a myle by it where by cummythe an armelet thorowghe a bridge of 2. arches. Ther cummithe one arme downe from Mayden Bradley v. myles

Wading beneath the bridge's arches you can also glimpse the 'mysterious' Frome tunnels, which require a short digression because they're probably not very mysterious. Once again, the answer lies in geology. The layers of clay in our local soil hold water, which bursts out wherever limestone hits a clay seam, powering mills and turbines, pouring down Cheap Street, filling garden wells and bursting out in countless cellars – the *Lamb and Fountain* has a maltings and an ice house in theirs. Again, over to Andrew:

> Frome is full of holes. The stone around here is really easy to get out, just get a crowbar and lever it out. They'd dig a basement – no need to quarry it, the stone was all broken up in the last ice age – then use the stone taken out to build the house. Basements were often knocked into each other for shared storage as a flying underground freehold is common, and then they make tunnels.[10]

But with woods nearby offering ready material, Frome's earliest buildings, apart from the church, are timber-based/framed and covered with lath and plaster.[11] Later build used the local stone, Forest Marble,[12]

---

of, and an othar from Hindon, and mete aboute a myle above the towne of From.'

10 The idea of an ancient maze continues to fascinate, however, and the tradition of Medieval morality plays inspired an amazing drama devised by Bo Bowman-Shaw and produced by Andrew Shackleton for the Frome Festival in 2013. 'Tales of the Tunnels' blended social & environmental history with pagan deities, with music and dramatic visuals. For added impact the audience was transported under the vaults by boat, but the producer himself says 'They're not really tunnels, are they, they're just holes in the ground – It's like Frome's Loch Ness Monster, this mythical thing that you get glimpses of but there's nothing really ... tangible.'

11 Wood remained easy to access for some time but the royal land-grab meant permission was required to hunt and even collect firewood, as well as to fell timber – and local lords were gradually acquiring it. By the end of the seventeenth century most of what was left was claimed by the Thynne family as the Longleat estate.

12 Forest Marble, actually Jurassic limestone, was so named in 1799 by William 'Strata' Smith, the first geological mapmaker of England who used the name of a quarry in Wychwood Forest in the Cotswolds where he found a 'pretty stone much in used in the villages of Somerset, Dorset, Gloucestershire,

which has the same pallor as the stone from Bath and Doulting that
created some of Frome's Georgian buildings, evoking the grandeur of
that genteel city, always aesthetically more highly-regarded. Victorian
homes had floors made of elm or blue lias, a kind of limestone – or as a
cheaper alternative, 'delves' dug up locally (just past the Mason's Arms),
stones with rippled surface caused by their formation under water.
Roofing often used pantiles, the red clay tiles that give the townscape in
some areas a Tuscan look.

More important than stone or wood in making and shaping the
original town was water. The 'sacred spring' from which water constantly
flows is almost certainly the reason a settlement developed here rather
than at the crossing point of known tracks – this would have been the
earliest object of reverence. There's a massive mythology, not to say
spiritual industry now, around the Chalice Well in Glastonbury, but no
reason to assume Frome's 'sacred spring' was not similarly revered in
pagan times.[13] The watercourse which flows down Cheap Street is only
one of a cats-cradle of culverts around the town, from medieval days
onward.[14] I'm much indebted to Colin Alsbury for showing me an 1812
plan of existing watercourses and projected additions when Bath Street
was built, and for explaining

--------

Oxfordshire, Northamptonshire, the Cotswolds and Wiltshire.' Smith never
came to Frome but is associated with High Littleton, about 12 miles away,
which excited him so much that he called it 'the birthplace of geology'.

13  The spring as we see it today is a consequence of the activities of the
energetic Vicar Bennett, relocated in Frome in the 1850s after banishment
from Pimlico for his 'Romish' predilections, who set about rebuilding St
Johns and restructuring the surrounding terrain. As well as demolishing
a row of buildings to insert the contentious Via Dolorosa, he adorned the
ancient spring with a lion's head and a Gothic arched canopy inscribed 'O ye
wells, bless ye the lord'. Incidentally the churchyard had previously caused
problems: in 1799 the retaining wall 'fell out, rolling forth numbers of dead
bodies,' and Bennett's alterations resulted in the loss of the wall originally
above Twattle Alley, which was eliminated, along with the folly and the first
blind house, so that the present wall actually rises up above the churchyard.
Hence the buttresses, originally intended to face the other way.

14  Other towns call them drains, but in Frome it's a leat. 'Cepe' was an old
English word for trade – this area of town has been trading since 1500 at
least.

When Cheap Street was built, this route from the spring line to the
well was cut and would originally have run behind Three Swans down
to the river, that was its natural course. The plan shows that when
they cut the 'new road' – Bath Street – they added new water courses
and diverted one along Palmer Street where there was another
spring, that's the one the YMCA Routes had trouble with. There are
so many springs and streams – we found another well-shaft in St
John's school playground, underneath the tarmac. If you look at an
aerial map of the town, you can see it's almost as though the roads
follow the spring lines – if you built along that line, you've got water!

You could almost say Frome rose from water like Atlantis in
reverse, and there's more about how water shaped the town in the
next section when the town began to turn things around and shape
the water. For hundreds of years floods were common: even as recently
as 1978 a rowing boat was called in to ferry people across the market
place. Old postcards feature flooded streets and reports of deluges were
commonplace: sometimes with a serious side. In 1932 four boys drowned
when the old stone bridge where they were playing collapsed into the
river while it was raging.[15] To quote lifetime resident Tony Bennett, we're
floating on water.

Frome is on an artesian well – it's riddled with wells all the way
through. Wells are part of the fabric of Frome. I remember in the

---

15 The boys, one of whom was celebrating his ninth birthday that day, were
watching the flood from the bridge, which had once been part of the
watermill, when the force of the water battered it into a sudden final
collapse. The river had risen eight feet in two hours after heavy rain, and
become what the local reporter described as a 'roaring cataract, swirling and
lashing itself into a frenzy of foam.' Five boys were swept away instantly,
their friends managing to grab and save only one, 11-year-old Dennis Moore.
PC Harold Olpin was nearly a victim too: as soon as he heard the alarm he
dived in fully dressed in a heroic but futile rescue effort, and was instantly
swept along with them into the dark tunnel below the houses. He was saved
by his cape, which caught on a branch on the bank, and was pulled to safety.
It wasn't until the next morning that the boys' bodies were found, down by
Welsh Mill. PC Olpin was awarded the King's Police Medal for bravery, and
the whole town turned out for the funeral of the four boys.

'60s, watching when they were raising the height of Christchurch Street West a few inches – the part below Wesley Slope – and the concrete mixer suddenly slipped down a well they didn't know was there. In the middle of the road one minute, next minute it disappeared.

Virtually every building had its own well, but most of them are covered over now – even, sadly, in pubs which used to feature them. There's a happy exception in Catherine Street, in the premises currently occupied by Bonbon Chic,[16] where the well is in the shop under a glass cover and you can see deep down the shaft to the water below – the stream flowing constantly beneath the hill.

The Wallbridge area, being beside the river, was particularly affected by flooding and when Asda promised to control the flood plain if allowed occupancy, the offer was accepted despite local scepticism. The supermarket chain had predictable difficulty in controlling natural elements but one condition of their arrival in 2004 was successfully achieved – the establishment of a dedicated nature reserve.

Glimpsed from the A362, the untidy alders around a quiet lake may look unimpressive, but this slightly sodden space is home to thousands of plants and insects – including very rare ones – with over a hundred different birds, again including rarities. The less specialist walker will notice swans, cormorants, and herons (evidence of good water as they prey on fish and small water mammals) and also nesting tits – great, blue, coal, long tailed – through peep-holes in withy screens. There are masses of wild flowers, including a 'local novelty' – the rare *corky fruited water dropwort,* one of the umbellifer family, but tiny not like cow-parsley or hogweed, which also grow in abundance here[17].

This richly abundant wildlife resource, accessed by the kissing-gate just beyond Asda's petrol station, is entirely managed by a team of

---

16 This iconic shop, on the corner of Catherine Hill and Paul Street, is locally known as The Wedge and has had various incarnations throughout its history, including a book shop.

17 So too does the *hemlock water dropwort,* which is even more deadly than its cousin the hemlock. The informative Wild Food online site notes in the 'Medical Use' category of its catalogue: 'Being the most poisonous plant in the UK, this is not used for medicinal purposes.'

volunteers: Frome Area Wildlife Group, local enthusiasts who took the
initiative at the start of Asda's occupancy to approach the supermarket
with a plan. Founding member Mick Ridgard gave me the potted history:

> I would see a lot of seagulls on my morning walk to get the paper, but
> one day a rare bird arrived – a Bonaparte's gull. People were coming
> from all over the country to watch it, and we thought, what's going to
> happen with this area? We formed a committee and got in touch with
> Asda, and they said they were looking for somebody to manage it. We
> got together a five-year plan of what we reckoned needed doing to
> the reserve, and we've been doing it ever since.

It's clearly a labour of love for the little group, and they've had
to make difficult decisions to maintain the integrity of the site. One
is to close it to visitors during the breeding season, which extends
from February till August. But a look at the roll-call of visitors on their
website[18] suggests that this trade-off is invaluable. Rodden Reserve
is now a Somerset Wildlife Trust 'Local Wildlife Site'[19] and a County
Wildlife Site.

> We've had about 140 different species of visiting birds. We have a
> chap to do a check on insects, he goes around with his net, swooping
> and catching, and he's found a lot of rare ones, beetles and bugs and
> butterflies – he'll find things you wouldn't notice.

A short insect-inspired digression from wet to dry land here: Frome
has an active Beekeepers Association with around sixty members, most
with a minimum of three hives, some with more than twenty. Bees are
massively prolific and queens lay up to 2,000 eggs a day in summer, but
as bees work themselves to death in two months they need that many

---

18  https://www.roddennaturereserve.org.uk/
19  No mere formality, this: According to the Wildlife Trust, 'Local Wildlife
    Sites are selected locally using robust, scientifically-determined criteria
    and detailed ecological surveys. As a result, these special and often secret
    spaces have a huge part to play in the natural green fabric of our towns
    and countryside. They make up a web of stepping stones and corridors for
    wildlife, forming key components of ecological networks.'

to keep the colony strong. 'They are completely expendable,' bee-keeper John Plaxton explained, consolingly, 'They're like little Exocets. It's a super-organism, basically, not an individual. The colony is a single animal, in a way, and all they care about is the colony.' Nevertheless, that's about 1,200,000 bees sharing the summer with us in Frome.[20] Hive-owners have a rapport with their bees that goes way beyond the honey-stealing, with an age-old tradition of introducing themselves to the bees, never shouting at them, and telling your bees of marriages, new births, and – especially – deaths.

BACK TO THE LAND, where it seems unlikely that Frome's water will ever be fully tamed. Wood has been easier to vanquish: throughout the centuries its trees have been felled in their thousands to make space for buildings, transport routes, and sometimes merely to 'landscape' gardens of the wealthy. Trees have always been significant in Frome's history, to create and furnish homes, provide tools and weaponry – and even to affirm the identity of the town itself: sallows – broad-leafed willow trees – are on the coat of arms adopted by Frome, and birch branches were traditionally used to 'beat the bounds', so everyone in the community knew where their boundaries ended. This not only prevented land disputes, it established responsibilities for paying tithes and distributing poor relief.[21] But from an area once densely forested and stretching for about sixty miles,[22] Selwood forest is now reduced to about

---

20  People are of course a massively-minority life form in the town, as in all healthy towns. Apart from the plethora of pets, from spiders and snakes to pre-loved ponies, the insects, birds, water-living creatures and wild mammals living in and around Frome here in every category far outnumber the 27,000 humans. We've got riverbank rats, cordial cats and brown-eared bats. We've got quite a lot of frogs, hedgehogs and obviously dogs, which in Frome have the status of a hindu deity in Agra.

21  St Johns in Frome is the only church in the country to maintain the tradition of decorating the aisles with birch branches at Pentecost, an ancient spring fertility rite from Saxon times. The vicar has suggested the rustling leaves perhaps sounded like the whispering of the Holy Spirit to the disciples but the custom predates Christianity and has pagan origins.

22  At its greatest extent, from the head waters of the Thames (near modern Cricklade) to the borders of modern Dorset. The forest was also home to many so-called 'outlaws', avoiding payment of taxes they saw as giving

two miles by one, and Frome, on the fringes of the still thickly-wooded
Longleat estate and with ancient Vallis Vale unfelled, is aware how
fortunate it is to have this proximity.

'Reviving Selwood' – or at least keeping a passion for trees alive – is
the mission of our renowned dendrologist Julian 'Bugsy' Hight, who has
travelled the world researching and writing about trees and is always
ready to step in when the town's most precious ones are threatened.
'England has less trees than most of northern Europe' Bugsy says,

> but they can grow very old – oaks can live a thousand years and
> they're hot-spots of biodiversity, homes for kinds of ecosystems, not
> only birds, bats and barn owls: an ancient oak supports hundreds of
> life forms – lichens, mosses, fungi, and certain beetles only live in
> decaying wood of oak trees – so we need to preserve them.

The plane tree in King Street was the first test. When an application
to fell appeared on this still healthy old[23] tree in 2013, Bugsy started a
petition to save it. 'Within a week 3,000 people had signed – that's 10%
of the population!' Mendip supported the protest and now, although
heavily pollarded, the tree is still there. 'Like Tony Benn said, you can
make a difference from the grass roots,' says Bugsy – 'but we weren't so
lucky with the copper beech in the churchyard, which was decaying and it
was right by Blind House Lane so in the council's view it could just fall on
someone's head. You win some you lose some.' The old beech was yarn-
bombed for an arboreal wake before in 2017 being reduced to an oddly-
shaped stump but still supporting wildlife – worms, insects and fungi,
lichens and mosses.[24]

---

nothing in return.

23 It helps if you have the knowledge to destroy the developer's case: the
claim was made that this tree was planted only 40 years before, and Julian
produced evidence that 'a conservative estimate for the age of the tree at
Kingsway must be close to a century old.'

24 The jury was still out when I wrote this as to whether another of Frome's
iconic trees would go too: the big sycamore on the Millennium Green lost a
limb in winter storms, and its wounded trunk revealed severe fungi so felling
might be unavoidable. It's recorded as an 'ancient tree' by the Woodland
Trust and as Frome Town Council is a member of the Woodland Trust Tree
Charter, we have to hope it will be saved.

In part due to Bugsy,[25] many people in Frome are enthusiastic about trees now and there's an annual competition to decide the town's favourite – it's currently the massive 'stoical and beautiful' Cedar of Lebanon on Bath Street, planted in 1843 by Thomas Bunn.[26] There are plenty of lovely non-ancient trees around too: Victoria Park has some splendid ones, including a Judas Tree whose lipstick-pink blossom bursts directly from the rugged bark in late spring each year.

> 'If trees are not our teachers, we are at least their pupils. They have given us shelter, medicine, shade, food and fuel. It is a mere two hundred and fifty years since wood was superseded by iron as the fundamental material on which the great human experiment was founded and for almost all of our cultural history trees and woods have played the role of provider and teacher.'

– Max Adams

UNTIL FAIRLY RECENTLY, fields remained a visible aspect of the town – the first Wesleyans preached under trees behind *The Packhorse* and there were other open areas for those physical sports and popular diversions so deplored by the Methodists. One noted preacher, the Reverend Griffiths, left us a vivid example: 'In the month of May 1810, hearing that a stage was going to be erected for single-stick playing at the Butts,[27] one of the suburbs of Frome and characterised by the

---

25  Frome's current arboreal champion has also identified our local heroes on the *Woodland Trust Ancient Tree Inventory*, There is in addition his facebook site *Revive Selwood Forest* to locate and promote ancient trees, and Bugsy is on a mission to re-foliate the area by 'guerilla-planting' open land with heritage oaks grown from acorns from the original trees.

26  The prolific diarist recorded apprehensively 'I have planted numerous cedars of Lebanon which have been destroyed chiefly by idle boys plucking off the leading shoot. One alone prospered and was become so large that I thought it was safe. Today I observed that this beautiful tree was despoiled of several of its spreading branches – my mortifications are so numerous that I will not attempt to recount them.' Despite his fears, the tree survived better than his grandiose plans to reshape Frome to rival Bath's Royal Crescent.

27  The Butts' may have been originally a field for archery practice, with 'butts' or mounds of earth as targets. A medieval law required all Englishmen between the age of 15 to 60 years old to equip themselves with a bow and

name of Hell-corner, I was induced to call the inhabitants together and freely give them my sentiments in a sermon on the subject.' (There will be more from the preachers of Frome in a later section. At one time they were as prolific in Frome as mindfulness teachers are now.)

Frome's medieval past is most evident on the south side, where the ancient 'great fields' can still be seen, shared spaces where men would all work together for the community. They used the old ' three field' system, allowing one in three to lie fallow each year to recover. Surviving examples are a rarity, as most were enclosed in the 18th Century, but the Mount estate is built on one of these, and the fields beyond, leading down to Longleat forest, are rare open fields too: medieval history, still vividly present in modern Frome.

Enclosure of common land has been a struggle throughout history, and was part of the growing divide between the owners and the owned. The 'Black Death' scythed the population by about 60%, thereby massively reducing the number of serfs available to work for lords who owned the land,[28] so after 1348 men could barter for 'strips' from the lord, and also charge for their labour. The elite retaliated immediately by legislation, and the 1349 Ordinance of Labourers barred peasants from moving around in order to stop them seeking areas of shortage to ask for higher wages.[29] Discontent at the growing imbalance of wealth, and

---

arrows, to act as an army if the king needed one. In 1363 a further law required them to carry out two hours of longbow practice every week, supervised by the local clergy. Interestingly, this law still appears to be valid to this day. 'Single-sticks', also known as cudgels, were a popular free entertainment and form of street play.

28 Ironically, these 'owners' of the land had acquired it from 'owners' who had simply claimed it. Our entire system of heritage and ownership simply means some people's forefathers appropriated other people's forefathers' plots of land. 'The first man who, having enclosed a piece of ground, bethought himself of saying "This is mine" was the real founder of civil society. From how many crimes, wars and murders, horrors and misfortunes might not someone have saved mankind by pulling up the stakes and crying to his fellows, "Beware of listening to this impostor; you are undone if you once forget that the fruits of the earth belong to us all, and the earth itself to nobody."' ~Jean Jacques Rousseau, *A Discourse on the Origin of Inequality*

29 At that time skilled manpower was in such short supply that the Act failed, and some of the previous peasant class did manage to make themselves yeomen farmers, but they were never accepted by the 'gentry'.

resentment at ownership by others, often *in absentia*, of the land they lived on, understandably never really went away: though not identified with specific uprisings like the Peasants' Revolt,[30] the history of Frome as elsewhere shows a social profile of haves- and have-nots, morphing into a divide that peaked in the Victorian era – about which more later.

Sizeable spaces now are limited and need to be maintained safely, but we're lucky to have Rodden Meadow and the Dippy. Within the town and quite close to the centre, we also still have about six acres of fields which were used until 2002 by the Cheese Show before it moved to East Woodlands.[31] The Town Council has responsibility for parks, aiming to please most of the people most of the time[32], and with the patrolling 'park-keepers' now replaced by a team of energetic young 'Rangers'.

---

30 After the Black Death, there was a shift in perspective among the serfs. Many challenged their status, demanding that all men should be free and equal, and campaigning for less harsh laws and a fairer distribution of wealth. In 1381 a group marched on London, and the king, Richard II – then aged 14 – agreed to meet their leader Wat Tyler. The Lord Mayor of London promptly killed Tyler, but the young king calmed the rebels by promising to abolish serfdom. They agreed to disperse. Perhaps Richard meant what he said, but he was still a boy: the lords and bishops who controlled the court sent troops after the returning men and most were hanged.

31 The Agricultural Society who run the Cheese Show had leased this land from Mendip who sold a section for the new hospital and Medical Centre. The remainder was acquired by the Town Council.

32 'We have to manage strategically' Chris Stringer said of his Environment role: 'If you design a park for young children, that might be at odds with dog walkers. With an area like the skate-park – graffiti and skating have gone hand in hand for so long – why resist it? Why not actually embrace it instead?' Compromise was reached on the dog issue when pro-dog protesters won continuing freedom of Victoria Park while pro-less-poo-on-our-toddlers protesters gained gated safety around the adjoining Mary Bailey Playing Fields. About the street art, I feel Frome could do better – we need more of it, and to accept the kind of expressive energy in which this form excels, rather than expect easy-viewing decor. It's a transient medium perfect for experimentation, and there are masses of unloved and undervalued walls around. Several notable graffiti artists have contributed terrific pieces both publicly and in the disused industrial site of Saxonvale – a glorious Hall of Fame for years, with Bristol veterans like Mutartis inspiring the next generation.

Frome's 'green' status is watched keenly by local conservation groups:[33] FROGS, the volunteer organisation referenced in the previous section, aims to ensure that the town continues to have non-specific open spaces: as spokeswoman Sheila Hedges says, 'You need a big area – just there, as a space to enjoy, to do what you want – sit, picnic, fly a kite – just breathe.' Natural open spaces are not only there for children to develop limb strength and dogs to run off leads, important as those are, but for us all to change pace and find a shift in perspective – Friedrich Nietzsche insisted all truly great thoughts are conceived by walking.

FROGS also engages in specific projects: Frome's pump track is one of their success stories, installed at Welshmill park[34] and opened in a carnival atmosphere in 2012. Sadly perhaps from a purist perspective, but happily for the many younger children who use it, the track had to be tarmacked as wheels on scooters and skateboards were digging ruts and making it unsafe. But the positive spin-off is more than skill and physical prowess as older children not only role-model how to use the track safely but also look out for the littlies, who watch their wheelies with awe, building social confidence and reducing the likelihood of bullying.

FROGS' current project is the Otherside, the previously undeveloped pathway along the west side of the river, now fully passable with a ramp and a round house, and raised beds of wild flowers and herbs.[35] On the other side to Otherside, the traditional river path from the Market Yard to Welshmill has a seat and four way-markers carved (incredibly, considering their intricacy) with little creatures by wood artist Anthony Rogers, using children's designs. Forty-two tiny lights visible only after dusk now illuminate the path so you can walk it even on the darkest night – I've often done so: with nothing else visible and the

---

33 New build encroachment worries many as houses are arriving, to quote from *Hamlet* – not in single spies but in battalions. There's a new estate overlooking Rodden and another above the Millennium Green, and an application to build on the medieval fields is currently shaking the *Keep Frome Local* group.

34 after fundraising nearly £50,000.

35 The Town Council, *Friends of the River Frome* and *Edventure* combined with FROGS on this community project with Incredible Edible and the Apothecary Garden. The Roundhouse garden is on raised beds because this used to be a rubbish site for Singers and the ground is designated low-level polluted.

sound of the weir so near, you feel like you're walking into a fairy tale...

Another significant environmental group is SOS (Save Open Spaces) Frome, a group which invested not only time but money: in 2015 when Whatcombe Fields were threatened by development, as their website explains: 'A group of 282 shareholders now jointly own this beautiful 34 acre stretch of fields and are very keen that the public continue to enjoy them as a community space.' [36]

So despite our famous heritage of stony streets and buildings, Frome is not as urban-minded as you might think. Frome's youngsters have an access to wildlife rare for town children: schoolchildren at Vallis reported seeing badgers, foxes, and otters as well as the bats that roost under the bridges and flutter down the river at dusk.[37] The river is reckoned one of the best in the country for diversity and fish stock – here, too, volunteer protectors have stepped in: *Friends of the Somerset River Frome* (FoRF) aim 'to see the river function as a corridor for wildlife, an urban open space and a recreational area.'

As well as the extensive greensward of Whatcombe Fields and the old Showground area to ramble, there are small and special spaces in the heart of the town only a few minutes walk away from the busy main road. One is the Millennium Green[38] with its long views and extracts from Christina Rossetti and Siegfried Sassoon carved on stones and

36  see footnote 33.

37  Six different types of bats breed in this area, and *Somerset Bat Group* organises walks in Vallis Vale, listening to their calls on bat-detectors to identify them and watching them fly through torch beams across the sky. You can adopt a bat, too, with *Frome Bat Care* which 'rehabilitates' injured bats before releasing them back to the wild. Bats eat about 3000 insects a night which is, BBC Somerset TV conceded, demanding. *Frome Men's Shed* has an ongoing project to create bird, bat and bee boxes for trees around the town, in projects with the town's Rangers and school children.

38  The opening ceremony for the Green was an early commission for *First Cut,* the children's theatre company I was involved with as writer. My concept was a mystic messenger, part Hermes part Oberon, called Hagadorn, given energy and voice by Annabelle Macfadyen. Dressed in green, half-hippy-half-outlaw, she led children dressed as sprites and elves with drums and other instruments, through the town and onto the Green. I have a very old newspaper cutting, with a picture by John Frapwell. Probably the only town in England where the Millennium Green was a wildlife area on a steep slope with a launch conducted by faerie folk. I am still proud of this.

benches, and on the other side of the main road there's another haven: the beech grove, thronged with wild garlic in spring, with its 'line of desire' footpath that runs parallel to the oblivious drivers on North Parade.

Another favourite of mine used to be the abandoned site of Saxonvale already mentioned, with its splendidly graffitied derelict buildings as well as ancient trees and wildlife: hedgehogs and birds like blackcap and garden warbler. Time has run out for this strange wild place, once a busy industrial estate: by the time these words are printed, this glorious wild heart of Frome will be history in its literal sense.

The graveyards of Frome are safe from development, and are delightful places to stroll and loiter: St Johns, being central, is often busy but if you want quiet contemplation, the Dissenters Cemetery always delivers. Here you can find the untold histories of people of Frome: the young servant girl whose family paid for her headstone, the boys who died skating on a Sunday when the ice broke, whose memorial still reproaches them 'Remember the Sabbath, to keep it holy'. The white graves are for soldiers: the Commonwealth War Grave Commission provides them for Frome men who died on British soil. James Parsons, Secretary of the Board of Trustees, ensures a wreath is laid on every soldier's grave or memorial on their death anniversary dates; this kind of careful attention shows too in the fruit trees and general tending that make the cemetery so special a place.[39]

---

39 The Dissenters Cemetery is unique in recording the names and plots of the many babies who died at birth or were still-born – infant mortality took a huge toll until sanitation was better understood, and most graveyards simply put these unbaptised – therefore not Christian – tiny children in an open grave. Also fascinating to those like me with a morbid turn of mind, graves in the 19th Century were designed to be capacious enough for family additions, and were offered for sale at depths of up to 16 feet – all dug by hand, and walled within. In 1854 this would have cost you 5 guineas. Thomas Bunn, although he encouraged the dedication of this cemetery to nonconformist burials, is not resting here with his sister: he 'went posh' according to my informant, and abandoned his Methodist roots for anglicanism and a grave at Christchurch. The small chapel in the graveyard is not currently in use although hopefully this information may soon be incorrect: it was used in the past for storage of gardening equipment and, at one time, an aeroplane. James Parsons explained 'A gentleman whose family are in the graves – he's

For those with more time, and sturdy boots, Vallis Vale is the place
to walk: the well-used pathway along the river with its abandoned lime
kilns and the remains of Fussells ironworks further along towards Mells.
You may or may not see a kingfisher but there's a sense of awe just to
stand on the old bridge where the Frome merges with Mells stream,
ancient woodland all around, the hillside dense with fans of harts-tongue
ferns (which a naturalist friend told me are usually rare, though profuse
here) and wild garlic, every branch and twig decked with that dayglo-
green moss so thick that it looks like you could spin each sprig into yarn
to knit mittens.

From the many allotments, including the organic community one
on the Mount, to volunteer clean-up groups, it's clear that open land
within the town is as valued as the buildings. *Al fresco* activities are
massively popular: as well as markets and car-boots, there are outdoor
gatherings to celebrate events in every season. Victoria Park, popular
for parties and fetes, has a thatched bandstand – uniquely topped by a
weathervane – which is widely used by young musicians as well as the
Town Band (and for many years the splendidly-costumed national Town
Crier contest), while a tour of the 'Hidden Gardens', those mini-paradises
created by personal imagination and skill, is one of the most popular
features of festival week. The ancient lanes around the town have been
donated by the bypass to walkers and runners, and cyclists hoping to
complete the 'missing links' of their SUSTRANS route[40] across the south
west.

THE LAND THAT WAS ONCE MARSH is now buzzing with activity:
hikers and bikers, strollers and shoppers, buskers and traders,
youngsters playing in precincts, oldsters sitting on the benches – and
overall a sense of a town owned by the people who live there. In part, this

---

an engine driver and also a T.A. – he likes flying microlights. So he built a
little aeroplane in the chapel, over a period, and whenever we wanted to do
anything he lifted it up into the beams. He still flies it now.'

40  The plan to complete the last leg of a cycle track into town is active at
time of writing, with an 'Ecology group' to observe and support wildlife
on the verges of the tracks. Frequent sitings include shrews, voles, toads,
slowworms, lizards and a surprising number of grass snakes – 'they seem to
love the sloping grass verges', the report notes.

has been developed and encouraged by the IfF party's hands-on approach of informing everyone of everything going on, via town noticeboards and online, but it's the same go-it-alone ethos evidenced by the number of organisations (like the Food Bank and U3A) deciding to re-invent the wheel and make it a better fit for Frome. From the retirees who confronted Asda's management with a plan to manage the nature reserve to the youngsters who twenty years ago argued their skateboarding demand into the council chamber and made it happen, there's an energetic and active sense of urban rights – a sense that 'this land is our land', not because we inherited it but because we care for it.

Sheila Hedges feels this innate independence is partly also a West Country trait.

> With no big industries, most people were working for themselves or their families, which was why Methodism took hold, because people thought for themselves. They had to – there was nobody looking after them. And that sense of 'not answering to anyone else' is what kept us going. We were that bit more independent because we had to be.

Frome has had scant connection to those claiming ownership of the town since its nominal founding (Aldhelm lived in Malmesbury and died in Doulting). Surrounding lands were claimed by kings[41], who lived nowhere near, and by 'the church', an abstract entity, and were leased often to associates, sometimes as debt payments.[42] Townsfolk had no reason to feel allegiance to a monarch whose foresters were constantly in conflict with them and regularly interfered with their means of survival – since although the king didn't own all the land, his deer roamed across

---

41 The king who famously died in Frome was Eadred, in 955, promptly removed and buried in Winchester Cathedral. He seems to have been a monarch of the wild sort, ransacking Northumbria when it decided to be ruled by the King of Norway, the delightfully Blackadderishly named Eric Bloodaxe, and his reign, such as it was, was characterised by much quelling and quashing.

42 For example: In 1361 Stephen Wynslade became Lord of Frome after his cousin Thomas Branch died with no heir, and he granted the manor to a London armourer in his lifetime, to go after his death to Guy de Bryene, to whom he owed £20,000. Edward III intervened to give the manor to his mistress, Alice Perrers, instead.

it.[43] Poaching seems to have been a way of life in the 12th and 13th centuries.

So it's not really surprising that the land seizures of the Reformation made little difference to Frome: everything had been leased out by the church in everyone's living memory, there wasn't anything to notice[44]. If you were a sublet tenant of an absentee landlord whose name you knew only by hearsay and had never met, would you really care when the licence changed hands?[45] This almost orphan-like civic status and ingrained self-sufficiency might account for both the disorderly behaviours and the indifferent 'apathy', as well as the egalitarian basis of Frome's recent development.

THE HISTORY OF FROME is traditionally told in industrial terms, but at heart, we are a country town in a rural area. Gipsy pony-and-traps still trot regularly along the main street, alongside buses to local villages and shoppers at the twice-weekly charter markets, and you can walk from the fields on the northern side to the lakeside meadow on the south in around an hour. The cattle market may have moved to Standerwick, three and a half miles away, but it's still Frome market, just as Frome Cheese Show kept its identity when it too outgrew its original home and moved three miles to West Woodlands.

A digression here about the market: Frome's cattle market began in the streets, and was formalised early on – the Domesday book of 1086

---

43  Hugh of Witham (later Lincoln) constantly challenged King Henry II on the iniquitous forest laws and the cruelty with which the foresters treated those who lived on the land near Selwood forest.

44  Because it was a chantry, St Katherine's land was not sold until 1548 when all chantries were abolished; Henry's son Edward VI then sold it to Sir John Thynne of Longleat. Fifteen years later the land was bought by Richard West of Frome, and this family began the development of the area for housing.

45  The principal difference in practical terms was that the Church, which had owned one fifth of all England, had at least provided hospitals and alms for the poor. Henry VIII's land grab was to finance his wars with the incomes, and without interim support at times of trouble, divisions in wealth would became exacerbated. One of the reasons the Parliamentarians had support in this area was their promise of equity if they came to power, but when they did, the royal land they seized back was instead sold amongst themselves.

records 46s. 8d. dues paid to the crown in that year. Alan Sandall[46] evokes these early days when 'a farmer would set out with perhaps three or four beasts, driving animals along the same road, joining with others on the way, reaching town footsore and weary with the first task to sort out the animals they had been herding and find their own!'

While the major move of out of town to Standerwick in 1990 is the one remembered by many now, as with so much in the town's history, there was a precursor. Until 1875 cattle were traded in the space outside the George Hotel, where the Boyle Cross[47] was erected in 1871 as a drinking fountain which must have added to the chaos vividly described by researcher and art historian Sue Bucklow:

> Cattle and sheep could be found tethered and penned, sometimes all the way up Bath Street. It was even more chaotic on 'Frome Fair' days as along with the bawling livestock, the market place and surrounds were filled with noise of small firing booths with rifles, vendors of fly sheets singing samples of their songs, the cries of 'quack' medicine men, a dancing bear to music accompaniment, and Punch and Judy shows.

It was Charles Cooper, founder of Cooper and Tanner, the firm who built and now operate the Standerwick Market, who had the idea of moving this scene of chaos to a designated site on the edge of the town beside the river, on Brownjohn's Mead, in an area covering three acres and two roods. It required the establishment of a Frome Market Company, the purchasing of rights and tolls from Lord Cork, a special Frome Market Bill brought to Parliament to enact, and formal Royal Assent, before the livestock market was moved to Justice Lane in 1875. Horses were stabled under the Science & Literature Institute, and the Black Swan doubled as a sales area for smaller livestock.

---

46  *Going going gone, the history of Frome's Livestock Market* (March Press, 1991).

47  Carved from a ton of red Devon marble by Frome sculptor Joseph Chapman, this monument was the idea and design of the vicar's wife E.V. Boyle. Permission to use the site came from Richard, 9th Earl of Cork and Orrery, Lord of the Manor of Frome, also her brother-in-law, not that many on the streets would have known much about that.

In a hundred years the spacious area chosen for the market to spread itself had become as overcrowded and chaotic as the main street had been, and the problem of transport parking was overwhelming and unanswerable. A move outside the town entirely was the only solution, and as auctioneer David Millard has said, without the decision to relocate the market in Standerwick, Frome would have gone the same way as so many other small towns and simply lost the market entirely.

While livestock trading was the primary initiative, Frome was also renowned as a cheese town – early markets were known as Cheese Fairs, and the arrival of railway prompted the first exhibition of cheese and butter by the new Frome Agricultural Society, founded 1861. Records show that this was a serious trade fair, with one sale alone recording 28½ tons of cheddar, and the Cheese Show continued to develop separately from the market with a range of attractions, from displays of rick-thatching to international show-jumping contests – and dog shows of course. After first establishing the Fromefield Showfield in town, where it was a popular family day-out for the whole town, the Cheese Show quit Frome for West Woodlands in the same year as the livestock market.

The loss to the town when the market was moved to nearby Standerwick was deeply felt by many: one older resident told me emphatically

> It took the heart out and killed the town. Wednesdays was the highlight of the week when all the farmers came in, and when it all moved out to Standerwick the town seemed to go dead. It affected the shops a lot, as people went to Mole Valley Farmers to buy their meat and never came into Frome.

The market has thrived in its new venue, but something indefinable left the town. The rural community no longer looked to Frome as their place of exchange, not just for money and goods, but for information and gossip – a place to meet acquaintances over a drink, or check out new trends, get a hair-cut, browse the shops… there are many ways to spend newly-earned money in a market town, and Frome lost them all in 1990.

Frome people live close to the rural community: houses, shops, schools and workplaces of Frome are surrounded by woodland, grassland, and agricultural land just as they always were, but the 2001 foot-and-mouth epidemic, when the Ministry of Agriculture followed a 'ruthless slaughter policy' left the the farming community devastated and distressed, and financially depleted too, by piles of slaughtered stock. Jude Kelly, now owner of La Strada in Frome and Lacock's King John's Hunting Lodge tea-rooms, remembers both aspects of life as a farm child on the edge of town, as her father looked after Orchardleigh estate, a farming estate in those days:

> It was fun riding my horse around, and as the first thing I learned
> to drive was a combine, I have no fear of driving anything! But
> I remember the burning – it was tragic. Horrendous. Every
> doorway you dipped your footwear in disinfectant, everywhere was
> disinfected, we lost all our dairy herd, our sheep, it was traumatic.

Frome is still set in among farmland, but the farming is changing, so with respect to all who work the land, this section ends with a case-study of one contemporary farmer. Ed Green is a sixth-generation farmer who lives in Frome but still works the land his family have owned and worked since the 1700s. If you ever meet Ed I recommend you sit him down somewhere with a pint of Guinness – preferably not a few feet from a punk band soundcheck, as I did – and listen to his story:

> When you're a farmer you have to be a jack of all trades – you have
> to work hard manually, have husbandry skills and people skills, and
> a strategic head for business. I never wanted to be a farmer, I wanted
> to be in a band. I had to put my foot down to do A levels and go to
> university, but then I went back home to work out what to do next,
> and before you know it, I was running the farm without intending
> to, really, and it turned out I was really good at it. The farm is in a
> small hamlet about 15 minutes west of Frome, 800 acres, and I built
> the herd up to 300 and built a new dairy. But prices weren't good

and milking is a pretty relentless and thankless task, so in 2004 I sold the milking herd and switched to a beef livestock herd, building up numbers. I focused on native breeds like Aberdeen Angus and Herefords, and sold them into high-end markets like Waitrose.

Then in 2012 I won a Nuffield Farming Scholarship to travel and learn about innovation and best practice around the world, to bring ideas back to the UK. My core study was the global supply & demand chain for beef and my trip gave me a huge insight into livestock production around the world, not just from a producer's point of view but from that of consumers, governments and NGOs (non-governmental organisation) and I came back really questioning everything. England is a small nation, and our farming reflects small island thinking – I had met people who were farming on such a huge scale it was mind-blowing. In North America I visited huge beef feed-lots with 100,000 cattle on them and, while the management was impressive from a purely economic aspect, I struggled with the effects of these systems on the animals, the environment, and the people. And in Brazil I met a New Zealander who had come because he analysed it as the best location for farming – it's got rainfall, sunshine, good land, was energy self-sufficient and had a big population as consumer base.

I came home with a mixture of feelings, thinking, where does my farm fit in with all this? In England you can't compete in a global market on a commodity basis, because of the scale of farming in North and South America and Australasia. So that was my challenge, to bring back a better model in the UK.

I decided what we should do is produce niche, value-added products.The beef feed-lots in America gave me a model - they didn't own the cattle, they were a service provider. Over here every farmer expects to own cattle, but the problem is that retailers are big and powerful and farms are small and don't collaborate, so farmers have to accept whatever the supermarket says. I saw a way to turn the relationship between farmers and retailers on its head, so we could be price-makers not price-takers.

So I started approaching retailers and processors. The proposition I offered was, a bed-and-breakfast service with high welfare and environmental awareness – so I would provide farmers with top-quality facilities and I could provide processors and retailers with a constant supply of consistent-quality cattle. I managed to get a contract with Waitrose whereby they bought cattle off the farmer, put them into my farm, and then took them out at the end. That was revolutionary. I built my farm up to over 2,000 cattle and it did well for almost ten years – it was a very good business model. I also gave a lot of talks, and set up the first on-line livestock auction, which was not only fairer for bidders and saved transport costs, also animal welfare improved because they spent less time in lorries, so it makes sense for everyone. 'Sell My Livestock' is now doing really well and has started to revolutionise the way animals are bought and sold in the UK.

Then a couple of years ago, I started thinking, I've been doing this for over twenty years and it wasn't what I ever wanted to do. People are becoming squeamish about getting their food from animals. Vegetarianism is normal, the vegan movement is growing – the zeitgeist is moving away from livestock production. We're a small urban country and the more stressful our lives get in this technological age, the more people need land as a leisure amenity – somewhere to go and relax, recover, and enjoy.

So what I've done now is a four-year contract to rent out most of the farm, and I'm using this time to become dedicated to eco-tourism. I've done a barn conversion for holiday lets and retreats and activities, I'm doing a major woodland replanting scheme, over quite a few hundred acres as I want to do large-scale art installations like the Forest of Dean trail, and have bike trails, and log cabins here and there so people can come and stay. And that will give me more time for music.

(Ed Green is also Captain Cactus, and returns in the section on Creatives)

# Nine Mysteries

## 1 The Buried Treasure

The most ancient of Frome's mysteries is still being researched by experts: the now-famous Frome Hoard of 52,503 Roman coins found in 2010 by metal-detector-wielding hospital chef Dave Crisp just outside the town. The coins, dated AD 253 to 305, were in a big ceramic pot and include five rare silver denarii struck in the reign of emperor Carausius. Commendably Mr Crisp was concerned they shouldn't be shifted from the county: 'The Romans had been there over 200 years, so they were more Somerset people than Roman really,' he pointed out, commendably, but other than a force field around it, Frome's elderly little museum couldn't provide a secure option so they went to the Museum of Somerset in Taunton for a purchase donation of £320,250. The mystery is why such massive wealth, with coin dates spanning decades, was crammed into a pot and buried. Such dramatic stealth suggests a violent social upheaval or danger to the owner but no research has uncovered what that might be…and furthermore, why was it secreted close to Frome, where there were no Roman settlements and the nearest Roman road is thought to have bypassed the present town on the Eastern side by several miles…

## 2 The Phantom Hitch-hiker

Not just a tale for a wintry night, a genuine bafflement to Frome Police, according to multiple reports. 'We've had people coming in here in a state of virtual hysteria' the duty officer told one researcher. The *Sunday Express* in 1977 featured the story of a Mr Evans, who claimed to have twice encountered a man on the road to Nunney who asked for a lift. The first time he obliged, but after repeating several times that he felt cold, the man in the back seat disappeared. In one version of this story, the second siting of the hitch-hiker caused Mr Evans to swerve and crash into a tree. Others using the road reported both seeing a man and also the sensation of a man in the backseat of their cars. The newspaper report stirred up other memories, and was developed by other papers even more dramatically. Ghost-busting historian Michael Goss went to 'the scene of the purported haunt' to talk to Superintendent Lee and was surprised to learn this was no press fabrication: there had indeed been many such reports.

What deepens the mystery is that this road leads to the area once known as Gibbet Hill, and since place names develop for a reason, it's likely there was a gallows here in days when roadside robbers were displayed after hanging at the scene of their crime. The ghosts of highwaymen are frequently claimed to haunt such areas, and a local name can be a clue. Cannard's Grave on the road to Glastonbury, for example, allegedly refers to a haunting by 17th-Century publican Tom Cannard, who moonlighted as a sheep-rustler and whose activities took him as far as Frome and beyond. He ended his life on the gibbet, the last man in England to be hanged for sheep-stealing. Tom has apparently been seen and heard in the area frequently since, the first report being in 1692.[48]

The spirit allegedly haunting Nunney Road however, is clad not in britches but jeans. No account has ever been discovered to explain his appearance, disappearance, or his constant complaints about the cold.

### 3    The Crop Circle

Wiltshire is the mecca for crop circles, with Cley Hill frequently visited, but if you google Frome you'll find we have one in the annals too, photographed on 17 June 2012. Not intricate enough for a record label cover but certainly circular.[49] I've decided not to discuss UFO sitings, but do talk amongst yourselves if they interest you.

### 4    The Underground Passages

Frome tunnels are famous for being... well, famous. There's a 'Frome Tunnel Team' but despite several 'digs' no conclusive evidence has been

---

48  There are other tales of hanged men walking in Somerset, but the most sinister and sad reports are not sightings but hearings: gasping sounds of choking men have several times been reported near Gore Hedge on windless nights, and are believed to be as the last breaths of long-dead victims of the Hanging Judge.

49  Steve Alexander, who researches crop circles, has an impressive image here: https://www.pinterest.co.uk/pin/346917977536753962/

found of any extensive linkage. Legend has it that the tunnels were to allow priests to hide from persecution during the Reformation era (the Thynne family, who had snaffled large chunks of dispossessed church lands, were notoriously rigorous in their support of this favourable new regime) but as their construction is medieval that theory does not convince. Exploration continues...

## 5    The Secret Bunker

A tale is told of a local caver who in the early 1980s during the time of the 'Cold War' came across a military bunker in the Welshmill area of town. His news was hushed and it was sealed up quickly after the discovery. One commenter remembered tales of a nuclear bunker just off Vallis Road, by the old Weston Vinyls site, with a visible entrance to "something that was sunk in the ground. It could have been local folklore and actually just a septic tank or something though....who knows!' Who indeed.[50]

## 6    The Seven Faces of Badcox

Peace, Plenty, and Mirth are large godlike faces, with more than a touch of Green Man about them, who – together with personifications of all four seasons – adorn the small row of shops on Badcox. Pagan-looking iconography is unusual even for a town notorious for nonconformity, and these stone faces have been there for a long time: Mr Hodder's pharmacy was built in 1890 and his business with its watchful god-guardians have survived more changes to the street scene than most other parts of Frome.
But no-one, not even current occupier Oakville Care Centre, knows why they are there...

## 7    The Disputed Murder

Methodist ministers were often called to the dying to facilitate a safe passage to heaven. In February 1801 the Rev Edward Griffith failed to oblige as he just didn't believe the sad tale of Betty Edington aged 80 who confessed on her deathbed that she had committed a murder. 'I said "You are dreaming" and treated it with indifference, supposing it to

---

50  See http://www.subbrit.org.uk/rsg/roc/db/988805870.010001.html.

be the effect of her weakness: "No, I am not dreaming, 'tis too true. My own child, when I was sixteen years of age" which was 72 years since.' Mr Griffith quizzed her about locations and argued a while ('perhaps it was in Ireland, or Bristol?') to test the distraught crone, 'but neither age nor sickness had impaired her mental powers and nothing I could say could move her in the least from the dreadful point; yet I still wished to disbelieve it. "I stabb'd it with a penknife, and buried it in the garden; and this is not all, I killed a young man, and pushed him down the rocks into the sea because I had sinned with him." ' Mr Griffiths found himself at this point unable to continue his interrogations – 'which I rather lament' – and merely 'pointed her to Jesus, and departed.' Betty died the next day, with her confession signed by five of her neighbours who were present at the time. The report, including the full argument, is reprinted in *Brief Annals of the Frome Methodist Society from Its Commencement* by Stephen Tuck 1814. But was the Reverend right to dismiss Betty's gruesome confession?

## 8    The white witch and the cricket ground

Belief in witches was once so widespread in England that hundreds of women were put to death for alleged witchcraft, immersion in water being the test and also the usual cause of demise. If she didn't drown, the devil had saved her so she'd probably be burned at the stake. At one point in history just about any woman who lived alone, had a cat, and knew a bit about medicinal uses of plants was deemed a to be witch, especially if she had annoyed someone – so it's surprising there's little history of witchcraft in Frome.[51]    Frome can however take credit, or should at least admit culpability, for the last recorded witch-murders in England, when in 1730 (fourteen years after the last official judicial sentence) an aged crone was thrown in a millpond to undergo the ordeal by water, watched

---

51 Frome did, however, have a demonologist with an obsessive dread of witchcraft: Joseph Glanvill, vicar of St Johns from 1662 to 1680, wrote a book on the evil powers of witches entitled *Sadducismus Triumphatus*. The most interesting, and sinister, consequence of its publication was that the alleged examples of supernatural disturbances were seized on in 1693 to justify the Salem witch trials. I say 'alleged' because there are several contemporary accounts of locals teasing the gullible reverend with spoof spooks.

by 200 taunting cheering spectators. She was eventually dragged out and dumped in a stable, but did not survive her rescue.

Being a witch is quite a respectable thing nowadays, and witches, like goddesses, are usually happy to proclaim their status. In 2004 a Frome witch, Titania Hardie, was brought in by Frome Town Football Club to sort out their losing streak in home matches. They were scoring well in their away games, but never got near the net at home and so feared their Badger's Hill turf was cursed. According to my informant, the witch of Sheppard Barton had put a spell on the ground after someone in the club bar was rude to her, and after inter-witch astral negotiations and an apology from the team, the curse was duly lifted.

## 9   The phantom bar staff

Spirits in pubs are frequently reported and the Ghost at the *Griffin* is notorious, attracting investigation by *Twilight Shadows/ Phoenix of Wessex Paranormal* who in 2009 arrived to investigate a shifting hat-stand in the attic. A long night ensued as some of the group communed with an irritable spirit called Albert who became excessively frank about his love life and after several changes in temperature and sound effects were noted, the visiting mediums managed to transfer him and his entourage to the other side but sadly the hat stand remained static and the *Twilight* reporter failed to get any positive readings on the EMF meter. The cellar more helpfully supplied another investigator with visceral evidence when his beer glass exploded in his hand: this spectre allegedly resisted exorcism and is now walled in.

Most of Frome's pubs, in fact, appear to have resident ghosts, as illustrated last year when a request on Facebook for paranormal experiences had a massive number of responses. Paul Kirtley remembered 23 Bath Street when it was the the *Wheatsheaves*: 'The cellar there used to be the mortuary as it was the coldest place in town. I practiced with a band one Sunday afternoon in the Loft and when we finished the landlord offered us a drink. As he poured I smelled kerosene, and he explained we'd disturbed old Fred who used to work there, lighting the lamps.'

The anecdote met immediate recognition: 'I had a funny one with old Fred, I was sat at the bar many years ago looking over to the table by the window. When I looked out the corner of my eye, I was sure I could see a old man, but when I looked full on he wasn't there. Joe (landlord) saw me doing this, and knew exactly who it was.'

This was confirmed by Joe, with ensuing debate as to whether the spectral smell is paraffin or kerosene. Paul concludes 'Our band practice must have disturbed Fred – we were loud enough to wake the dead that afternoon! I'm sceptical about spirit stuff but I'm certain that we had Fred for company that day.'

*Gentle Street*

# 3   STREETS AND BUILDINGS

*– no coast to guard, no castle culture, no Roman roads, no*
*Herriot hype, no university challenge –*
*disappearances and changes: trees, water, jewels in our crown*
*– Trinity debacle, Piggeries recovery –*
*– temporal layering – sacred edifices and sublime entropy –*
*highlife & lowlife glimpses – Case Study: the street –*

'Architecture is the very mirror of life. You only have to cast your eyes on buildings to feel the presence of the past, the spirit of a place; they are the reflection of society.'

– Ieoh Ming Pei

'What goes on around us is the product of innumerable forces – some are, of course, created by design, in both senses of that word. But they are

the exceptions. Accidents – chance juxtapositions, fortuitous collisions – some happy, some not – clashes of style and material, harmonious elisions of contrasting idioms, stylistic hostilities, municipal idiocies and corporate boasts, the whimsical expressions of individuality made by the patronisingly-named man in the street or by Jane Doe or by Anon – these are some of the more salient determinants of our urban and suburban and extra-urban environments – they are accidents.

Buildings are of course the major components of these environments'

– Jonathan Meades

THE BUILDING OF FROME is a complex story, a blend of geology and sagacity, personalities and passion, misfortune and mismanagement, and quite a lot of luck. I think we were lucky that the romantic poets confined their laudanum-inspired reveries to paths further north in the county, that Jane Austen preferred smarter locations for her social parodies, and that we lack heights that wuther,

or coastlines for smugglers and swaggerers. Frome has never become
packaged as a heritage venue, like 'Brontë Country', Du Maurier's Fowey,
Wordsworth's Lakes, or James Herriot's Yorkshire. Frome had no reason
to establish to Grantchester-style tea-rooms or Coleridge Walk trails: We
have no such cultural icons to dominate our town's branding.[1]

First we had mills, and a thriving town of independent artisan
workers. Then we had foundries, and print-works, and all the network
of resources big successful businesses need to thrive. And in the 1990s
it all died. Industries had failed, England was in recession and Frome
could no longer rely on any of its retail trade to survive. If you talk to the
older inhabitants of any town you will hear tales of dramatic changes and
helter-skelter declines. There surely can be few metamorphoses to rival
Frome in the roller-coaster decades of the end of the 20th Century.

The next section looks at how that happened, this one is more about
the impact of its history on Frome structurally. The story is scribbled
everywhere, tagged on every street name: the bartons of the rich, the
trades of the poor. There's a traceable time-line from medieval timber-
frame, through urban vernacular[2] and Georgian stone to contemporary
build, mostly in traditional style apart from the Steiner school which
opted for a sauna look. You can track the changes in collections of old
photographs online, in the museum, and in collections with captions
which, like the images, are now poignant memories. You can take an
imaginary walk, referencing informative plaques about places of interest,

---

1　The poet Elizabeth Rowe, 1674-1737, while much admired in her time, was
　not a writer with lasting appeal. She does, however, have a birthplace plaque
　in Rook Lane. I should also mention, although perhaps not in the same
　breath as Elizabeth, a Mrs Tuck (apparently closely related to the Wesleyan
　historian) who in 1823 published a collection called *Vallis Vale and Other
　Poems*, featuring the legend of Edmund Leversedge, who reputedly was taken
　for dead in 1465 after a particularly debauched night. Think McGonagall, but
　without the interesting line variations of that great purveyor of doggerel. For
　44 pages Edmund's recovery was at the time attributed to a return from 'the
　other world', visions of which were popular among the curious dwellers of
　this one, presumably hoping for greater equity.

2　Houses built from locally available materials and reflecting custom and
　tradition rather than fashion. They're considered essential contributors to
　local distinctiveness, documents of times that may have left few other traces.

via the *Frome Heritage Trail* [3] or *Discover Frome,* but instead of any these sensible approaches I'll begin by talking about some things you <u>won't</u> see – some of them once-features of the town, some simply projects never realised – as a way to explore how Frome stubbornly shapes itself always from a different perspective – aided by that powerful evolutionary force we call change.

The first significant absence is trees. Before the arrival of cars, and consequent road widenings, there were many more trees, and early aerial views of Frome show the town virtually nestling in woodland. Trees lined most of the streets, encroaching so close to the town centre that the toll house [4] at the top of North Parade in an early photograph looks like a cottage in the middle of a wood. The Leys, a path to Vallis Vale now part of the East Mendip Way, in 1905 ran through double line of trees now reduced (by disease) to only one, the wide-spreading horse-chestnut you pass if you walk to Vallis Veg over the fields from the new housing estate called, appropriately, Ley Vale. Most arboreal losses are due to redevelopment but as discussed in the previous section, the primary emphasis now is on preservation and renewal.

Another thing there's less of around is water – surplus water, that is. We no longer see the level of interruption to the working day once commonplace in that area, as evidenced by this off-the-record tale from the carpet factory.

> I was factory manager in the '70s and if there was a lot of rain it was
> my job to find out if they'd closed the gates at Bristol, which they
> did if they were getting high tides, because if they did that, a couple
> of hours later we'd have a flood and all the tufting machines on the
> ground floor would have shorted out, because we couldn't shut them
> off so they would have kept on running and jamming up. Once I

---

3   Published by Frome Society for Local Study, available at the information centres.

4    Frome Turnpike Trust was established in 1757 – roads throughout England had fallen into a bad state, having had no major investment since Roman times, and cart wheels caused further damage so these toll roads were controlled by gates (originally pikestaffs) which were opened after payment to allow horses and vehicles through. The Trusts eventually became no longer viable when usage shifted to railways and canals.

ended up throwing rolls of carpet across the road to stop the flood, which got me in a lot of trouble, then the managing director called me up and he said, 'Next time that happens… do it again, you saved us thousands of pounds worth of machinery damage.'

Spillages like this in the Wallbridge area, which were background to the creation of the nature reserve described in the previous section, were not the only flood points. Frome's livelihood was built on water, but at one time its power seemed untameable. Residents remember the floods of 1968 when the river burst at Pensford, and times when the whole of Willow Vale was flooded and families routinely moved upstairs in heavy rain. The reason we no longer see water filling the main streets is the flood alleviation scheme[5] constructed between 1971 and 1984. This consisted mainly of channel improvement, major realignment of the river's route, re-grading and widening, and work on bridges and weirs. The river continued to elude control alongside Rodden Road despite Asda's alleged flood plain: The Devon and Somerset Fire & Rescue Service were called out twenty times in three years, and in 2008 engineering consultants were again involved. Passability is now largely improved, although in 2012 Wallbridge was once again under four feet of water with press pictures of stranded vehicles towed out and a jet ski doing laps up and down from Rodden Road.[6]

DESPITE THE CONSTANT AVAILABILITY, not to say profusion, of water there's another notable omission: If you've ever wondered why – with so many canals nearby and since waterways are an easy, pollution-free, way to transport heavy materials – Frome never had a canal, the answer is: there was supposed to be one. The Dorset and Somerset Canal was intended to link Poole to the Kennet and Avon Canal up by Bradford on Avon, with a branch to link Frome up with the Somerset coalfield at Nettlebridge. Construction started in 1786, not at the logical end on the coast but in the middle of the branch line –

5  You can see more by googling *A portrait of Frome* December 2008, an account compiled by Mendip District Council with a map showing the old and new routes of the river.

6  http://www.itv.com/news/westcountry/update/2012-04-30/mans-rides-jet-ski-in-street/

apparently hoping to create a coal route between Nettlebridge and Frome to bring the company some early income. The big problem for engineers was that the eleven-mile line had a contour drop of 210 feet from west to east, and ingenuity was needed to overcome the problem of locks. Local engineer James Fussell responded with a design he called the Balance Lock which he patented and built at his Mells ironworks in 1800. This ambitious solution became a huge tourist attraction with hundreds coming to watch his testing, which was so successful that work promptly started on the other four required. And then... just short of two miles from Frome, the company's funds ran out, partly because of increased costs due to the war in France, and no further money was ever raised. Work was never completed on the branch or any other part of the canal and the project was abandoned in 1803.[7]

A LOOK AT BUILDINGS NOW, still with an eye on what has now vanished from view. This is not to imply that conservation *per se* is a Good Thing, or that all losses were caused by planning decisions. Fires were frequent in earlier centuries, and timber-beamed houses were naturally vulnerable. Cheap Street suffered a major fire in 1923 – the burnished colour-change of the brickwork on one side of *The Settle* shows how close that building (at that time a pub called *The Albion*) came to incineration.[8] Once insurance of property and contents became

---

7   Another abandoned scheme was the Funicular Railway, suggested in 1997 as an asset to Green Tourism and intended to run from Monmouth House up the steep garden into the United Reform Church cemetery, thus gaining level access to the shops on Catherine Hill without the laborious climb that might deter visitors. Both the Millennium Lottery and Heritage Lottery funds rejected versions of the plan, and piecemeal selling of the relevant land eventually prevented the plan being re-presented. Thanks to Jean Lowe for the insider view on this particular non-event.

8   Three shops were destroyed and had to be entirely rebuilt, including two at the top: luckily the adjoining building with its jettied upper storey, one of the oldest in the street, was saved – all are now occupied by Amica. Damage limitation was credited to effective intervention by the Fire Brigade, captained by one John Hiscett whose statue is built into the wall of the new fire station. It was built as a figurehead at the old fire station but nearly overlooked in the move, so that's the only place they could find when they remembered. I heard that from a fireman.

more common, so too did conflagration, and payments became tailored to probability of owner complicity. Rob Gill, a long-serving fireman who keeps a personal archive on Frome's flaming histories, described a substantial fire he was called out to at the Pine Factory in Keyford. The main building at the back was fully demolished but fire-fighters managed to stop it from incinerating the shops along the entire front by creating a fire-break which halted the spread. There was a widespread belief that it was arson, and the insurers, apparently, said that they were 80% sure he'd had the business torched, so they were only going to pay out 20%. 'Because that was the second fire – he'd had a pine business previously at the top of Catherine Hill and that one was definitely arson – the guy he paid went bragging round the pubs saying he'd been paid to torch it. So that was all considered part of the evidence for this one.'

Fires, whether accidental or deliberate, are not the only way Frome's skylines have changed, and some planning decisions do seem regrettable – like the tiny clutch of pointy-roofed cottages on Gorehedge, looking in a 1905 image as if they came from a fairy-tale, which were sacrificed to over-enthusiastic road-widening and replaced by grim-looking toilets which are now permanently locked.[9] At least the triangle of land next to them is pleasantly grassed with seven trees and a glorious daffodil display in spring. Here, in living memory, was the 100-foot high chimneystack of Lambs' brewery[10] with its walkway to the bottling plant and barrel stores beside the pub itself. Robin Lambert, who remembers the event well, showed me a photograph of the crowd watching demolition in 1959 to make way for the current fire station to replace the original one on Christchurch Street.[11]

Other than road widening, profitable developments seem to have been the main reason for clearance, with shared community spaces

---

9   The entire row sold by Lord Bath for £175, apparently.
10 The brewery was built in 1858 but this chimney was apparently not added until later.
11 The Old Fire Station is now owned by Luke Manning who has retained the fireman's pole and converted the upstairs into Pencil Studio where he works on branding and marketing projects, while the ground floor is the superbly effective studio of Visual Radio Arts, Frome's innovative Facebook-based broadcasting company.

particularly vulnerable.[12] A public swimming baths[13] and no fewer than two cinemas were demolished in living memory, and are still mourned by several people who talked to me. Tony May, who went swimming in the river also as a boy before its course was altered, loved the swimming club there and went every night after work. He remembers Victoria Swimming Baths, up the alley off Rook Lane, where Gala Night races were so popular the queues went from the baths right round into Bath Street.

'It was gorgeous,' Mike Witt confirmed: 'It was about the only place you could get a hot bath. Glass roof leaked like a sieve. You had two-hour swimming sessions, we queued up in the street. If it wasn't too full you could get another hour if you ran round to the back of the queue half-dressed. Mr Sweet must've taught most of Frome to swim there. They were brilliant days.' [14]

---

12 The Swan on Badcox was demolished in 1963. Pictures show this popular pub, built in the mid-1600s, had a small garden with benches in front of it where people could sit and chat, and the bland housing development replacing it was seen by some as another example of what you might call unresolved-conflict-of-interest on the council. 'The grip the council had on the town while I was growing up was phenomenal,' one local told me, 'some of the men on it was notorious.' I was given their names but it would be injudicious to list them here.

13 Built in 1899 to commemorate Queen Victoria's Diamond Jubilee, the blue-and-white tiling with its circular window and gilt lettering was acclaimed at its opening as 'probably the finest public baths in England.' It wasn't just for recreation, there were plenty of bathrooms for the many in Frome at that time who otherwise relied on the tin bath in the back yard for ablutions. They cost sixpence – two and a half pee in decimal currency. The abandoned baths apparently became a mecca for developing street artists: with police apparently turning a blind eye -'all the kids were in the same place, so they knew what they were up to,' I was told -'I call that sensible policing.'

14 Basically I found when I talked to people who grew up in Frome, memories were all of a vibrant town with children playing freely in streets, full of lively neighbourly conversations, feuds and banter and rumour all enjoyed and generosity abounding. A fun place, safe for children to explore, a river for paddling and fishing, skating in winter and swimming in summer, scrumping apples in autumn, sweetshops and ear-boxing for minor misdemeanours – a town of bike shops and pie sellers, with ale in barrels and sawdust in butchers shops where everyone knew who was selling them everything because it was the name over the door. You'd almost expect the firemen to be

Mike talked also about *The Gaumont*, a thousand-seater cinema with tiered seating at the back, opened in 1939 and in 1967 renamed *The Classic*, then demolished three years later to make way for the Westway shopping mall. There was a massive public outcry. Press photographs show men, woman and children marching in the street in protest, holding banners all demanding KEEP THE CLASSIC OPEN,[15] and Robin Lambert showed me cuttings and memories of all the cinemas:

> Beautiful place the Gaumont was, and it smelled nice too, sort of perfumed air, something they used to put in the air system I suppose, and when we was kids we used to go to the children's club there. Uncle Charlie, the cinema manager, used to organise it all and Auntie Nellie played the piano – that was old Ellen Bray, one of the founders of the stationery shop – and they do flash the words up on the screen and you had a singsong before you had the film. Before the Gaumont, there was a cinema at the bottom of Church Steps – the old Palace Theatre[16] but Bray's animated pictures, back in the silent times, actually started in the auction rooms – You wouldn't recognise it now.

The shift to home entertainment, as televisions became part of household furniture, was cited as a justification for the closure of the *Classic*, but the much-smaller *Westway* which opened 1974, has survived[17] converted in 2017 to an excellent little three-screen cinema

---

called Hugh, Pugh, Barney McGrew, Cuthbert, Dibble and Grub. Of course it wasn't always exactly like that. Especially when it rained...

15 Some of the banners added, somewhat mysteriously, AND DEATH OFF THE ROADS, while others more politely explained WE PREFER IT LEFT ALONE.

16 *The Picture Palace* opened around 1915 and was continually in use until 1939 when the new *Gaumont* opened in Cork Street. The Gaumont British Theatres chain had been running it for a decade by then. The *Palace Theatre*, as it was by then known, was converted for retail use and burned down in 1961.

17 Dennis and Dolores O'Connor ran the cinema for more than 20 years and their daughter Martina took over at their retirement. Martina successfully negotiated the costly change from 35mm to digital and won Person of the Year award for her persistence in maintaining the cinema as well as her charitable commitments, but damage caused by a fire later put future survival of the cinema at risk until Pat and Beryl Scott, who run the Ritz at

charging just £4 for any seat in the house and one of only a very few in the UK with a licensed bar.

So despite these lost originals, Frome does have now an independent cinema, and also a swimming pool in the sports centre which is run by Avalon Leisure, 'independent provider of leisure management solutions in the South West of England.' Some functional buildings however have gone without replacement. The Magistrates Court on Oakfield Road, for example, was recently demolished for housing. While this building[18] was not a thing of beauty, its demise in the 'rationalisation' of courts has had an impact on Frome. Bob Ashford gave me this insight:

> I was working in London at the time and ironically happened to be at the presentation from the Lord Chancellors department by a civil servant who amazingly used Frome as his example. Needless to say I didn't accept his argument as Yeovil, which was proposed and accepted, has virtually no travel links – it just looked fairly close to Frome on a map. There was, and is, almost no public transport and the earliest train doesn't arrive until after the court begins. It also means defendants and witnesses travel on the same train. This came following the closure of the custody suite at Frome and downgrading of policing in the town which has continued. John Killah was an ardent campaigner against the closures.

John Killah, Frome's much-respected criminal defence advocate, did indeed make a strong plea for the survival of the court 'that has been sitting in Frome for hundreds of years – it is about to go and it will

---

Burnham on Sea, bought the building and converted it.

18 A previous Magistrates Court in Justice Lane had been replaced by the magnificent Gothic-style 1857 Grade II listed building on Christchurch Street West designed by Bath City Architect Charles Davis, shared with the Police Station for almost a hundred years until 1952. It's now the Bo-Jangles dance studio (and said to be haunted). From here, both police station and court were relocated in a flat-roofed red-brick edifice on Oakfield Road now razed and re-filled by a small housing estate. Subsequently, with no Magistrates Court with which to twin its building, the Police Station was temporarily sited above the Pizza Hut and now police formal presence appears reduced to a desk when the library is open.

never come back', pointing out that Lord Justice Goldring himself had said there was no justification for its closure and that other towns were applying for a judicial review while neither our local MP (Lib-Dem David Heath) nor Mendip District Council had bothered to do so. The response from Mendip's leader was that having an accessible court in town was not considered 'good use of taxpayers money.' No answer to that really, although it does beg the question of what better use was made of the taxes instead...

Changes in policing practice came late to Frome, as the next section will discuss more fully, but in the context of disappeared buildings it's disappointing that both our ancient overnight lock-ups have succumbed. The Guard House which adjoined the Blue Boar is now only a trace memory on the wall: it became a toilet and was later demolished. The Blind House in St Johns churchyard built in 1798 although a Grade II listed building is now used as storage for rubble, and virtually inaccessible.[19] Its original location was on the corner of Church Street and Vicarage Street, but in the 1790s it was deemed a traffic obstruction and relocated, with the Bishop of Bristol arriving to reconsecrate the churchyard.

Frome was never hit much by WWII war damage, but we had a one-night blitz: my data here is again supplied by Hilary Daniels:

> *We had two lines of bombs one night, Easter 1941, which I spent under the kitchen table. One came down in Nunney Road – it took out several houses, you can see where the road was rebuilt in quite a different style – it was a delayed-action bomb and went off 24 hours later. The other line of bombs went over the Mount – one dropped 200 yards from where I was standing on my front lawn. I was eight and I had time to run upstairs, get my little book of planes and watch it come over – it was a Heinkel 111.*

STRUCTURAL REPLACEMENTS and alterations are inevitable in any town that has survived for centuries, but you only have to look around the wonderful higgle-piggle of the town, magnificent, grimy, insouciant and sublime, with its jettied roofs and lichened walls, its

---

19 The Blind House in nearby Nunney is well maintained and has the dignity of a plaque.

splendid churches and sly alleys, bartons and steps, cobbles and pavings, lamps and signage, curiously named roads and crested doorways, arches and carvings and sudden unexpected glories, to see that in Frome far more has survived than has been lost.

Frome boasts, truthfully, more listed buildings than any other Somerset town with a total tally of 370. By my calculator's calculation, even if you located a dozen a day, it would still take you over a month to view them all. They include walls, lamp-posts and war memorials, pubs and warehouses, gates and fountains, three telephone kiosks and the entire bridge, as well as cottages, mansions and churches. And of course Frome railway station, one of the oldest surviving Brunel designs in the country, still with its iconic wooden roof – one of only two roofed stations in the country.[20]

Being 'listed' can be something of a poisoned chalice, as Jude Kelly found out when she bought 'the Pepperpot', claimed to be the oldest house in Frome, to convert it into a café in 2000.

> It took me nearly two years to sort. It's medieval building, and English Heritage wanted expensive archeological drawings. I said, "I am not doing that – it's been bastardised over many years because there was no legislation to stop people bashing around in the old days! I am restoring it to its former glory as much as I can." I found the stone wall at the back was only held by a bit of cement which was resting on soil – I had to go down a metre to bring a foundation wall in. I remember my building reg's guy standing under the beams looking up, and I said, 'What's the matter?' He said, 'I'm just wondering how the building is standing up. But it's been here this long, Jude, I'm sure it will be fine.' It's all been passed now.

---

20 Great Western Railways acquired the authorisation in 1850 and the line completed in 1857 originally as a Wilts, Somerset and Weymouth railway link between Chippenham with Weymouth. Originally, as envisaged by Brunel, it used broad gauge, but in 1874 the whole track was converted to narrow – against the express wishes of Brunel and despite all research on safety, speed, and general convenience. Narrow was of course cheaper. Sadly the Frome-Radstock-Bristol line suffered from increasing trend to road haulage and eventually closed, though in 2014 a charitable trust was set up to reopen it.

Structurally, Frome's story is one of random adaptation. There's not much in this town you could call 'purpose built' – the museum began life as a Literary and Scientific institute and the Old Fire Station is now home to a recording studio. Churches become bakeries and community centres, many smaller buildings have become private homes and most of the old factory sites are now housing estates.[21] Derelict buildings may linger for years, buildings still in use may be suddenly demolished like the swimming pool. Reasons seem sometimes unfathomable: 'They just seem to want to get rid of things sometimes, don't they?' one ex-councillor I asked suggested, but there were, of course, conspiracy-theories around contractors and back-handers.[22]

Changes were mostly piecemeal and, in the days when planning permission was not required by the wealthy who owned the properties, both building and demolitions were carried out without any overall concept agreed, or even known about, by the people who lived in the town. The most significant absence in terms of history and heritage, is a big bit of the oldest industrial housing estate in England, demolished in a fit of 'slum clearance' fervour in the 1960s allegedly inspired by a tidy-minded town clerk.

Dwellings had been constructed randomly since the 1500s in the area known as Woadground (or Oadground) in the Manor of St Katherine, as increasing numbers of workers arrived in Frome in response to the developing cloth trade. This had become[23] the main growing area for the woad used in wool dye. Cloth-making was done by home-workers, and as the trade grew so too did the houses, throughout the 1600s, with no other planning than the lease of a plot that fitted the existing tracks and hedges of the old field strips. By 1725 a tight network

21 The notable exception is Saxonvale, once home to Notts Industries. Jonathan Meades with his lust for entropic beauty of wastelands and debris would have been enchanted by this derelict riverside area as indeed I was, with its crushed debris carpet, furniture of rubble and rooty stumps, walls of eloquent apocalyptic graffiti.

22 Several people I spoke to were ready to name a cabal of councillors who controlled the town as tightly as the Mafia in the 1960s.

23 Cloth making for trade originally developed along by the river, where Willow Vale is now, but the shift from water power to steam power opened up other areas of the town to the industry.

of streets on this grid-plan contained over 300 houses.

The 1960s demolition frenzy took out about half: Rosemary Lane, The Mint, Kittle Alley, Barren Alley, Limerick, and Bell Lane where Lewis Cockey had set up his bell-casting foundry in 1685. Bull-dozers arrived in 1968 and *Frome Standard* maintained weekly reports with photographs to graphically illustrate captions like 'The area of Frome bounded by Milk Street Selwood Road and Trinity Street together with areas beyond Duke Street are rapidly developing all the aspects of a battlefield! Soon this old-world part of Frome will only be a memory.'

The first phase was complete before any serious protest began but a delay before the second phase got underway gave protesters a chance. In 1975 the papers were full of a different side of the story: A 'Save Trinity' campaign now had the backing of many of the council, and to the fury of the pro-demolition councillors, the plan was now under additional scrutiny by the housing committee and furthermore attracting wider interest of an annoyingly derisory nature: A Bristol newspaper reported that 'It took four newcomers to wake up sleepy Frome to the possibility of losing a unique part of its heritage' – referring to two couples who had come from London to work in Frome. The Civic Society produced a rehabilitation plan approved by ministers yet still not accepted, the Department of the Environment designated the area a conservation area of special merit, the Historic Building Council was involved, and for one reason or another the never-ending saga was front-page local news for years.[24]

In another twist, squatters from Camden had arrived in 1977 and,

---

24 'We were just fed up', one ex-resident told me, 'We just wished they'd make up their minds and do something. It dragged on and on till 1984. The majority of people just stayed waiting for a decision.' The council's recalcitrance had supporters in the wider community however. One angry letter in the paper from a Mr Walker of Styles Hill suggested 'a referendum would show that not more than ten percent would be in favour of preservation.' Mr Walker's own view was 'the area had very little (if any) historical value... cramped, insanitary tumbledown houses infected with woodworm and dry rot, leaking roofs and damp stonework. There is nothing here that Frome can be proud of, in fact, quite the opposite... I see no merit whatsoever in spending ratepayers' money preserving the rubbish of the Industrial Revolution.'

with previous experience of such situations[25], they encouraged residents to form Naish's Street Housing Association. A social centre was to be set up in a house on Somerset Road (number 36)

> as soon as we get our acts together – The Frome Autonomous Zone
> can offer meeting and arts spaces – Just look for the huge banner and
> the red and black flag fluttering proudly from the roof! If you're in
> the area and looking to squat, drop by – there's plenty of empties to
> go round! No Cops – No Journos – No Fash. [26]

Eventually the impasse was resolved only by the 1975 local government reshuffles, according to historian David Pierce, when the new District authority declared all Frome an outstanding conservation area. The Department of the Environment increased its usual allocation to include a 5-year £3.6 million scheme and a £337,000 historic buildings grant.

To be fair to the over-enthusiastic slum-clearance planners, the area wouldn't have looked like a model plot of 17th century cottages, as infills and random adaptations over the years would have effectively hidden the real significance of the oldest industrial housing estate in England – and some of those rehoused were probably glad to to move to somewhere with a bathroom. Steep stairs were also quoted an issue by pro-bulldozer

---

25　The squatters movement was active throughout the UK from around 1968 to the late 80s, shifting from their initial position of confrontational opposition of welfare institutions and policy, to working within welfare and state provision. Without visibility their obvious impact decreased, but their legacy had immense social and political importance. Many participants went on to work in influential roles, retaining their ideologies to influence the development of urban environment.

26　The mission statement of 'The Frome Squatters' Network' was 'to connect with squatters and everyone interested in squatting, in order to create a social, political and practical network for the promotion of squatting in the Frome area.' You could say they were re-envisaging the right to forage when there is need, which Frome's ancestors had struggled against kings to claim, but apparently that wasn't the general view. However some squatters fell in love with Frome anyway, and stayed: one ex-commune hippie bought a 4-bedroom house for £4,500... ('Fash' btw wasn't short for fashion then, it meant fascists.)

councillors but the people I spoke to who lived there remembered the area fondly.

Tony, retired butcher born in 1937, recalled the area vividly. I met him at the top of Badcox, in Baker Street[27], and he was keen to put his view.

People seemed to think Chinatown was a bad place, but I was brought up here and it wasn't – that's a myth. That was a nickname, because it was a rabbit-warren of little lanes and streets. This used to be a thriving area. There was lots of shops, and Milk Street School, quite a nice school, where I went to. And there was the church, and a butchers, and on the corner there, a fish-and-chip shop, and the Co-op, a couple of greengrocery shops, and a bespoke carpenter who used to run the Boys Brigade – and during the war there was a well-known naughty-ladies' house. After the war there was lodging houses, that was when a lot of the Irish navvies were brought into Frome.

This was the hub of the town. It really was. That used to be a bicycle shop, and people coming in from the villages on a Saturday, used to store their bikes there while they went to town. Over the other side of the road was Scotts Garage – when we were young we used to take our radio batteries there and get them charged up. There was never any trouble here. I never heard of any woman accosted, any children assaulted, no. People used to say, oh you couldn't leave anything out in Chinatown, it'd get pinched, but as far as I'm concerned that's a total myth.

Roger, a generation younger, also had direct experience of the loss.

I lived in Union Street, which was all ripped down. Between the Griffin and the print works, all the houses were knocked down as slums. Today, they wouldn't have knocked them down, but the big trouble was what they built in its place. They built houses that were

---

27 irrelevant but fascinating, Baker Street only acquired this name in 1904, being previously Brandy Lane, called after not the spirit but the smithy there which made branding irons. This and much other intriguing data can be found in the excellent and aptly titled book *Frome Place Names*.

rubbish and they've since knocked them down again – my gran lived in one of them. Concrete, absolutely awful.

The flats that were built in 1963 to replace housing dating from the time of Stuart kings were all demolished in 1998. There's no doubt that the Trinity clearance meant the tragic destruction of the earliest industrial housing in England, comparable from a conservationist's viewpoint to ethnic cleansing, but as these were technically slums it was probably hard to realise their value – and some people who lived there admit they were looking forward to being rehoused somewhere with a bathroom indoors.[28] (That's not heresy, just fact.)

It seemed to take a while for Frome to realise, as Jonathan Meades argues in *Museum Without Walls*, that 'Demolition does not destroy just buildings, it destroys the sentiments we attach to buildings, it destroys a little bit of us....' but by the time phase two was launched, the bleak images in the paper, the empty spaces, and doubtless quite a lot of poignant reminiscence, may have all contributed to a change of heart more effectively than outrage from beyond the town.

Sun Street was one survivor of the storm of new planning, avoiding demolition due to the resilience of one resident. Percy Cooper owned numbers 14 and 15 combined into one private house: most of the others in the street were council owned and so unable to take his defiant stance, but it only needed one to make the street safe. I heard this story from the current resident, Sally-Anne Fraser. The houses were nearly all one-up-one-down cottages, and Percy acquired his extension in 1947 when his neighbour covered a debt by donating his property. Percy planned to modernise, but the council decided to knock down the entire street to build a road from Badcox through Castle Street, down Zion Path, into Cork Street, obliterating all these unwanted houses and replacing them with service yards and a multi storey car park. ('I have the plan!' Sally-Anne told me.)[29]

---

28 The 'tin bath in the back yard' does however seem for some a symbol of a lost world, remembered fondly as a deprivation more than made up for by happier times and a kinder society.

29 The draft apparently dates from 1963, but it was 1972 when Somerset County Council planned to build an inner relief road around the town centre, parallel with Catherine Hill and through the market yard, demolishing the

Percy ignored all the compulsory purchase letters and when pressure mounted, he barricaded himself and his wife in their house, going outside for nothing. Neighbours brought them food. The long siege caused a delay which, perhaps with other issues, led to the road being officially deleted from all plans in 1983, at which point Percy renamed his house, appropriately, Reprieve Cottage.[30]

O NE VALUABLE CONSEQUENCE to the town of these Trinity debacles was the determination of residents and planners to ensure nothing like this ever happens again. Hilary Daniels believes

> We were one of the first towns in the country to say, we're not going to have this done to us! Because after he'd knocked down one block of the Trinity area, we said 'Enough, no more!' And what is interesting, driving up from the town you see more or less where the bulldozers were halted in their tracks – the architectural change.

It might have also helped this change of heart that Frome was outed to the world in 1975 as an awful warning by that national treasure Sir John Betjeman, in his forward to *The Rape of Britain* which documented the worst examples of Britain's urban heritage destruction. The report was gloomily factual and philosophically frantic. 'It seems unlikely that Frome will survive the present-day spate of improvements.' the authors lamented, 'The Council has little feeling for the historic nature of the town.' The new road planned was deplored as 'ludicrously destructive' and doubts about its morality implied.[31]

---

*Black Swan*, the Museum and the Masonic Hall. Properties were acquired to build this, causing further blight by yet more empty buildings decaying as they awaited demolition.

30  Sally-Anne moved into the cottage in 2014, when she discovered Percy's passion for modernising had extended to boarding up the 1690 Inglenook fireplace and fronting it with a gas fire. The row of houses on the opposite side of the street, by contrast, were all bought cheaply and restored in original style with Stanley stoves and traditional utilities – 'They're not very comfortable, it's a historical street. Mine is the only one not listed.'

31  The planned route supported a large new commercial development, financed by Commercial Union Properties Ltd. to provide 70,000 square feet of shopping space in the town centre.

Some of the losses feared in this sad and anxious look at Frome
have been avoided, although Badcox Chapel on Catherine Hill, built in
1711 for a splinter group of Baptists, was indeed knocked down for a
temporary car park. But the urge to demolish had dimmed. As cultural
historian François Hartog explains, 'The 1980s saw the idea of memory
unfurl like a giant wave, accompanied by its more visible and tangible
alter ego, heritage, and the issue of protecting, cataloguing, promoting
and rethinking it.' After the vandalism of the 60s, Frome caught onto
the zeitgeist of regeneration. The next area of the town coming up for
development had very different treatment from the streets of Trinity:
'Piggaries' was the generally-used local name for the zone of back-
gardens behind Catherine Hill, the working zone behind the street
frontage, and the problem was that nobody seemed sure who owned
which bits so it took over fourteen years to get all the permissions
before the District Council could activate their planned compulsory
purchase. The subsequent estate, which includes a range of housing, was
finally completed in 1998 and won the 1999 RTPI award for Planning
Achievement, with special commendation to 'the teamwork between the
architects, council officials, contractors and the housing associations, and
the care taken in dealing with the local community.'

Frome started to look carefully at its developments, and began to be
thankful that, like some of the smaller medieval towns in France, it had
been saved by neglect.[32] We had entirely swerved the '90s obsession with
multi-sectioned chainstores and lacked the space for supermarkets with
vast car-parks to distort the quirky charm of the town centre. Although
councillors were suspected again of blocking their arrival so that their own
retail outlets would thrive, there is a simpler explanation: shop units were
simply too small for the big chains to be interested. As Lyn Waller told me

---

32 With the cloth trade in tatters and emigration to Canada seen as a rescue line
   by many of those fit enough to leave, population as recorded on the census
   fell from 12,240 in 1831 to 11,057 by 1901, and remained under 12,000
   until the 1970s. Those interested in demography might like to know that in
   the 2001 census, 67% of Frome people of working age were in employment
   with only 3% unemployed – the rest were apparently 'economically inactive.'
   68% of workers had jobs in the service industries, the rest in manufacture.
   I work that out as 32% of the working population still involved in industry,
   which is more than I expected.

I'd sit in meetings where people would say, 'Oh why can't we have
Top Shop'- or whatever – and those shops all wanted specific square
footage, and ours just weren't big enough. And that's actually turned
out to be its saving grace, because now that is what actually attracts
people to Frome.

By now the emphasis was all on saving and mending. Mendip
District Council's list[33] of successfully saved Frome buildings comprises
a cottage Button Street, Garston Lodge (previously the vet surgery, the
original building dates from 15th century with an 1835 facade which is
a rare example of Gothic revival in Frome), Whittox Lane Sunday School
(that's the tiny octagonal building outside the HUBnub, now an artist's
studio) and the Feather Factory. This last is on Willow Vale, dating
from early 1800s and with an unusual gambrel roof[34], 'one of the best
surviving examples of a pre-factory machine workshop in the area'.
Frome now recognises that good preservation doesn't need time-
freeze: *The Lamb* Brewery's old bottling plant and barrel stores (on the
corner opposite Gorehedge) and the original *Selwood Printing Works*
have both been converted into flats and both developments look good,
blending tonally and enhancing their sites. In the words of the *Academy
of Urbanism* report on Frome in 2015 'There are good examples of new
buildings in the town that manage to avoid pastiche and fit well in
scale and materials.' Despite 'not being a picture postcard town with its
rough edges and run-down areas', developments like these combined
with positive social factors contributed to Frome being awarded the
prestigious title "Great Town."[35]

---

33 *Historic Buildings At Risk Register,* 2012
34 A gambrel roof has two symmetrical sides, each with two sloping surfaces,
   the lower one using a steeper slope than the upper one which joins the
   structure at the mid point.
35 Among all the positives that brought Frome this commendation there
   was one specific concern identified: 'Sustaining the social diversity is an
   issue, and there is a concern about changes in the schools provision from
   a three-tier system to competition from a nearby academy school and the
   first publicly-funded Steiner Free School in England. The original education
   structure worked well because everyone, irrespective of background, went
   through school together, which helped reinforce a close-knit community.

'Rough edges and run-down areas' in my opinion are no bad thing. As dangerous as razing ancient buildings is what has been called the Disneyfication of cultural memory.[36] Every town needs 'edgelands', the term given by Robert Macfarlane in *Landmarks* to those messy, inconspicuous hinterlands, disruptive of the picturesque, dismissive of the sublime – the unseen landscapes.[37] There are a lot of them in Frome: those strangely useless corners between converging walls, the bits of wasteland where brambles dangle and tufts of grass burst inexplicably through the tarmac (have you ever noticed how much grass there is around the centre of town? scruffy little patches of verdancy), moss riming kerbs and snickets, stone walls daubed lizard green with lichen, old painted doors crackled into intricate mosaics, rusted hooks and rings now unused but still hanging... Jonathan Meades writes of the glory of decay, decrepitude's pattern-making, entropy's sublimity – and Frome is full of such secret gems: did you know there's a faded shield, featuring a chevron, three stars and three lions, on the guttering outside the Pet Shop in King Street, or that the wormy wooden beams in Amica's shop window date from the 1500s and are carved with tudor wooden roses?

R ECLAMATIONS AND RESTORATIONS are now part of the 'look' of Frome. Their histories have been researched, and reported extensively – once again I refer you to the bibliography and will reference just a few examples. There's a good deal of support for such recoveries generally: the Town Hall recovery was urged by a banner-waving protest on the steps, and the Blue House survived by a series of public appeals throughout its history: I'll start with a quick look at these two buildings:

The Town Hall on Christchurch Street West, built in 1892 and iniquitously lost to Frome as recounted in the first section, was built to

---

This is a national issue that is particularly affecting Frome.' Just saying.

36  The historian François Hartog has written of what he sees as a trend from history to 'history-heritage' – 'an identity in search of itself, to be exhumed, assembled, or even invented...The 'ardent obligation' of heritage, with its requirements for conservation, renovation, and commemoration is added to the 'duty' of memory, with its recent public translation of repentance.'

37  'not the unseen world in a psychic sense, they belong to the world that lies, visibly, about us. They are unseen merely because they are not perceived...' – Paul Nash

an Italian Renaissance design and retains many original features: mosaic floors, ornate fireplaces and a surprisingly avant-garde air-conditioning system. The Blue House with much older origins has also stayed close to its founding purpose – in this case, the concept of community support. The original almshouse on this site was established in 1461[38] by William Leversedge, then Lord of the Manor of Frome, 'for the relief of the poure people'. This building seems to have had structural problems from the start, and in the 1720s it was completely rebuilt, incorporating a charity school.[39] The benefactor was a solicitor called James Wickham who is thought to have collaborated with his mason Richard Coombes on design, choosing a style Nikolaus Pevsner[40] has termed 'oddly disjointed' but which seems to suit Frome.[41] The most noticeable features are the

---

38  That's according to a deed of 1621 but dates on these documents seem to have been penned as casually as Shakespeare's signature – William didn't succeed to his father's title until 1465. But it was definitely a very long time ago.

39  Education was a costly luxury to most in an era when child labour was an essential part of a family's income but, as work became mechanised, schools included industrial training in their schedules. Frome was actually well-served for schools for 'the poor' including a free Grammar School in Vicarage Street and Keyford Academy in Sunnyside from 1810 till 1930. For the more well-off families, many women home-owners offered 'boarding schools' of varying quality. Sunday Schools were the main official source of tuition for many children until 1880 when education became compulsory for children aged five to ten, extended to thirteen in 1899. This new emphasis was a consequence of the emerging mechanical age: as sociologist Alvin Toffler pointed out in 1970 in his seminal book *Future Shock*: 'Industrialism demanded skills that neither family nor church could, by themselves, provide. Mass education was the ingenious machine to produce the kind of adults it needed. The problem was how to pre-adapt children for a world of repetitive indoor toil, noise, machines, crowded conditions, collective discipline, in which time was regulated not by the cycle of sun and moon, but by the factory whistle and the clock. The solution was an educational system that simulated this world.'

40  Nikolaus Pevsner was the 20th century England's Baedeker, his opinions on architecture ground-rules for middle-class travellers. His judgements were often personalised: Rook Lane Chapel he found 'surprisingly self-assertive', and considered the West Front of St John's 'pitiable'.

41  'The doorcase is imposing and has a fashionable pediment and bolection moulding. A hipped roof with cupola crowns the whole imposing edifice,'

two stone figures – 'Nancy Guy and Billy Ball up against the Blue School wall': they represent the elderly women and the young schoolboys who between them shared the charity's funds, and that imposing azure-blue clock was made by one James Clark. The school closed in 1921 and the Blue House is now adapted for individual residence with eighteen flatlets and has been Grade I listed since 1949, so the future looks secure.

S OME OF FROME'S MOST ADMIRED BUILDINGS have survived by changing role completely. To quote Jonathan Meades again: 'a structure's purpose is ultimately provisional: the mosque becomes a cathedral, the warehouse is transformed into a skating rink, the old abattoir is now a boathouse.' The *Black Swan* on Bridge Street is one of Frome's prime examples of such adaptation. Built in the 17th Century, it was a thriving public house until the first world war and, with a prime location near the cattle market, it's strange that the business then failed. By 1955 the pub was closed and Frome Urban District Council bought it in 1961 as a listed building, then equally mysteriously allowed it to decline into such dangerous dereliction that by 1974 it was scheduled for demolition.[42] In the early 1980s the building was still standing, just about, and a small group of public-spirited locals raised funds to repair and reopen it as an Arts Centre to enhance the town and also to provide affordable studios for the artist community already growing in Frome. Black Swan Arts opened in 1986, combining with the Round Tower[43] and providing workshop space, point of sale, cafe, and frequent exhibitions. Black Swan Arts today is one of the success stories of the town, and

---

explains the Blue House website, adding loyally 'It would not be out of place in Bath, Bristol or any other Georgian city and has been described by Bryan Little as "an admirable work of vernacular baroque".'

42 The yard was used on market days as a point of sale for chickens, geese, rabbits, pigeons, ferrets, and other small creatures. One of the traders, a well-known local called Bob Joyce, apparently had a habit of selling pigeons without mentioning that they were homing pigeons, and was known to laugh with friends that on market days they were home before he was...

43 The 'Round Tower' was built in the mid-18th century as a stove to dry out the dyed cloth. Some conservationists were disappointed that the new complex had completely linked it physically to the connecting passage rather than leaving a slight space so that it retained its claim to be one of the last surviving separate round towers in the country.

in terms of Frome's structural history, is a very good example of the palimpsestic nature of the town's development.

Another instance of the layering of eras in the fabric of Frome is the Silk Mill – one of the best preserved textile mills in the area, now providing studio spaces for working artists and a large gallery space for exhibitions, performances, parties, and other functions.

The Silk Mill is particularly interesting among the mills of Frome since whereas wool was worked from very early eras, successful silk-making was largely unknown in England until Sir Thomas Lombe in early 18th Century visited Piedmont and managed to steal the secrets of 'silk-throwing' by luring some of the specialist craftsmen to his mill in Derbyshire. This new craft was lucrative but predictably unpopular with local cotton and worsted spinners who opposed a renewal of his patent in 1732: Lombe was compelled to comply with an order to share models of his machinery, and three more mills were built. The north of England remained central to the English silk industry, yet Frome had a thriving mill by the end of that century and despite industrial unrest the Silk Mill maintained its role[44] till 1926. The building was then bought by Notts Industries which, despite being over 30 miles from any coast, became the major manufacturer of Carley Life Floats and Buoyant Apparatus, known locally as Carley Works. In 2005 Damon and Kate Moore revived the name and restored the building.

Among other notable buildings[45] to have survived and thrived, Rook Lane Chapel, the amazing building at the top of Bath Street, is probably one of the best known of the altered-role renovations.[46] Built in 1707 as a Congregational Church (and unusual in that era of small chapels

---

44  Silk had a boom in popularity when Queen Victoria's mourning habit made 'widow's weeds' a fashion statement, but WWI put a stop to that, and to the English silk industry.

45  Pedigrees for most of the many interesting buildings can be found not only in printed literature but online via a quick google search. For that reason I am only mentioning here those that have changed function particularly distinctly.

46  Those who revere Pevsner might like to know that he reports Rook Lane 'exceptionally handsome, it's size and pride remarkable at so early a date' and his reviser, Andrew Foyle, applauds the renovation: 'a steel and glass link to a rear wing with a monopitch roof; admirable and uncompromisingly new'.

for its sheer scale) it was occupied for over 260 years despite the split in 1773 to form an evangelical wing named Zion Congregational Church.[47] It closed for worship in 1968 and, despite being Grade I listed, soon became dilapidated. In 1991 SCC used compulsory purchase to acquire it, and after a couple more sales and a bit of repair, it was still empty until 2001. When I arrived in Frome in the late '80s, Rook Lane was a popular place for parties and used by Artspark[48] for events as it was cheap to hire because there were absolutely no facilities. Laurie Parnell remembers 'It was just a shell – restored and then left, with no floor, no water, no power.[49] One multi-media event we did as an Artmusic collaboration, with Rowena Pearce, Alastair Goolden and Helen Ottaway, was Lacrimae – falling glass teardrops.'

Rook Lane is now home to NVB Architects above and the Rook Lane Arts Trust below, hosting art exhibitions, concerts, choirs, performances, and talks. It has been beautifully restored by the architects themselves.[50]

-------

47 This was a big time for establishing solid structures for the dissenting groups: several Nonconformist churches were built in the early years of the 18th century, the most important of which were the Rook Lane Congregational Church and also Badcox Lane Baptist Church in 1711.

48 Artspark, based in Bradford-on-Avon, offers creative arts projects around the southwest. Much of Laurie's work with them was influenced by 'Common Ground' – a national organisation formed in 1983 to encourage people to engage more with their local environment. One artist they supported was Andy Goldsworthy, now OBE, who describes his work as 'tapping into change, light, growth and decay... Process and decay are implicit. Transience in my work reflects what I find in nature." Not unlike graff, really... They also provided the inspiration for the Mount Parish Map project, referenced earlier.

49 At the end of the century, visual artist Helen Langford organised a memorable masked ball as a Millennium party. 'It just seemed like a good idea. I hired a Portaloo and an industrial heater like you use on building sites – possibly terribly dangerous with children running around but otherwise it would be freezing – and had lots of chandeliers strung from the ceiling, made of pieces of wood with nails to hold the candles – terribly unsafe but it looked very beautiful – we had a huge fishing net filled with balloons too, and some great masks....' I remember them, and the flamboyant costumes, and the candlelit gloaming...

50 NVB Architects came up with the rescue scheme: renovation of the old chapel plus an additional extension including a cafe for community use, in return use the upper area as their own offices. This, since 2003, has not only

Another deconsecrated success is the metamorphosis of old Whittox Lane Zion Chapel to the HUBnub Community Centre, completed in 2017. New owners Ed and Io Fox-Roberts asked Minerva Conservation, local restoration specialists, to salvage both the exterior – needing extensive stone replacement – and the extraordinary interior, with its high balcony and vast organ in a vaulted alcove. The only solution to saving this was steel joists, which Minerva craftswoman Nell Pickering has disguised with gilded stars. It looks gorgeous. Rye Bakery currently occupies the main area, the balcony is a gallery and the back rooms are extensively used for various sessions and classes.

WHILE MANY OF THE TOWN BUILDINGS that changed their role are religious ones resigned to a more secular society, some are simply working areas which have changed hands. A look through old postcards of Frome will show variations in ownership even when the building itself survives entirely recognisably.[51] The pet shop in Kingsway precinct was built around 1700 for the Sheppards, major cloth traders of Frome, and the interior today retains virtually every key feature including the elegant hall chandelier: the ornamental moulding on ceiling arches, blue lias floor, cornice and stucco pilasters, mahogany stairs and bannisters, even the window frames, are all original. The terrain around the house has changed since it was named Iron Gates because of the massive ones enclosing a sweeping carriageway that then surrounded it – the traces are still visible in the car park. 'Above ground archaeology' is the term used for these secret corners by stonemason Andrew Ziminski, (who also showed me that coat of arms on the Pet Shop rainwater hopper.)

---

saved the building but given Frome another 160 seater venue. For more information on conservation in Frome there's a useful pdf summary of salient points by John Peverley here: fcs_conservation_in_frome_feb_09.

51 Cheap Street is particularly good for this, as most of the buildings look pretty much the same: Charles Hart jewellers, for example, has retained the lift of the original cheese shop. Shops have changed role but are still mostly independent: organic food from *Frome Wholefoods* and *Sagebury Cheese*, a local baker between the two coffee shops at the top, clothes shops using eco products, two independent bookshops, and *Raves from the Grave*, where famous musicians happily busk, and not a single Ye Olde sign anywhere. Cheap Street and Apple Alley date back to the 13th Century, although most of the buildings seen today are from the Tudor era.)

Perhaps the strangest shift of function in Frome is the old toilet in the market yard which now serves food. 'Loop de Loop' is a candy-striped ex-toilet row now housing a mini art gallery, the free Community Fridge, and a hot food service, and the seed for this conversion was planted by an image posted on Facebook in 2012 showing the several dejected-looking abandoned toilets in town. Katy Duke, knowing that this particular dejected-looking one had a wall containing glass blocks made by artist Helga Watkins-Baker and embedded with artefacts from Frome's lost industries, mounted a rescue. Refused on her funding bids, and with irreplaceable art work as well as a still-solid twelve-year-old building both at risk, Katy started a crowd-funding scheme and raised £11,000 in 13 weeks. Loop-de-Loop was cleaned, painted, and ready for the world in time for the 2013 Frome festival. As Katy told the BBC 'It's another of those Frome projects which show that passion and creativity can overcome enormous hurdles in dealing with buildings and bureaucracy. Frome is a bit of a hotbed of this sort of activism.'

THE BEST WAY to find out more about the town's structures is of course to invest a pound in the map-dispensers dotted around town and start walking. Guides all say no impression can be formed by car, which isn't quite true as an impression of annoying perversity can quickly form. Names are not necessarily helpful – *High Street* for example is so named simply because that part of town is quite high up in relation to the river – and tarmacked roads with encouragingly traffic-related kerbside lines may end abruptly in a barton with only a flight of steps as exit, while what seems like a passable route to the central car park becomes a dead end because the road bridge over the river has been replaced by a footbridge.[52] Parking in the old town, and many other

_____

52 A change which puzzled many, not least Jenson Button, after whom it is ironically named, who allegedly pointed out 'I'm a racing driver' to explain why he declined the honour of opening it in 2010. National media found this risible too, the *Guardian* (Jan 2010) speaking teasingly of the glitter of the accolade and *The Scotsman* milking it further: 'TV comedian Charlie Higson also hails from the town, so presumably a lamppost will be bearing his name soon enough.'

I'm indebted to Jean Lowe's thorough documentation of council cogitations for the background here. The original 'Bailey bridge' dating from WWII was getting rickety and the options were to repair or replace. The first

areas too, is creative to the point of anarchy: pavements, verges, and churchyard access all become overflow car parks. One resident told me he thought that the double yellow lines had been as detrimental to town trade as the loss of the market.

Shortage of car-friendly routes around the old town is inevitable of course, since none of them were designed for anything wider than a horse-drawn carriage.[53] The area around the market place was up until 1810 a labyrinth of courts and passages, with a slaughter-house just beyond the church: as there were also houses in the churchyard at that time, this left 'no very large space at the church doors.' Eagle Lane, King Street, Cheap Street, and Apple Lane are virtually unaltered,[54] which gives you an idea. By the time *Rees' Cyclopædia* was printed in 1819 Frome was considered 'greatly increased, to about 38 streets which are in general narrow, irregularly built of rough stones, and covered with heavy stone tile dug from the adjacent quarries.'

Until 1791 these streets, and other small alleys now disappeared, were the only way to negotiate Frome. Bath Street, now the main connection for road traffic between the three south-eastern routes to the north, wasn't built until 1810 and followed the plan of wealthy

---

option had a lot of support but failed to attract National Heritage subsidy because of a minor modification to the classic design, and rising costs became an issue. Public opinion continued in favour of a road bridge but 'luckily EMCP had already agreed the previous November that a vehicular crossing, which the townspeople preferred, was unnecessary.' So the next step was the arrival of 'a very grand cable stayed suspension bridge with an improbable spike... ...signed off by two Frome Town/District Councillors undiscussed at Town Council. In Bradford-on-Avon the same design had been put to town referendum and rejected.' A further attempt to get Frome's Bailey Bridge listed failed because by now it had been given to a Wiltshire Canal Trust for a farm crossing at Semington. Just one of the many insights into life behind the scenes, perhaps in some small way explaining the swing to Independents on the council in 2011.

53  In 1810 the widest streets were only 16 feet 7 inches wide, most being 13 feet 10 inches including footpaths.

54  From a lecture on 'The Street Names of Frome' by the late Rev. W. E. Daniel, delivered at a meeting of the Holy Trinity Young Men's Institute. King Street, he surmised, was probably connected to 'the coming of the Great Deliverer in 1688' – that's the Dutch husband of James II's protestant daughter Mary, established on the throne after the 'Glorious Revolution of that year.

diarist Thomas Bunn,[55] in the first known example of the gentrification of Frome.[56] (The next was to be a sweeping Grecian crescent to outclass Bath but funders were not forthcoming – luckily, as the vista Bunn aimed to achieve would have required destruction of most of the old town.)

The *Wagon and Horses*,[57] still a serving pub until 1959, retains some of its interior dating from 1568 or earlier. It was from here in the 18th century that the Frome Flyer stagecoach set off on its two-day journey to London each week – and also seven wagons laden with cloth for the London market. Horse-drawn carriages didn't have to cope with Gentle Street: they used the stable yard, accessed from Christchurch Street East – then called Behind Town – between a tithe barn and Rectory Farm at about where St Johns school is now. Gentle Street was known as Hunger Lane from the 1300s, then renamed by common usage after the Gentell family lived there. Its current cobbles[58] were laid in 1987. I remember watching

55  The then-vicar of St Johns, the active W.J.E. Bennett, took the opportunity to rebuild access to his portal as a gothic arch and to redevelop the churchyard, with space for his own memorial. This ambitious edifice, due to an error over weather-resistance of materials, survives only partially and very messily. The contractor, anticipating such an outcome, wisely returned his fee shortly after completion.

56  Originally there were railings on the garden walls all the way up Bath Street. Hilary Daniels recalls their confiscation for the war effort in the 1940s: 'The Government decreed that all unnecessary metal anywhere should be brought in, and they went round with blow torches and took all the railings from all the houses – you can still see the little metal stumps of where they cut them off. Then they found that kind of metal was no practical use in the war and they were used as ballast on ships, which is why if you go to places like Cape Town or Melbourne they've all got elaborate ironware balcony rails because the ballast of returning ships was all unloaded there.'

57  The Wagon and Horses was still a pub until 1959, and I have failed to find out when the bollards at the top and bottom of Gentle Street were constructed. Rumour has it that these were added in early Regency days to prevent young blades racing their horses down the steep slope for bets, culminating one dreadful night when two light carriages made the dash together, colliding tragically at the bottom and causing the death of all the horses and at least one of the drivers. Well that's what I was told when I arrived in Frome anyway, though I can find no trace of the story recorded anywhere!

58  Cobbles are traditionally round(ish) stones, so there's some debate as to whether the ones in Frome are actually setts, as they are flattish and more rectangular. However, setts are usually laid to give a flat surface while

this steady progress on my walk to college early each morning and back in the late afternoon, marvelling at the craft and the patience of the two men, Brian Mahon and Michael O'Loughlin. The hill looks so authentically ancient that BBC chose this area to film scenes for *Poldark* in 2015, and days after the crew had left you might have collected souvenir strands of straw on which Aidan Turner, sexiest man on the planet,[59] had strode.

Y OUR '*DISCOVER FROME SUPERB 3-D TOWN CENTRE MAP*' will show you quite a bit more than the 1774 map of Frome, drawn when the town basically consisted of the area between *Ring O'Bells* on Broadway to *The Three Swans* on King Street from east to west, north to south span being from *The Griffin* on Milk Street down to *The Lamb*, now *The Cornerhouse*.[60]

Pubs were a natural marker: they were integral to the life of Frome – as everywhere else in England. At one time Frome's pubs each had their own brewery.[61] Ale and beer were considered part of a staple

---

cobbles are deliberately bumpy to give better grip on slopes and in bad weather, so the commonly accepted term 'cobbled' for these roads is what I've chosen.

59 He was officially awarded this title in 2016 by *Glamour* magazine. Aidan has a slender connection with Frome via the 2009 BBC series about the Pre-Raphaelites, *Desperate Romantics*, in which he played Dante Gabriel Rossetti, brother to Christina who for a while ran a school in Brunswick Terrance in Fromefield with their mother. (I still think his best role was the vampire in *Being Human*, but that was filmed in Bristol so extolling their gothic humour is beyond this remit.)

60 *The Crown* and *The Three Swans* both date back to around 1600 or before. The present *Three Swans* is a 19th Century combination of the old building with its neighbour, with the alley that once divided them now integrated. By the 19th Century, it had a reputation for being massively rowdy and full of 'disorderly' ladies, while the *Crown's* notoriety was for Sabbath-breaking and political activism. *The Griffin* was irreligiously serving on Sundays from 1717, and though *Ring O'Bells* was first mentioned in 1721 it had been around for some time, similarly incurring regular constabulary intervention for drunkenness and assaults on the premises: sadly it was sold by Ushers Brewery in 1992, and lacking investment from subsequent buyers, closed in 2014.

61 *The Griffin* still has: Milk Street Brewery regular wins awards, and the pub is one of only two in Frome on the CAMRA *Good Beer Guide* -the other is the Old Bath Arms.

diet, often safer to drink than water from unprotected wells, and when cheap gin entered the economy in the early 1700s, the government actively encouraged drinking of beer as a 'wholesome and temperate beverage'. Pubs were places where people could meet and socialise,[62] sharing information and ideas, natural hubs for developing networks and strengthening community identity and the places where visitors of every social status went on arrival for information as well as refreshment. 'There is nothing which has yet been contrived by man, by which so much happiness is produced as by a good tavern or inn.' said Samuel Johnson in 1791 and others, George Orwell[63] included, have echoed the sentiment of Thomas Burke who wrote in 1930 'To write of the English inn is to write of England itself – as familiar in the national consciousness as the oak and the ash.'

Consequently the social history of Frome is written most vividly in the stories of its pubs, and it's really hard to stop reading the *Historic Inns of Frome* once you start...

To give you just a taste, consider the *Artisan*: previously *The Olive Tree*, which served excellent meals (not Greek but Thai) and before that notorious as *The Ship,* this pub's early history is fascinating even by Frome's weird standards. Built before the main Trinity development at a time when Badcox was known as Seven Dials from the number of streets meeting there and the Leversedge family were Lords of the Manor, it was owned by various of their kin over the years including in 1738 one Lionel Seaman who owned the *Packhorse* too and was also vicar of Frome. Rev Seaman accepted the rent paid by the landlord but his conscience apparently forbad him to support them and he actively prosecuted those

---

62  The collective name 'public houses' came into common use in Henry VIII's time: previously there was a distinction between taverns & alehouses, which provided food and drink, and inns, which also offered accommodation to travellers. The Beer Act of 1830 granted permission to brew and sell beer, at the cost of 2 guineas, to any home-owner, which increased the number of ale houses everywhere. Licensing restrictions were finally brought in by the 1869 as landlords were beginning to find it impossible to make any profit with so many outlets competing.

63  George Orwell was a regular frequenter of pubs, and a keen commentator too on their wider social role. He called the pub 'one of the basic institutions of English life', which 'carries on despite the harassing tactics of Nonconformist local authorities'.

guilty of Frome's favourite crime: drinking on a Sunday. This infuriated the publicans who wrote him a letter to put their point, which began *The people of this parish say that thou art a damnable wicked villain to use the parish as thou dost and that thou art no more fit to go up in the pulpit than the devil himself...* And thus, with disorderly ladies lingering late and frequent bar fights, the *Ship's* colourful history continued, just one more microcosm from three hundred years in Frome.

To END THIS FOCUS on buildings and their usage, a short case-study of a factor which has altered the pattern of daily life perhaps as significantly as the loss of industry: the closure of local shops in residential streets has happened in living memory, changing community interaction radically and resulting in neighbours who may no longer know who lives next door. The fact that Frome has changed its character so much in so short a time may go some way to explain the unease people feel at the prospect of more housing. It's not the property-value worry of an affluent town going all NIMBY, it's the shuddering of a town that has seen the fabric of its life alter dramatically. I could have chosen Badcox or any of the other places once bustling and now mainly residential, often with shifting populations as tenants come and go, but I've chosen Keyford,[64] from the Beehive crossing to Gorehedge, because that's where I live.

*'We depend on our surroundings obliquely to embody the moods and ideas we respect and then to remind us of them. We look to our buildings to hold us, like a kind of psychological mould, to a helpful vision of ourselves.*
– Alain de Botton, *The Architecture of Happiness*

CASE SRUDY: KEYFORD Keyford was originally a separate hamlet mentioned in the Domesday Book of 1086 and, as you can see from the leafy-gardened mansions of what we now call Lower Keyford[65],

---

64 It was an area rich in timber – 'keys' were wooden pegs, valuable for use and trade.
65 Benjamin Baker, Frome's most famous structural engineer, was born here in 1840 but never designed anything in Frome. He started his career in London, where as one of the planners of the Underground system he made the Central line 'undulate', and is of course most famous for the 1.5 mile long

smarter than this part of town. The name Keyford now refers to the short link road between the top of the southern hill and the scooping valley to the Mount and the industrial estate; it would be a rat-run at rush-hours if it hadn't been from half way along designated one-way, out of town only, in recognition of the narrowness of the road. The process of connection began in the 17th Century, as several houses on this street date from that era although most now have later frontages, and only the pub, mullioned and gabled, shows its real age. Mendip's 'Conservation Area Appraisal' of 2008 could find only one point of interest in the entire street – the defunct George V postbox in the wall beside a drainpipe – but it fascinates me that along this three minute walk you pass around 350 years of build and change.

Sioux How, historical researcher, lives in one of the older houses, with a front door directly onto the street and a thickly walled alley with curved sides at the back, designed, she believes, so that coaches could drive into the yard – 'there may have been a pub there at one time. I love that sense of all the things that have gone on in Frome – this house was built in 1656, so when the Monmouth's rebellion was crushed and the men were hung, whoever lived here would have seen it from this window!' Sioux indicates the fire-station, with its little bronze fireman surveying the town below, which is where gibbets were erected to give the widest possible view of the rebels' dreadful deaths.[66]

There was also a pub at this end of the street until 1968 when

---

Forth Bridge, completed in 1890. The first steel bridge in existence, it was widely hailed as the eighth wonder of the world although William Morris gave it the alternative label of 'the supremest specimen of all ugliness'. In 1840 Keyford wasn't part of Frome, Mr Baker Snr. worked at Tondu Ironworks in Wales, and Benjamin was educated at Cheltenham Grammar School, so strictly speaking he's not a child of Frome at all but I felt he had to go somewhere.

66 These were no ordinary hangings: the sentence was worded 'that you be drawn upon an hurdle to the place of execution, where you shall be hanged up by the neck, but cut down alive, your entrails and privy members cut off your body, and burnt in your sight, your head to be severed from your body, and your body divided into four parts, and disposed at the King's pleasure. And the Lord have mercy upon your soul.' Folk-lore had it that Gorehedge got its name from the blood that flowed from the quartered bodies of men, but gore is actually an ancient name for a triangular field.

it was demolished and replaced by the fire station: *The Unicorn* dated
back to 1770 and was one of the principal inns of its day although like
most of Frome's pubs, it had troubled times: In the mid 1820s it was
the base for striking weavers and in 1880 the publican, William Knight,
went bankrupt owing the bank £8,000 – around £100,000 in current
reckoning. The next landlord cut his throat in1902 and the last man to be
landlord had some trouble with the police and gave up the lease in 1948.

Keyford's surviving pub, *The Crown,* is far older, built probably in
late 1600s – a Charles II era coin was found in the garden – and was at
one time also owned by the Knight family. Back in 1876 landlord William
Knight (not the one who lost *The Unicorn* but his father) hosted a political
meeting which caused defamatory rumours, which he refuted in a letter
to the *Daily Post* insisting it was 'orderly and quiet – in fact there never
was a more orderly meeting.' *The Crown* was designated for preservation
in 1938, and is now considered a quiet pub for locals, which puts on an
old-fashioned sandwiches-and-cake street party outside on the Queen's
birthday.[67] The Crown features frequently in local research[68] and is a
favourite with the local gipsies, whose trap can be seen parked outside on
summer evenings, their patient horses tethered to the lamp post nearby.
Crown Gardens, next to the pub, was at one time a community garden –
we had anti-war vigils there in 2003 – but is currently fenced off for new
building.

Aside from pubs and hangings, Keyford's other claim to interest
in a social history sense is the sawmill which once filled the area now
containing the 51 houses of the Cooperage estate. Robin Lambert

---

67  This in 2017 contrasted with the Queen's birthday party we had on
    Catherine Hill with a Majesty lookalike twerking on the cobbles to sounds
    from Covers Vinyl, and several glittering Freddie Mercuries.
68  This was the alehouse where poor Sarah Watts's parents stopped on their way
    home to West Woodlands after a Wednesday market in Frome in September
    1851. They arrived back to find their child strangled, having been first raped.
    The details of the case are sordid but the culprits were nailed... though
    ironically, their lawyer successfully dismissed the evidence as circumstantial
    and all three walked free. This was the same era as the notorious Rode Hill
    House murder, the case in which Mr Whicher's solution was ignored by local
    police for years, so it appears London-imported detectives were not popular
    with the people of Somerset. (There's more on this later)

showed me his file of newspaper cuttings,[69] mostly his own contributions as memories, and one picture from the 1920s showed 'a familiar scene at Gray's Sawmills – horses delivering a huge oak tree trunk on a large timber carriage.' Eleven men in shirts and braces plus a boy with a dog pose proudly in front of it. The mill's machinery was steam driven, and in these pre-chainsaw days, it would have taken many man-hours using two-man cross-cut saws and axes to fell a tree of this magnitude. I'm torn between admiration for these fit young men in their Peaky-Blinder caps, and sorrow for the loss of this noble ancient healthy tree – it's girth is easily two foot more than the height of the man standing beside it on top of the carriage, and to have a diameter of around eight feet it must have been 400 years old at least.[70]

Charlie Gray's saw mill[71] closed in 1934 and was taken over by Wilson and Scotchman and bigger saws powered by electricity were brought in. In the early 1930s, a huge order of 60,000-gallon vats for the Guinness London brewery just about cleared the area of big oak trees and the saw mill fell idle. The army took it over in WWII, solving the mud problem by bringing in tons of rubble from bombed areas of Bristol. And now I live there...

Opposite the Cooperage is *Domesticare* independent electrical stores, one of only four retail outlets in Keyford – the others are a betting shop and two take-aways. When I first moved here there were also two small general stores and a post office. One by one they disappeared

---

69  *Somerset Standard* at one time had a section edited by Dan Biggane called *Looking Back*. It provided a fascinating pool of local history and is much missed.

70  Multiply the oak's diameter in inches times the growth factor to get the approximate age of your oak. Use 4 if unsure of oak type. So 96x4=384 – at least! Could be over 576 years.

71  Reader Arthur Williams responded with more fond memories of those early days: 'It was good to watch the horses bring a big tree up Locks Hill, you could hear hooves and shouting long before they came up the hill. I remember watching them working with a mouthful of nails and a hammer – men who worked in the timber industry didn't often show a full set of fingers; safety wasn't such a priority as it is now: Charlie Gray himself had a thumb and little finger only on one hand. It used to puzzle me how he missed a clean sweep.'

and the properties became residential.[72] I wondered if there had once been more shops, and put out the question on facebook. By next day I had over forty responses, and learned that at one time you could buy dresses, shoes, knitting wool, baby-clothes, toys, fruit&veg, fish&chips, ice-cream, sweets, cakes, fresh fish, electric goods, and newspapers – all from independent shops with named owners still fondly remembered. There had also been a Co-op, a Spa, a VHS rental and (in the 70s) a 'Channel Jive' CB shop. There was a hairdressers, a barbers, a DIY shop, builders merchants, pet shop, second-hand shop, and 'a tiny antique shop where my new boyfriend bought me a glass paperweight in 1974. I am looking at it now on my coffee table and my boyfriend is now my husband, together for 44 years.' Conversations followed as connections were renewed. 'It was a friendly sociable street...' 'There used to be shops along most of Keyford and we didn't need to go into town...' 'we had it all on our doorstep.'

It is somewhat sad, as some commented, that this local buzz has gone, but reassuring that Keyford was a happy experience for those who lived, worked, or walked through here. Alain de Botton wrote 'We owe it to the fields that our houses will not be the inferiors of the virgin land they have replaced.' It's probably not always possible to keep such a pledge to fields, but we should certainly promise the people who settle that land that they will not need to grieve that prioritising community has been replaced by prioritising developers' profit.

On the town side of the Cooperage estate is Linwood Motors, housed in a shed that looks more temporary than it is. Originally this was one of the garages of M H Scott & Sons in a thriving business of converting early Ford cars into delivery vans to meet the growing need for commercial transport. Behind this garage is the Drill Hall[73], built in

---

72  Reasons for this change aren't unique to Frome: life-style values were changing everywhere from the '70s: more availability of hire-purchase, more working women more cars, more TV adverts raising aspirations, all led to the shift towards bigger shops with more choice and lower prices, which left the small local shops unprofitable. The 1975 Equalities Act changed everything: women didn't need a man to buy on credit, so shopping malls were taking over as main trading areas.

73  Originally used by 4th Battalion Somerset Light Infantry and 2nd South Western Mounted Brigade Field Ambulance – it has rather nice 'half moon windows' apparently typical of Somerset.

1914 and still used by the Frome Platoon of Somerset Cadets and also as a polling station, and next to it the fire station, on the site of the Monmouth hangings.

The fascinating history of fire-fighting in Frome actually begins in St Johns Church, in what is now known as the Ken Chapel, as vestry minutes reveal that in the 18th Century the pumps were stored there. As Cheap Street seems so prone to conflagration this must have seemed reasonable, but in the 1820s the bishop wrote to churchwardens requiring them to move them out into a proper building. So the first Fire Station was built in 1828, and housed manual fire engines – basically a pump on wheels, with a lever to fill the buckets – which were used on a help-yourself basis, a bit like Boris bikes. The next advance was a steam fire engine, pulled by four horses, using a hose rather than buckets.[74] When new fire engines were acquired it was clear that a bigger base was needed, and Keyford Fire Station opened in 1971.

Keyford was also the scene of a serious fire in 1889. As noted earlier, the arrival of insurance had increased the risk of fires, and Charles Garratt, brush-maker, was either unfortunate or careless: in 1886 his Keyford premises suffered quite a big fire, but there was another worse one during a night in 1889 in which a servant girl died. Annie Moore was roused and warned of the danger but apparently didn't want to leave her room in her nightie, and was overcome by smoke before she could finish dressing. Mr Garratt's son ran off to report the blaze and 'With great promptitude the firemen were on the spot' – but the shop was gutted and 'nothing whatever was saved.' The coroner's inquest on

---

74 The Frome Fire Service had been formed in 1861, earlier than many other towns and though still a volunteer group, it was well organised and ambitious. The steam engine they decided to buy cost £500 – a lot of money in 1896 – which they raised in a highly original way, by setting up a Japanese bazaar in the Cheese & Grain to run for three days. 'Everyone was fascinated by the Orient,' Rob Gill explained, 'but nobody knew anything about it.' So a village of bamboo was created, with stall holders in Japanese costumes, there were theatre shows, music and food, and even discount train excursions laid on to bring people from surrounding towns. The firemen raised over a thousand pounds, enough to buy a 'Rolls Royce' fire engine, half a mile of hose, brass fire helmets 'and the captain had a silver plate one.' And also to put some money towards buying a new fire station, as the old one was now too small.

poor Annie was clouded by the insurance issue, especially as this was the second fire there. But at least, as the Somerset Standard reported 'The inhabitants of Frome have cause to be proud of their Fire Brigade. The alacrity, bravery, and self-denying efforts they displayed in the early hours of Friday morning will for ever rebound to their honour and credit, and the deputy coroner complimented them in a most graceful term.' [75]

The other major fire in Keyford was more recent, in 1991 when Pine Range – virtually opposite the Fire Station, was completely gutted. Rob Gill played an active part in controlling this dangerous blaze, managing to create a fire break and stop it spreading down the adjoining buildings. The business was never rebuilt and the space now belongs to Selwood Court.

S O THIS BORING LITTLE STREET, with apparently only a defunct post-box to commend it, is not your normal suburban street. But then nowhere is, in Frome.

---

75 The inhabitants of Frome were not in fact always fully appreciative of the efforts of their brave team. In 1901 the steam hooter woke the town early when a fire was found at Keyford Terrace but the blaze was quite small and inquisitive onlookers became noisy in their disappointment: noticing a nearby pile of coal, the Standard reports, 'the crowd grew sarcastic' and urged the firemen to enhance the blaze.

**F**ROM THE ARCHIVES – media headlines, local and national. Enjoy!

## A NEW TWIST TO TRINITY SAGA

The seemingly never-ending saga of the Trinity area at Frome has taken a new turn. Squatters from London have moved in.

– Somerset Standard & Guardian – August 1977

## TORY HESELTINE IN THE HOT SEAT AS BENN LIGHTS UP

Tim King reports on Friday's Any Questions? from Frome.

… It was Tony Benn who won adulatory whoops of welcome as the panel came, one by one, on stage, followed by chairman Jonathan – that's-the-younger-one-with-the-glasses – Dimbleby, ducking and skipping like a boy scout taking a Gang Show curtain call.

– Guardian, December 1989

## TOWN COULD BECOME HIPPY HAVEN.

A Stonehenge-style amphitheatre could attract hordes of hippies to Frome, traders fear. 'Travellers will smoke happy weed and run around naked' claims trader.

– Somerset Standard, 1991

## UNDISCOVERED COUNTRY: FORGOTTEN FROME

Modern day bustle has passed this Somerset town by, leaving its pretty streets and historic houses undisturbed. Frome, flung far to the east, almost lost to Wiltshire, is inexplicably the Cinderella of Mendip's five towns. 'Don't pass me by' reads the wistful plaque on a chapel wall, curtained by an ancient vine. But they do.

– Country Homes and Interiors, 1994

## END OF THE ROAD FOR FROME SWEET FROME

For centuries the inhabitants of a small Somerset town have proudly boasted that there's no place like Frome. But all that changed recently when the BBC moved in and reduced the streets to chaos while filming their latest period drama *Harvest Moon*. I have sombre news for the

townspeople. If you think that was bad, wait for the real horror to start when the series is broadcast, and Frome becomes 'Harvest Moon Country.'
– Daily Mirror, July 27 1996

## ONE WORLD EVENT MAN IN COURT
Solicitor says everything that could go wrong did go wrong for organiser
Mr Killah, solicitor, said 'This was not a fly-by-night event, but had been carefully planned by the organisers. The police had been warned that a convoy was on its way but only two police officers and a patrol car had been available to attempt to divert it... and the sewerage plant due to take the waste had closed for the day because of Princess Diana's funeral.'
– Somerset Standard May 1998

## SKATEBOARDERS TELL WHY THEY NEED TO GET OFF THE STREETS
Jack Lundin reports on harassment
Inspector Desmond Flood was surprised to hear that teenage skateboarders are being attacked on the streets of Frome. "The skateboarders are not any less valued members of the public than any other section. Not at all. If anything our actions ought to be diverted towards helping these kids get facilities. We want them off the streets."
– Somerset Standard, February 1999

## WE DO NOT NEED AIRY FAIRY PLANS
YOUR ARTICLE 'Office ruled out for the Hill (Nov 28) makes me wonder what kind of dream world Lyn Waller and her ilk live in. Queuing up to open a shop selling what? It's about time the district council stopped frittering taxpayers' money on subsidising airy fairy projects in this area. Here was a tenant turned down by a council which can be best described in the words of the late George Carman QC 'who bury their heads in the sand and expose their thinking parts'.
– letter from 'Peregrine Simcox' (aka anon) in the Somerset Standard 1999

## SO GLAD YOU FOUND IT, DARLING
Why are A-list celebrities suddenly flocking to buy houses in a sleepy Somerset town? Resident Ivan Massow has some answers ...I recall with

some nostalgia the time when someone shouting 'I've just seen Madonna at the cash-point machine' got everyone excited. Nowadays, her loitering outside the supermarket stirs up as little local interest as finding Neil Morrissey has behaved badly at the Sun Inn, or Frances de la Tour has been bed-and-breakfasting at the Melrose guest-house, or that the Prime Minister and Roy Strong are having a multi-cultural chin-wag in the Blue Boar Inn... What makes this more interesting is that the Frome phenomenon is not simply about 'Cotswolding' a new part of the West Country: the draw here is the town itself.

– Daily Telegraph Finance/property supplement September 2001

## WHERE THEY GO – FROME SOMERSET, ENGLAND
Who goes there? Madonna, Neil Morrissey, Ewen McGregor, Sting, Johnny Depp, Zoe Ball and Norman Cook, Gary Lineker, Chris Evans, Kate Moss, Jude Law and Supergrass all escape from the Madding London crowd to find solace in the quaint environs of this sleepy Somerset town.

What's the hype? Frome is in the vicinity of Babbington House (where Zoe and Norman got married) and Beckington Recording studios so there's often a spillover of stars roaming the town's winding roads. Quintessentially British, Frome offers privacy and peace and quiet.. Tony Blair chinwags in the Blue Boar Inn...

– Heat Oct/Nov 2001

## LAURA HOLT IN THE SLEEPY SOMERSET TOWN OF FROME
This tiny market town is never going to win awards for its thriving cultural scene, but its undulating cobbled streets make for a scenic stroll on a Saturday afternoon. There are bargains to be found in the arty shops of St Catherine's Hill, where you can rummage through vintage clothing and accessories... The Georgian charms of Bath are just 20 minutes away.

– Independent June 2013

## FROME: A WONDERFULLY WEIRD MARKET TOWN
We're milling around a lush green synthetic 'lawn' as a glitterball twirls and little hands waggle in the air, disco pumping from a mobile sound system. The aroma of freshly ground coffee beans peps up the smiling crowd on their quest to find treasures among the flea market stalls. And

the third person we've spoken to that day has told us that they came to Frome for a party... and have never gone home.

Talk about a wake-up call. When it comes to buzz, most towns should want what Frome is having. It's well worth joining the revolution – even if it's only for the shopping.

- Oxford Mail December 2013

**HOW FLATPACK DEMOCRACY BEAT THE OLD PARTIES IN THE PEOPLE'S REPUBLIC OF FROME**
On 7 May, a small Somerset town voted against traditional party politics and gave a coalition of independents control of all 17 seats on its council. As the crucible of 'flatpack democracy', Frome is leading a small-scale political revolution – and it's one that is spreading.

– Guardian May 2015

**VA-VA-FROME**
- there's no getting round the fact that eastern Somerset is trendy, and Frome has come a long way in the past 10 years. Once more rough scrumpy than craft beer, it has reinvented itself as an artsy-foodie hipster haven thanks to an influx of young families. What the locals say: We moved from London and never looked back.

– Sunday Times March 2017

**TIRED OF LONDON? – HERE'S OUR GUIDE TO THE BEST PLACES TO LIVE OUTSIDE THE CAPITAL**
FROME, SOMERSET - How Frome has changed. Twenty years ago, this market town of about 25,000 people was in decline. But the 1998 opening of Babington House, the nearby boutique hotel, put it on the radar of a cool crowd, who could see its potential. The artsy-foodie-music vibe is worthy of Hackney. . .

– Sunday Times July 2017

**LET'S MOVE TO FROME, SOMERSET: 'YOU WANT COMMUNITY? YOU GOT IT'**
When the revolution comes, it will start here, a small historic market town deep in wildest Somerset. Frome's got form. It rioted time and again in the 18th century when the wool trade slumped and the price

of gruel skyrocketed. Nonconformism flourished. By the 1970s it had become one of those spots where hippies escaped the rat race, a utopia gently scented with patchouli oil.

– Guardian November 2017

## THE TOWN THAT'S FOUND A POTENT CURE FOR ILLNESS – COMMUNITY

Frome in Somerset has seen a dramatic fall in emergency hospital admissions since it began a collective project to combat isolation. There are lessons for the rest of the country.

– Guardian February 2018

*Frome Street Bandits*

# 4   WORKING LIVES

*– what do people do when there's nothing to do? –*
*– wool and other industries – new industrialists and traders –*
*– law and disorder – dissent in church & state –*

*'Things men have made with wakened hands, and put soft life into*
*Are awake through years with transferred touch, and go on glowing*
      *for long years.*
*And for this reason, some old things are lovely*
*Warm still with the life of forgotten men who made them.'*
          *– D H Lawrence*

FROME HAS LONG BEEN an artisan town. The wool trade was dependent on home-working spinners and weavers, and even jobs in print-works, leather-works and foundries require craftsmen. Previous sections have referenced trading briefly: this section aims to focus on the working life of Frome's community as its cultural focus shifted through the ages.

To begin at the beginning, we need to go back to sheep.

Spinning wool and weaving cloth is known to long predate the Roman occupation: sheep had been reared for wool and food since Neolithic times, and the cloth industry was a cornerstone in local economy from at least the 14th century – the land around Frome was ideal for sheep, and cloth from Somerset wool was highly prized.

By the 18th Century, with water to power the mills, woad to dye the cloth and London only two days' coach drive away, Frome was all about the wool. There were other trades – there were brewers and preachers and a regular market – but Frome seems to have been known to the world as a massive hive of cloth-making with men, women and children all stained blue by the woad dye. The report by Daniel Defoe[1] from a visit in the early 1720s gives a picture of an extensive trade by an impressively organised economic network:

---

1  *A tour thro' the whole island of Great Britain* is Defoe's account of his travels, first published in three volumes between 1724 and 1727

The town of Froom, or as it is written on our maps Frome Sellwood, is a market town principally employed in the clothing trade, namely fine medley, or mix'd cloths, such as are usually worn in England by the better sort of people, and also exported in great quantities to Holland, Hambugh, Sweden, Denmark, Spain, Italy, &c. The spinning work of all this manufacture is performed by the poor people, the master clothiers sending out the wooll weekly to their houses, by their servants and horses, and at the same time bringing back the yarn which they have spun and varnished, which is then fitted for the loom (and) if their trade continues to increase, it is very likely to be one of the greatest and wealthiest inland towns in England.

I've been trying to think of a contemporary example of this kind of concentrated work, but there is no modern equivalent. The factory model has taken over large-scale manufacturing. Cloth-making in Frome was largely a cottage industry: many clothworkers used their own equipment at home independently though relying on the millowners and traders, creating the original 'gig economy'.[2] Neil Howlett has suggested to me the analogy of Uber drivers.

By 1790, according to *England's Gazetteer*, around 13,000 people in and around Frome were making enough broadcloth to fill seven wagon-loads every week in a trade worth £35,000 a year.[3] Yarn had been made by hand in Frome throughout the centuries on a drop spindle which

---

2   A 'gig mill' was a machine with a rotary drum covered with teasel hooks used for raising the nap on woollen cloth.

3   The *Gazetteer* says 700,000 shillings and I can't find a reliable cost comparison, but the weekly wage of a labourer in the mid-1700s according to Doctor Johnson's London was nine shillings and cheese was 4d a pound, so two months wages and six pounds of cheese would take you up to 20/- (i.e. £1). 'Spinsters' were untrained and poorly paid, even though the yarn had to be very even and fine for the quality of cloth that the merchants demanded. Frome museum has a display recalling days when children as young as eight worked in the mills from 6 am till 7 at night, with three-quarter-hour breaks for breakfast and dinner, for a weekly wage of between two shillings and half a crown. (That's between 10p and just over 12p, for readers who don't remember currency before 1971).

twirls the dyed & combed wool to twist the thread,[4] and in their cottages the weavers and their families transformed raw wool into fine cloth which went for sale at the markets across England and, even by the 15th century, also abroad.

As well as sheep providing fine quality wool, the area around Frome was a natural growing ground for two other vital elements in this trade: teasels, which grew wild in profusion, and glastum – more commonly known as woad – to dye it. Until 1856 natural dyes were used for dying the cloth, with other natural dyes added to give a range of colours: privet gave a dark green, heather a paler green, and lichen created a purple tone.[5] But Frome was particularly famed for its blue cloth, used throughout the Napoleonic wars, apparently by both sides. Equally important were the teasels used to tease out loose fragments of wool before the development of wire combs, known as cards, in the 18th century. Frome then became a national centre for carding, at the peak of its trade using eighty miles of wire a day.[6]

And the land around Frome, as well as good for sheep and the plants, provided water in abundance to power the mills.

It was perfect. . .

In 1796 Frome was the largest clothing town in the country and Defoe's prediction seemed to be proving correct. Frome was a model of prosperous industry. The *Monthly Review* of 1803 includes Richard Warner's often-quoted comment about the woad-coloured workers he saw milling about, literally, in his 1801 *Excursions from Bath*:

––––––––––

4   The spindle wheel, a very early Chinese invention, was in common use until the 19th century. 'Fulling' mills from medieval days washed the wool in Fullers earth (from Midford and Wellow) and smaller clothiers neither owned nor rented a mill but owned tools of the trade and carried out some of the processes themselves. They owned the materials at all stages of manufacture, and sent their cloth to be fulled and dyed on commission at local mills, often walking there with a heavy chain of yarn.

5   *Woad to this*, by Carolyn Griffiths, gives a full account of the history of dying in Frome with maps of the mills and woadgrounds.

6   Again from the *Gazetteer*: 'more wire cards for carding the wool for the spinners were made here, than in all England besides, which was for the most part supplied with them from hence, for here were no less than 20 master card-makers, one of whom employed 499 men, women, and children in that manufacture at one time.'

Frome, a town of no great name, furnishes Mr. W with an account
which is honourable to British industry: 'Here an agreeable
appearance of bustle and business catches the eye, every thing
indicates the presence of manufactories and trade; and the labouring
men, women, and children, as deeply tinged as ancient Britons with
a dark blue, discover the nature of the employment by which they get
their bread –the dying and scribbling of the wool, and the weaving
and shearing of the cloth of that colour. Frome has for many years
been famous for working Spanish and English wool into broad-cloths
and kerseymeres.[7]

*The Review* continues to quote Rev Warner's observations
extensively:[8] 348,000 weight of wool in 1789 was 'wrought' into 160,000
yards of broadcloth by 233 scribblers and 223 shearmen though – more
crucially than either the writer or the quoter may have realised 'The
quantity of wool manufactured here is since considerably increased
but the number of people employed is diminished, the introduction
of machines having lessened in a prodigious proportion the need for
manual labour.'
   The Napoleonic Wars of 1803-1815 were particularly lucrative
for traders as both French and English armies wore blue uniforms and
Frome was happy to oblige both sides. No wonder Defoe had foreseen
prosperity continuing into a golden future.

B Y 1830 WILLIAM COBBETT was describing a very different scene:[9]

At Frome they are all upon about a quarter work... These poor
creatures at Frome have pawned all their things, or nearly all. All
their best clothes, their blankets and sheets; their looms; any little

———————

7   Kerseymere is a fine woollen cloth with a fancy twill weave, broadcloth was a
    slightly more rugged clothing fabric of fine twilled wool or worsted.
8   A detailed account is given of the full process from sorting and cleaning
    of fleece, through dying, scribbling, carding, spinning, twisting, weaving,
    burling (nipping off knots and burs) milling, 'dubbed with cards of teazle,
    stretched on tenter hooks' dressing, shearing, pressing 'between heated
    planks and press paper' until finally packed for market.'
9   http://www.gomezsmart.myzen.co.uk/places/frome/cobbett.htm

piece of furniture that they had, and that was good for any thing. Mothers have been compelled to pawn all the tolerably good clothes that their children had. In case of a man having two or three shirts, he is left with only one, and sometimes without any shirt; and, though this is a sort of manufacture that cannot very well come to a complete end; still it has received a blow from which it cannot possibly recover. The population of this Frome has been augmented to the degree of one-third within the last six or seven years.

What happened? Up north, the cloth industry was booming, with the introduction of new machinery like the Spinning Jenny, patented in 1770 by James Hargreaves. The answer doesn't seem to be particularly mysterious. While the industry in northern counties buzzed with eight times the output of previous looms, Somerset saw anti-Jenny riots in Frome and local weaving towns. Women apparently played a key role in the protests and in the attacks.[10] In 1775 Frome magistrates were fearful enough to call in the military, and had to be restrained from doing so again in 1781 by the War Office requesting them to hold back 'until every effort of the civil power has been exerted and proved ineffectual.'

Weavers and shearmen of Frome played a major part in the 1776 riot in Shepton Mallet, when they 'proceeded to the town with the intention to destroy under the cover of night a machine lately erected by the clothiers for the advance and benefit of the manufactory and to pull down the houses and take away the lives of those persons who encouraged and promoted the use of it.' The dragoons were called in but the mob lay in wait and then in the early hours of the morning attacked the machines suddenly 'and before the soldiery could be had out to oppose them, not only destroyed the particular objects of their resentment but committed other injuries to a very considerable amount.' They also drank two hogsheads of beer they found. (Quoted reports are from contemporary accounts in the local press. Personally I'd imagine the hogsheads were always higher on the agenda than the murders.)

The saboteurs' main objection to the new machinery was the consequence of its efficiency. If one machine operated by two people can spin as much in a day as eight 'common spinners', they argued, then

10 Adrian Randall, *Before the Luddites – custom, community and machinery in the English woollen industry* (2003)

six out of every eight women would be out of work and hence 'a burden on the Parish for support.' Their appeal was ineffective, and the mill-owners' warning that, by losing competitive edge, the entire trade would see ruin 'which would involve themselves and their families in the most calamitous circumstances' was likewise ignored. However benevolent and benign the big cloth-trade families might have been, they clearly did not inspire the confidence of their workers that they would 'discount the use of machines if after a proper trial they shall be found prejudicial to the poor' – nor that their introduction would cause only a 'light, inconsiderable, partial inconvenience.'

The clothiers persisted, despite a trial which showed adaptation would be required for local wool,[11] aware that 'unless such machines be adopted the manufacturers of the North will enjoy such great advantages as cannot fail to secure them the preference at all markets.' They tried another Jenny in Frome in 1781 and it was promptly smashed up.

It was not until the late 1780s, over a decade later when much of the cloth trade had already diverted to Yorkshire[12], that the Jenny managed to infiltrate southwest England, instantly fulfilling the workers' worst fears. The by-employment of out-spinning, a key underpinning of family economies, was wiped out instantly, causing a rapid rise in poor rates. Historian Adrian Randall, researching the geographical shift prosperity in the wool towns, concluded:

> The rebellious culture of the West of England workers undoubtedly had an impact upon innovators. Their violent response to new machinery deterred all but the most determined from such confrontations, as repeated reports made clear. Woollen workers from the Frome area started the riots… Worker resistance may thus have been responsible for depressed trade and not the reverse as economic historians have often concluded.

---

11 It was finer than northern wool, and broke on the machine
12 Leeds, Bradford, Halifax, Huddersfield & Wakefield were becoming major cloth manufacturing areas, filling the West Riding with 'dark satanic mills' and effecting a rapid transformation from cottage industry to factory production. It was surely this aspect that independent Frome workers were resisting, and the inevitable shift from uniquely 'skilled hands' to interchangeable machine operators…

The economic collapse was not a steady decline nor were the anti-Jenny riots the first. Failing markets and rising prices in previous decades had caused intermittent food shortage from 1727 onwards. Dealers were accused of stockpiling to maximise profits, and disruptions were frequent in the southwest. In 1739 after what looked like a good harvest, sudden bad weather froze the corn mills, and riots about hoarded grain being routed to more lucrative markets in London and Bristol continued all year until the next harvest. Rioters were specific in their revenge: this was consumer retribution, not wholesale destruction, and some mill-owners in self-protection posted notice in the local papers that they took no part in the wheat and flour exports depleting local communities.

Throughout these difficult times, according to Randall again,

the more extensive disorders had their origin in communities of industrial workers and miners. Such groups living in large and surprisingly cohesive communities shared a common exposure both to the vagaries of the food market and to the vicissitudes of the trade or industry. This forged a strong sense of unity and a common purpose to resist those who threatened their 'rights'.

Mendip miners were frequent initiators and so too were the textile workers. The extensive food riots in Somerset in 1757 started in Frome and spread rapidly wider when riotous colliers demolished one mill and marched off to fight a pitched battle at another. Frome's rebellious role as an epicentre for violent protest was widely known, as this report even reached the *Manchester Mercury* : 'On Wednesday, I had the disagreeable Sight of the two Men that were killed, and four wounded, in the Riot of the Colliers that Morning aside Off Frome, where, in a Quarter of Hour's Time, they entirely pulled down and destroyed a Flour Mill.' As in the later textile industry protests, women too played a prominent role in disturbances.

Food riots continued on and off for a decade, as impoverished workers were constantly antagonised by the continued practice of stockpiling grain for more profitable sale. In 1766 a serious disturbance was once again initiated in Frome when a large crowd assembled intending to march to Trowbridge to attack dealers' houses. They were met en route and apparently appeased by promises, diverted instead destroying a mill at North Bradley. This was quite a battle: they were 'resisted with firearms by the persons belonging to the mills and several were wounded which so exasperated the rest that they immediately made a fire with sticks and throwing firebrands onto the mills soon burnt them to the ground.' One 'mobber' wrote an account of his own participation, without the deaths which embellished later versions, but with the information that 'a considerable number of us consisted of disciplined militia.' [13]

This 'Battle of Beckington' was extensively reported in local and national press, largely due to curiosity about the identity of the articulate 'mobber' (never revealed), but this was only one of many violent conflicts between the mill-owners and the hungry poor throughout the century. The anger ethos that developed at this time is seen by some historians as driven also by desire to protect the traditional rights and customs which were being undermined and eroded. In other words, not a mob-jerk reaction, but collective activism: the 'moral economy' model of marketing, underpinned by local statutes, had always emphasised that food should be traded locally, and these new profiteers were not only trading elsewhere but totally unscrupulously using food vital for local sustenance as stock for personal profit. In this context, the picture of 18th-century Frome as a town of ill-behaved ruffians would seem over-simplistic. As with their later struggle against factory machinery, this was a fight to retain the fabric of their community, and ensure that local crops fed the town rather than filling the purses of investors.

The cloth trade had long dwindled to insignificance by the time the last mill closed in 1965[14] and the population declined – even in 1930 it was still considerably lower than it had been a hundred years before[15]

---

13  The militia were founded in 1757 and by the end of the 18th Century numbered around 100,000, a strong presence in rural communities, and considered by many an unwelcome burden. Without barracks they were billeted cheaply in inns, so their cost was resented. Pay was poor and recruitment was largely from 'the lower orders'. They would be trained to use the musket, a slow-loading weapon notoriously inaccurate in its fire.

14  The Wallbridge factory, manufacturing cloth from about 1870.

15  The original Poor Law had been modified in 1834 as the wealthy were objecting to their taxes going to support the poor. Not specified, but the basic actuality. The workhouse now became the point-of-delivery for clothing

– but Frome's renowned resilience ensured that the town entered the 20th century as still an industrial force. Printing, light engineering, metal casting, carpeting and dairying were all significant employing trades.[16]

Printing presses became major employers as the 19th century saw the creation and distribution of literally hundreds of periodicals covering all aspects of cultural life, some like *The Spectator* still continuing today. In Frome, Butler and Tanner, founded 1845, was the main name for books and a major employer: by 1892 there were over 400 men in their Selwood Printing Works,[17] and even more when in 1907 they moved to the Adderwell site where the firm lasted into the new millennium in the rescue-package deal of flamboyant Felix Dennis[18] but beaten eventually by market forces.

--------

and food. Work there was hard, rules were strict, diet was bad, so fear of the workhouse became a powerful force of social control. Emigration seemed a better option to many and was to become for many families their only option. The Children's Friendly Society was founded in 1830 to promote the emigration of children and in 1879 the Poor Law authorities had official permission from central government to use local rates for that purpose: Dr. Barnardo's Homes was prominent in the transport of children from Great Britain to the dominions, sending between 1867-1910 over 22,000 children to Canada alone.

16  The shift of work-base in the town did not mean Frome became docile: the General Strike in 1926 had support from several unions, notably those involved with printing: the Typographical Association, National Union of Bookbinders, Machine Rulers, Paper Workers: also ASLEF and other rail unions.

17  Still locally known as the Selwood Steam Printing Works, from early days when steam drove the generators for the electric to work the motors on the machines. Tales are still told of the clocking-in door which the gateman would close on the dot, to make latecomers lose a quarter hour's pay.

18  Felix didn't long survive the closure of his final enterprise. Anyone of my generation will remember him with great affection for the role he played in the 60s-defining counter-culture magazine OZ – and the obscenity trial caused by the School Kids issue. All three editors were found guilty but Felix was given a lighter sentence than Richard Neville and Jim Anderson, as the judge deemed him 'very much less intelligent.' The Court of Appeal quashed the prison sentences and Felix dedicated the rest of his working life to 'proving the old fart wrong.' Mr Justice Argyle meanwhile dedicated his to campaigning for the restoration of the death penalty.

Another strand of emerging industry was foundry work. Singers was started in 1848 by Joseph Singer and is known now mainly for casting the lions in Trafalgar Square, and Charlie Robbins our Frome war memorial soldier. (In fact the lions are a misattribution: Landseer, who designed them, had them cast by one Baron Marochetti in 1867, but the figure of Justice on the dome of London's Old Bailey, designed by F W Pomeroy and erected 1906, was definitely cast at Singers.) After a merger with Morris Art Bronze Foundry, Singers continued to take on major commissions until forced into administration in 2010, though no longer a local employer since 1927.

Also metal workers, the Cockey family employed 76 men in their Palmer Street foundry opened in 1816 and specialising in street furniture – especially 'art nouveau' lamp holders which are still in use around the town,[19] many of them listed, although the firm wound up in 1960. Fussells ironworks went bankrupt in 1894, partly due to slow response to developments in iron manufacture and also from the knock-on negative effect of difficulties in the agricultural industry on the market for edge tools. Frome's dairy farming tradition meant it was, and still is, a renowned cheese producer, and cream cheeses and yoghurts were also made at Staplemead creamery after the Express Dairies relocated out of London at the outbreak of the second world war. Current production rate is massively reduced, with a focus on desserts instead of deliveries of milk as in the 1980s.

Other industries have come and gone. Beswicks, once a big employer, transferred to China, Notts Industries and Wellington Weston

---

19  Cockey's street-lamps were designed for gas, which came to Frome in 1831, but are now converted for electricity, which arrived in 1903 when a generating station was built and cables laid. Robin Lambert, who worked for the Electricity Board from aged 17 to retirement, described the big exhibition of 1908 to encourage people to buy products and start using this new power: 'The houses only had oil lamps and candles, so having laid all the cables, you needed to convince people to have electric put in their house. And to sway them to do it, they said "You can have it with two lights and a plug free." Right up to the 1930s some still had oil lamps – a lot had gas lighting too, and gas stoves. In fact the power station nearly didn't get built. The council paid for it all to be installed but they never had the expertise to run it, so they handed it back to the company that put it up, Edmundsons, and then in the '40s it became Southern Electricity Board.'

(who had employed around 900 people) closed, and Cuprinol had to vacate its premises in 2000 after toxic chemical contamination at its Adderwell site.[20]

I don't really want to spend too much time on the background stories of any of these, as Frome Museum has such excellent displays so, perhaps controversially, I'll move on to the demise of the town's industries in the 20th century, which is when Frome regained a distinctive identity and became interesting again. The loss of so many major employers may be regrettable but there isn't really much mystery about it. Some made managerial mistakes, some were too small to compete on the increasing scale or lacked funds to adapt to new technologies and increasing material costs, but it was the same story all over England. Changing buying habits and altering social expectations began the move away from traditional products, and the banking crisis of 2008 and following recession hit the whole country.

For the first time since the collapse of the cloth trade – and a new notion for its current population – job security had become a major concern for Frome. One by one the factories closed, with Butler and Tanner the last to go.[21] To compound the sense of loss, Frome cattle market, for over 100 years a weekly focus of trade and activity in the centre of the town, moved to Standerwick in 1990, taking with it the chattels market, the auction, and Mole Valley Farmers (suppliers of not only farm equipment but clothes and household goods). The steady footfall of farmers and their families arriving in town to trade and use services like pubs, barbers, cafes, and shops, disappeared at a stroke. All the shops felt the loss, especially the butchers and cooked meat shops. The move of the Cheese Show to a bigger site in West Woodlands Showground nine years later was another success story that felt like

---

20 Cuprinol was at that time using Lindane, now known to cause leukaemia which was said to have affected several workers. The ingredient is now changed to a water-based alternative, but toxic leaks had raised concerns as the production site was near the river, on a steep bank. Once the danger was acknowledged, all machinery was removed and the site shut. 'It was killing fish, and frogs, and loads of people were getting quite ill,' I was told by one of the team sent in to take out the corroding tanks.

21 'Working Memories' produced by the *Home In Frome* community group gives a vivid picture of life for workers in manufacturing industries.

a loss to the town. Although only happening once a year, the Cheese Show featured much more than cheese and was seen as a big part of the community identity.

The old industrial sites mainly went to housing[22], but the seeds of revival were already sown, in the regeneration of Catherine Hill already described, and by the gathering group of artisans and artists who will be the focus of the next section. Drawn by low house prices and Frome's still-considerable quirky charm, the 1980s and '90s saw the arrival of people keen to contribute to the next stage in Frome's history. Just as 'Frome Independent' is the latest incarnation in a series of craft markets, and Frome Festival continues the long tradition of town celebrations, so too the 'new' ethos of cafe society and innovative creativity grew from the determination to make something wonderful grow in this bedraggled-looking town. You could call it the Chumbawamba factor: 'I get knocked down, but I get up again – you're never gonna keep me down. . .'

SO NOW, WITHOUT HARD INDUSTRIES, Frome has developed creative alternatives – individuals and small teams working in offices like *Forward Space* or the new Commerce Park on the north side of town. The focus of trade has shifted from agricultural to niche, and the cafés, bistros and bottle shops generate a new income as widely-used places to socialise.[23] It seems almost as if Frome has its own secret seeds of regeneration. With the era of job-for-life expectations inevitably destabilised, Frome returned to its traditional survival skills of making, trading, and nonconformist resilience. We shouldn't perhaps

---

22 with notable exceptions like the Silk Mill, featured in the previous section.

23 Identifying names in a book is like scratching them in wall cement: relevance passes leaving only a reminder how important individuals are, continually, to the fabric of our surroundings. At the time I'm writing it seems to me that part of the café culture success is down to the tribe of young people at point of counter-contact – Tillie, Dan, Jacob, Terri, Izzy, India, Ollie, Tom, Django, and all the others who support the owners, managers, and chefs by making relationships which feel like real connections. We've all got beverages at home – what we want from these 'houses' is a sense of belonging in our community. Frome's personable young professionals in the 'Service Industry' seem to appreciate from the outset that this expanding strand of local employment needs many skills but none of them servility.

be surprised that the last factor has been crucial in Frome's current
perceived renaissance.

Gavin Eddy, already quoted, bought the old Wesleyan church school
in 2007 to develop it into 'a shared workspace for free-lancers and
small businesses – 'creative people who were doing things, but probably
in their back bedroom' – to create a space where they could come
together and collaborate.' *Forward Space* currently provides a working
environment for 120 members – and a cafe area open to all. Even in the
ten years this project has been thriving, Gavin has seen a shift in usage:

> Initially we attracted the more traditional businesses of a market
> town – book-keepers, a local estate agent or letting agent, and now it's
> brand companies, graphic designers, web designers, software designers
> – companies working with huge global brands, so we've got ambitious
> companies here, aspirational people that would not have lived in Frome
> ten years ago. We have responded to the way Frome has changed.

Gavin identifies his demographic as youngish, ex-citydwellers
– 'they've moved to the southwest from a larger area to settle down,
they've chosen this place because it's beautiful, for all the life-style
reasons we all want to live here, and it's a chance to become self-
employed, and start their own companies.'

Small businesses and individuals using creative skills... could this be
the new 'cottage industry' for Frome?[24] The jury's out on this one, as the
final section will discuss.

Seeds of regeneration were growing from those early days when Fay
Goodridge and Lyn Waller began to wipe the grime from Catherine Hill.
Fay recalls

---

24 The new commerce park on the north side of Frome has attracted a wide
range of small companies, many of them – such as innovative multinational
firm DNA Worldwide and Dennis Maps, UK's leading map printer with a
tradition traceable from 1850 – operating internationally mainly by mail
order so they can keep the cost of premises low. The new Vallis Mills estate
also hosts significant and creative projects: Protomax, who first designed
how to recycle plastic waste into usable building materials, is based there,
and the renowned Mark Bruce Dance Company has a purpose-built studio
for their small multi-national creative team.

I was what you could call the second wave, about five or ten years on. People like Jon Evans from the Garden Cafe were already here, we had Black Swan Arts and the Merlin Theatre so things had started to happen. Frome attracted artisans because it was affordable, you could pick up a cottage and could do it up – and you could find workshops! So there were a lot of us artists and artisans, and we had the idea of putting on a show together. Kate Semple, who was a Labour councillor then, organised the original 'Made in Frome' exhibition in the Cheese and Grain, and later we had one in the Black Swan. We took exhibitions out to the twin towns. The council gave us a small grant, and we had jumble sales to raise the rest of the money, and made banners, and put it all in his van and took it over to France on the ferry – it was fantastic.

The *Made in Frome* group included a brewer and a blacksmith as well as makers of textiles, glass, paper, pottery and musical instruments,[25] and the criterion, Laurie Parnell told me, was simply to be using your craft to making your living.

It was partly a professional mutual-support group, and partly to say to the council "There's a lot of good skills here already!" because every time they wanted anything, they'd get it designed out of town. We raised the profile of Frome makers, especially when we all went to

---

25  Butler & Tanner produced a superb souvenir booklet of their trip to Château Gontier in 2000, listing: Christopher Barlow (harpsichords), Nick Bramwell (beer), Pie Chambers (weaver) Annette Gabbedey (jewellery), Fay Goodridge (framing), Gonique Hol (glass-blowing), Arwyn Jones (clay pots), Chris Jones (glass-casting), Sonja Klinger (glass-blowing), Katie-Jane Letch (knitwear), Ann Muir (paper-marbling), Charlie Oldham (woodcarving), Laurence Parnell (stringed instruments), Alan Patterson (ironwork), Jez Pearson (blacksmithing), Corinna Sargood (illustrator – who also provided Virago with the images for Angela Carter's fairy tales), Kate Semple (stonemason), Richard Wallace (furniture) and Robyn Wilkinson (clay pots) Some of these pioneers have left Frome now: others continue to contribute to the town's artisan tradition – Charlie's benches, with their carved epigrams, can be seen by the river in Rodden meadow. Local antiques dealer Tim Snell, who volunteered the van, is also part of the complex story. His daughter Amy with her husband Stuart now runs the High Pavement restaurant just off the hill.

Murrhardt with our families: they put us in caravans in the Municipal
Campsite by a lake and we had the use of the exhibition centre
which is a converted monastery with a commercial kitchen, so we
ran a Somerset Cafe for a fortnight. We'd taken out cider, and local
cheddar, and cream and jam from Frome WI market, and made cream
teas in the afternoon –serving from Mark Melbourne's specially-
made teapots. We played concerts and had a great time out there, but
what was much more valuable was the publicity when we got back.

Another example of Frome's exuberant festival spirit, on this occasion
shared abroad.

The *Made in Frome* group, with its wide variety of contributors
and lively self-presentation initiatives, was not only a precursor to the
festival – and to the series of the flamboyant markets for which Frome
is now famed – but it also renewed and reaffirmed the town's ancient
connection with artisan trades, which had become diffused by the
interim period of industries requiring routine skills and interchangeable
operators. Once again Frome has seen a wave of new residents, attracted
by the town and finding it affordable. Those already retired from work
usually donate time and energy to support an ethos they value, while
many of those earning now, as in the deep past, are individuals or small-
group operators engaged in creative, self-designed, work. Outcomes
and ethics may have altered in Frome after the days of wool wealth
and independent weavers, but much of what goes on today trails a long
history. What is particularly interesting about that history is its breaks
and recoveries. The post-WWII decline is strong in living memory – even
in the memory of recent incomers – but the 19th century too was a
particularly difficult time for Frome. After this quick trailer to the future,
we're going back in time in another digression to give a wider context of
social life and growing divisions.

After the end of twelve years of wars with France, England was
left with hundreds of homeless, penniless, vagrants. Their solution was
to illegalise them. The Vagrancy Act of 1824 made it an offence to sleep
rough or beg[26] with a possible penalty of up to one month's hard labour.

---

26 It apparently remains in force today, so anyone found to be sleeping in a
   public place or trying to beg for money can be arrested. I bet there's a few
   thousand who would love to claim that right on a cold night.

(This was amended in 1838 – to include acts that were deemed at the time to be likely to cause moral outrage, which was used to prohibit street performances of a lively nature, as much that had been accepted in previous eras was now considered bawdy and obscene.) So there was an increasing concern over lawlessness everywhere, and of course also in Frome. The Magistrates Court discussed in the previous section was a comparatively recent addition, as for most of its history Frome would have been served by a system of crime limitation unlike policing as we know it. Early crime control throughout England had relied on 'hue and cry', calling for pursuit and capture,[27] and later conscription of a *'posse comitatus'* – a group of men who were summoned to repress riots or other crimes. Wrong-doers were pushed overnight into one of two lock-ups mentioned in the previous section, and then next day taken to the mansion of the nearest available magistrate, a local of some standing who would dispense judgement in a 'hearing' on the spot. If prison was decreed the miscreant would be despatched to Taunton or Shepton Mallet. In more complicated cases, local pubs acted as Magistrates Courts, as they were the only buildings with rooms big enough – with the advantage of refreshment available to the avid audience.

A gripping account of town life before official 'policing' is provided by the *Journals of Isaac Gregory,* Constable of Frome for double tenure: 1813-14 and then again three years later, standing in for his reluctant brother. Mr Gregory, middle-class and doing well in the leather trade, was strongly opposed to drunkenness and non-observance of the Sabbath: when these two habits coincided he became especially irate. He certainly didn't pre-empt gender equality in his views (he was happy to see a murder charge changed to accidental for a man who 'threw his wife over the stump of the bedstead…. her liver was torn apart,' since 'the man had an undoubted right to force his wife to bed, especially if she was very drunk') but he was often compassionate with pragmatic wisdom too, writing 'Some tell me I am too mild. But who can govern a drunken man? He is dead to everything he does and I always find mild treatment at such times the best.'

When the County Police Act was introduced in England in 1839, Wiltshire had seized their chance immediately but Somerset for some

---

27 In former English law, the cry had to be raised by the inhabitants of the hundred – i.e. local area – in which a robbery had been committed or else they would become liable for the victim's damages.

reason waited until 1856, when such provision became compulsory, before acquiring its Peelers:[28] a superintendent, two sergeants and eighteen constables for Frome. Up until that time the town constables like Mr Gregory had authority to quell petty disturbances without involving the Assizes by use of whipping, putting in the stocks, or incarcerating in one of the lock-ups previously described, where the over-inebriated and over-excitable were thrust to await transport next day for fining. The lockups were notoriously disgusting places, damp, rat-infested and filthy in the extreme, but their use seems to have been accepted as a matter of course for some revellers, whose friends would follow and find ingenious ways to smuggle more liquor. Their use was abandoned after the Peelers arrived, and reported them 'of the most wretched kind, and perfectly inapplicable to the requirements of the Police Acts.'

Forty years after Isaac Gregory wrote 'goodbye to Constableship forever' after for the last time dispersing 'some dirty chaps at Whatley corner', Frome Police became embroiled in the biggest murder case of the century, a thriller still read about, and viewed on box-set, today. The murder at Rode was solved by one of the newly-formed London detective squad, whose lowly origins combined with his outrageous suspicions challenged social assumptions of the era – and also kick-started a national obsession with crime stories. The real-life Mr Whicher became role-model for the detective-hero, using psychology as well as physical clues to solve the case.[29] Rode Hill House is three miles beyond town, but Frome police often worked with their Wiltshire colleagues and were called in to assist when young Saville Kent was mysteriously murdered in 1860. Saville's father was already unpopular in Frome as the man responsible for implementing the 1833 Factory Act which

---

28  As you may know, the first professional policemen were known as 'Peelers' or 'Bobbies' after Sir Robert Peel, the Home Secretary who set up the force in the Metropolitan Police Act of 1829.

29  With newspapers now widely available, this case gripped the nation so intently you could almost say it changed the face of popular literature: Wilkie Collins, Charles Dickens, G K Chesterton, and most famously Arthur Conan Doyle between them creating the trend for crime mysteries and detectives who used what Agatha Christie's Hercule Poirot summarised as 'little grey cells' to solve the case.

while improving safety also slowed production, and so was resented by workers as well as owners. With this background, Frome people were intently following the case and *Frome Times* reports feature prominently in Kate Summerscale's brilliant reconstruction of how the *Suspicions of Mr Whicher* uncovered the culprit – although snobbery overruled his solution until, years later, when it was confirmed by confession. It was a Frome policeman who provided the vital evidence: 'James Watt, Police Sergeant of Frome had found a woman's shift wrapped in newspaper in the kitchen boiler hole… "It was very bloody" he said, "I handed it over to Mr Foley." John Foley, leading the investigation, promptly suppressed this evidence, which would have closed the case in a day, lest it was menstrual blood and therefore too 'shameful' to examine. He was later 'castigated by the magistrates but forgiven, as his error had been prompted by feelings of delicacy.'

James Watt, the astute policeman from Frome, had been involved in another child-murder case nine years earlier, even closer to the town in West Woodlands: *The Awful Killing of Sarah Watts,* by David Lassman and Mick Davis, relates another tragic case though with less mystery, but what is fascinating about this admirably narrated account is its vivid picture of the lurid side of 19th century Frome, where ruffians would steal anything from watches to potatoes and cheese.

Much of the undoubted lawlessness in Frome in the 18th and 19th centuries can be attributed not only to the poverty caused by repeated crop failures but also anger at the erosion of autonomy. Until the era of unions and votes, rioting was the only way an opinion could be visibly expressed. I'm indebted to Neil Howlett for the following example of attitudes at the time. In 1822 ten weavers were arrested after a dispute, and a further eight also jailed for involvement in the protest while having work on their looms. Their official report explained the men's houses were 'opened by force, from whence some riots ensued, which were not terminated without the interference of the yeoman cavalry.' The Home Secretary was moved to write to the Magistrates commenting

> You state that, at the instance of the masters, you had been induced
> to issue warrants for the preservation of the master's property
> although such warrants were not authorised by the law. Mr. Peel

directs me to remark that however desirable it may be to preserve
the property from deterioration, it is vastly more important that
magistrates should act strictly within the law; and he thinks the
tendency of the measures you adopted is rather to ferment than to
allay the existing discontent.

Apparently unconvinced and unabashed, the Frome Justices
responded defending their action loftily: 'We are confident that although
the law may not strictly sanction what we have done, our acting in the
emergency of the case was the means of preventing outrages...' [30] Their
next letter reported the situation calm, attributing this to the arrival of
the cavalry and the weavers weakened by starvation and demoralised by
hard labour sentences of their colleagues, and concluded 'We have weighed
out justice impartially, eighteen weavers in gaol, one master fined £20 for
breaking the law relating to truck.' Impartial indeed. The response from
the Home Office applauding their 'determination to pursue the sharp path
of administering the law equally to a parties' must surely have been ironic.

F ROME AS A TOWN is nothing if not resilient but this particular
era was definitely a low ebb. By the middle of the century, in a
population of around 12,000, less than 200 had work – an estimated
3% of those able. Against a backdrop of handsome new housing for the
affluent, and cosmetic changes to the architecture of town, for most of
the population these were desperate times. William Cobbett returning
to Frome in 1826 saw 'between two and three hundred weavers, men
and boys, cracking stones, moving earth, and doing other sorts of
work, towards making a fine road into the town.' The workhouse on
Weymouth Road became something to be aspired to – as was prison,

---

30 The tendency of authorities to support the wealthy over the poor wasn't
   new then, and subsequent history suggests it's still well ingrained. After the
   Brixton riots in 2011, for instance, when protests at police racism, escalated
   by effects of recession on employment in the area, led to widespread anger
   expressed in looting, the jail sentences imposed on those involved were on
   average four times as long as usual for such offences. The Justice Minister
   defended this hard-line response saying 'the disgraceful behaviour was
   wholly intolerable.' The presenting agenda is public safety, the hidden agenda
   might be seen as the priority of property and the formal re-assertion of a
   dividing line between the haves and the have-nots.

both offering at least subsistence diet, and the amount spent on poor relief escalated from under £2,000 in 1792 to nearly £12,000 by the middle of the century, and the Poor Rate was used to send as many as possible to Canada. Yet as historian Michael McGarvie wryly comments 'If the bodies of the poor were neglected, much thought was given to their souls.' There were embellishments on the various churches, with St John's virtually rebuilt by the Vicar Bennett who arrived in 1852 from Pimlico.[31] Bodies though certainly were neglected: A report on sanitation before 1845 revealed no baths and the river too polluted by clothiers to be fit for bathing, no sewerage and no public water supply (until 1880) – death rate unsurprisingly above the national average.

Mansions and workhouses, prosperity and poverty – these tend to be the balustrades of Frome's perceived edifice.[32] Industry divides a community: there are those who organise and those who operate, in a hierarchy headed by owners who usually neither organise nor work but simply profit. You could say that Frome's history was inevitably laced with conflict from the time the cottage industry described by Defoe started shifting to a more factory-based pattern.

In this context, the 'dissent' of formal separation easily merges with social dissent at being controlled by others. There was at that time as yet no organised socialism, but the proximity of France and the successful rebellion against monarchy by the French would have long been well

---

31  William James Early Bennett: 'the only vicar ever prosecuted by his own parishioners for heresy' as he was described to me by historian Nick Hersey, was accused of ritualism after affirming the communion ceremony represented 'the real, objective, Presence of our Lord, in the form of Bread and Wine, upon the Altars of our churches... whom I myself adore.' He was acquitted by the Privy Council who apparently decided that proxy cannibalism of an adored body fell within the range of anglican views, but resigned his London post after dispute with the bishop and came to Frome.

32  Actually of course for a much longer period of time, this area like every other part of Britain had none of the monetary values that now dominate our reading of the past. To go back again to the long era of hunter-gathering communities, their connective network would be kinship or friendship, not status. The shift to 'haves and have-nots' came about ten thousand years ago, when people first created agricultural communities, replacing foraging with storage, and so introducing the concept of ownership. 'Inheritance' came inevitably next... and the story of 'class' was invented.

known in Frome, with its long-established trade routes. Less and less does it seem likely that the town which declared a rebel king against a Papist monarch, the town which surprised Cobbett by its political awareness, whose townsfolk literally fought for the right to elect a political representative of their choice, would ever have been apathetic on any but the more socially irrelevant issues. Not much surprise either, then, that many in Frome embraced the doctrine of a direct route to Christ offered by non-conformism, preferring open-air preaching which affirmed the individual over the hierarchy of the existing church, and the autonomy of bible-study in a house to services that so often underlined their debased status. A popular hymn from 1848 typically sanctions the social inequality of that era:

> The rich man in his castle, The poor man at his gate,
> God made them, high or lowly, And ordered their estate.[33]

Dissent, the term for Protestant non-conformism, plays a massive part in the history of the church in England, as big as the rift with the pope in 1534 and as important as the Reformation itself. There were many dissenting groups in England, although Frome is unusual in actually having a cemetery especially dedicated to them, and in today's secular society many people don't realise that the dissenters were not opposed to Christianity, only to the official Anglican interpretation of worship. So here's a bit of background:

Dissension as a movement was triggered in 1662 by the Act of Uniformity, the last of several such acts making the book of common prayer an essential component in worship and the one which finally caused the rift that has divided the church in England ever since. On St Bartholomew's Day 1662 around 2,000 ministers were ejected from their churches (and thereby from their homes) for refusing to accept embellishments like altars, candles, crosses and vestments, and – most

---

33 I remember this hymn well, we used to sing it in Assembly at my Primary school in South London (though apparently it was banned by ILEA in 1982) and my father comforted me by assuring me the poor man had come to the gate only because the rich man was going to give him food for his family and nice warm clothes...

specifically – rejecting compulsory use of the prescribed prayer book.[34] One of these original dissidents was John Humphry, vicar of St Johns, who thereby started what became Rook Lane Congregational Church, preaching initially in local cottages until the chapel was built in 1707.

The following decades saw a plethora of non-conformist alternatives emerge throughout England. From Protestant agrarian communists like the Diggers to the puritan Calvinist 'Countess of Huntingdon's connexion', they shared a belief that there was a more direct way to find spiritual truth than by the ritual and routines of the Anglican church. Some, like the Grindletonians, faded from the scene before the end of the century, others like Quakers survived. Some seemed to have little connection with christian beliefs: the Ranters were pantheists while the Muggletonians avoided all worship and were prone to curse those who opposed them, including apparently Sir Walter Scott. The most significant and long-lasting is Methodism, which had a difficult passage in Frome after its first introduction – allegedly by a Bristol rag-collector in 1746 singing Wesley's hymns.

John Wesley, founder of Methodism – a 'method' to connect with Christ through bible study and prayer rather than through the Anglican hierarchy – came to Frome himself several times. He didn't think much of it at first,[35] but in September 1778 he noted with satisfaction 'a very numerous congregation. . . stood as quiet as those at Bristol' in the market place of Frome.

Wesley's gratification came at a cost. An account[36] of the experiences of the first Methodists shows that they were persistently

---

34 The objection to peripherals came from a Puritan conviction that such treasure should not be hoarded in the house of God, and the objection to using the book of Common Prayer was because it was written in Latin as a handbook for priests and monks not intended for the laity. The over-riding reason for dissent, however, was resentment at officers of the state telling people how to worship. Having already rejected the idea of a Pope as intermediary between themselves and Jesus, people had no desire to insert a king.

35 'March 1753 I preached at Frome; a dry, barren, uncomfortable place' he recorded.

36 *Brief Annals of the Frome Methodist Society from its Commencement to The Present Time* (Printed for the Author by J L Vardy, and sold by J Tuck, Frome 1814).

treated with dedicated brutality, and the treatment of victims by the authorities was equally outrageous. One record of bullying in 1751 had tragic consequences for three of the women involved: two were imprisoned, one of whom died, and another, the widow who owned the house where the bible-study group met, was fined so grossly she lost her home and livelihood.[37]

With Baptists attacking them like Chelsea football supporters, it's surprising Methodist numbers swelled but they did, and in 1779 supporters built the Wesley Chapel just beyond Keyford, on what's now called Wesley Slope. The 1814 history notes some difficulties in completion, resolved by 'the timely intervention of Mr Wesley.' The difficulty turned out to be that the person entrusted with all the funds had absconded with them, and the intervention was not a donation, but a canny financial manoeuvre to connect all Wesleyan chapels in trust, so any loss was carried by the group.[38]

'Unpleasant altercations' continued between leaders, with people expelled and membership numbers yo-yo-ing up and down – whoever said Frome was apathetic? – but the general picture is that the religious life of Frome was dominated by personalities not doctrines. 'Dissent' was ingrained in the fabric of the town.

Again, we need to see this in the context of the economic history of the 18th century, which was a golden age for open-air preaching in England. 'Taking a living'– i.e. in the established church – had become nothing to do with religious vocation[39] but as the blasé phrase reveals was a means to secure a dominant place in the hierarchical society, and so consequently church attendance meant giving affirmation and support

---

37  Their principal persecutors later met divine justice from a clearly very wrathful God: one fell in a furnace of boiling tallow, recovering with such terrible ulcers he had to be removed to a place near the poorhouse where he drowned in a flood, another died drinking gin, and the worst of the bullies was frightened to death by a cat.

38  Clive Murray Norris, *The Financing of John Wesley's Methodism c.1740-1800* (Oxford U P, 2017)

39  When a wealthy man died, the eldest son inherited his estate and the second son 'went into the church' gaining a comfortable living, a home and status, and hiring a curate to do the tiresome business of involvement in the parish. The despicable Wickham in Jane Austen's *Pride and Prejudice*, seducer and opportunist, was expecting to 'gain a living' from his benefactor.

to the wealthy in power. The 1851 religious census revealed[40] 'a sadly formidable portion of the English people are habitual neglecters of the public ordinances of religion… it is observable how absolutely insignificant a portion of the congregation is composed of artizans… this growingly important section of our countrymen is thorough estranged from our religious institutions', and concern was expressed that working men were deterred by the pew system (payment for 'best' seats), didn't want to spend their one day off in proximity to 'persons of a higher grade', and disliked 'having pressed upon them some memento of their inferiority.' All these were doubtless true, but tinkering with church service would make no difference: rivalry between church and chapel had less to do with belief than social aspiration, and non-conformism was a response not so much to Church of England practices but to the class system it represented.[41]

By the mid 19th century the notion of social control by ownership and wealth was leading to a new concept: the 'criminal class'. Partly because of the reluctance of the poorest in society to report anything for fear of police indifference and even mistreatment, criminal activity was becoming associated with the 'lower orders' – not as a consequence of social inequality, but as a moral problem: Victorian social reformer Edwin Chadwick perceived offenders as refusing to do 'an honest day's work for an honest day's wage', preferring to wait for an opportunity for disorder and plunder.[42]

Frome had some fine examples of individuals from the 'Haves' who showed concern for the 'Have-nots' and offered practical help and

---

40  James R Moore, *Religion in Victorian Britain* (Oxford U P 1988)

41  There are many surviving examples of Victorian sermons and papers deploring working-class irreligion based on church attendance but it seems more likely that the hierarchical nature of society at that time had led to alienation of attendance. Anglican clergy were overwhelmingly upper-middle-class: Historian Richard Brown quotes the Rural Dean of Kennington in the 1890s: 'Working men don't go to church for the same reason that I don't go to the races.'

42  'By the middle of the century the term 'criminal classes' was in vogue; it was used to suggest an incorrigible social group – a class – stuck at the bottom of society. Intrepid explorers of the slums and the 'rookeries' of the poor, like Henry Mayhew, often wrote of this 'class' as if its members belonged to some distinctive, exotic tribe of Africa or the Americas.' – Clive Emsley, *Crime and the Victorians* (2011).

support,[43] but the overall ethos wasn't helped by the constitutional powerlessness of the worker community. It's easy to forget, when the suffragette struggle for women's emancipation is still in the lens of public awareness, that most working men had no right to decide who represented them in Parliament until 1867[44] and the following year saw more than three times the number of votes cast than the previous one. Frome's notorious election riots had represented strong convictions for which no expression was permitted. Ballots weren't secret until 1872, so feelings would be running high throughout the day of the election, especially as money was known to change hands at such events. As an example of passionate involvement, when popular Radical Liberal Donald Nicholl lost to the wealthy Tory candidate by a single vote, not only women but strong men burst into tears and sobbed aloud.

As soon as the franchise changed, men in Frome mobilised themselves to focus on other ways to represent their political feelings and formed a Working Men's Liberal Association, followed in 1874 by the establishment of Frome Liberal Association. Six years later the Tories followed suit, and in **1882** Frome Working Men's Club anticipated the forming of the Labour party by eighteen years.[45]

---

43 Thomas Bunn (d.1863) is a frequently-quoted philanthropist and certainly saw himself in that virtuous role, though his diaries also reflect the underlying judgements of his era: he commented after meeting an impoverished man with thirteen children 'the people complain of their poverty and go on creating more' (1838) and when two men caught after breaking into his house and stealing eggs and drink were sentenced to ten years transportation, his response – as well as feeling 'obliged' they had taken nothing he valued – was 'I only regret that our beautiful colonies should be peopled by the worst of mankind.'

44 Before 1832 voting was essentially a rich man's privilege, allowed only to men of property. The 'Great Reform Act' widened the definition of property to include landowners and shopkeepers, and allowed a vote to householders paying more than £10 in annual rent. Even though the age and property value was reduced in an 1867 amendment, non-householders (domestic servants, soldiers in barracks, those living with parents or the homeless) all had to wait till 1918 to get the vote.

45 This wasn't the first time Frome had shown itself politically at the forefront of contemporary thinking: back in 1825 – only two years after the Anti-Slavery society had been founded in London – a meeting in support of the 'Abolition of Slavery throughout the British Dominions' was held at The

Nicholl finally achieved success in 1857 and represented the town for two years, but in 1885 Frome lost its status as a parliamentary borough as a result of the Redistribution Act which disenfranchised towns of less than 15,000. It became a division of Somerset, and was served alternately by Liberals and Conservatives (sometimes called Unionists) until 1923 when the first Labour MP was voted in. Conservatives reclaimed the seat until the end of the war, but Frome joined Labour's post-war landslide victory with Walter Farthing's election. He was the last MP for the Frome constituency, as it was transferred to the Wells division in 1950 and then in 1983 wedged into the top nub of a new 'Somerton and Frome' constituency which stretches down nearly to Taunton and has been solidly in Conservative hands ever since the amalgamation – apart from going briefly to Liberal David Heath until the Coalition.

Frome town however still manages to go its own way. In the County Council elections of 2017, two of the three councillors elected represented the Green party, and for the District Council the ratio was three out of nine. And as we all know, the Town Councillors stand for none of the national parties at all – at least, at the present time. . .

THIS SECTION HAS LOOKED mostly at the reasons Frome acquired its reputation for dissent and rebellion, and touched only lightly on the most important aspect of the town's self-assertive energy: the next section will focus on the creative community.

---

George. Supporting names included the mill-owning Sheppards and Thomas Bunn. The Act was passed in 1834.

# FALSE NEWS

**The subjoined account of a riot at Frome is extracted from a Bath paper:**

'On Sunday morning , between seven and eight o'clock, an express arrived at Bath from Frome with the unpleasant intelligence of a riot having taken place in that town on Saturday evening.

A number of persons early in the afternoon showed symptoms of discontent at some additional advance in the price of potatoes. Their numbers increased to between two and three thousand by seven o'clock and they then proceeded to acts of violence. The magistrates, with the utmost promptitude read the riot act, and the Frome cavalry having assembled to preserve peace, was immediately assailed with follies of stones, brickbats, &c.; we lament to say, in this conflict Colonel Wickham received a severe wound to his head which caused him to be led from the scene of action; seven or eight of the cavalry have been wounded or bruised, and as many horses,

**This account is reported in *Cobbett's Political Register* 1816.**

Cobbett quotes at length, deconstructs the language and writes sarcastically about cavalry being 'a match for all the disloyal old women and boys in the county, especially when the latter have neither food in their bodies nor arms in their hands.' Then he offers 'a true account of the affair at Frome. It is a letter written from the spot, and signed with the real name of the writer':

July 17 1816    '. . . I find that the public have been led into some error from the accounts given in the newspapers, which appeared long before it was noticed in your Register. The true state of the case is this: Some person in the Market having demanded 1s.5d. per peck for old potatoes, which was a rise of 5d. since the preceding Market day, the persons who came to purchase were dissatisfied, and, during the altercation one idle young man pushed another over the market-woman's basket and overturned it. These young men were immediately seized by a constable. They were taken without opposition to the Guard House. The news of this soon spread about; a great concourse of people assembled, and demanded that the men should be discharged out of custody. The Rev Henry Sainsbury, a Magistrate of Beckington now arrived and, the people still demanding the one having his eye knocked out. At four o'clock on Sunday morning, a detachment of the Inniskilling dragoons arrived from Bruton, and shortly after some degree of order was restored. The Bath cavalry have received orders to hold themselves in readiness, and are now assembled opposite the Guildhall. The rioters first proceeded to rescue three men that were taken into custody early in the day, but were defeated in their purpose. They next proceeded to the factory of Messrs Sheppard, with the intent to destroy the same, but through the prompt exertions of the magistrates and the cavalry, all was saved. Great praise is due to the meritorious exertions of the Frome cavalry on this occasion; and we understand the whole of North Somerset yeomanry are under arms to aid the civil power, as these deluded men have threatened to repeat their depredations on Wednesday next.'

July 30 1816 – *The Edinburgh Annual Register*

liberation of the young men, he read the Riot Act and called out the Cavalry. Things now began to wear a serious aspect. The Cavalry were assaulted with stones and brickbats and many of them, to the amount of 17 were wounded, among which number was the Commanding Officer, who got a very severe wound in the face. I have just seen him and he now has a large black patch over the wound, the mark of which he will carry with him to the grave. At about ten o'clock at night, when the tumult was at its height, Mr Champness of Orchardleigh, another of the Magistrates, arrived and, as I am informed, demanded of some of the people what they wanted. They returned for answer, 'the liberation of the young men who are in custardy.' Mr Champness then had them brought to him and finding no one to prefer any serious charge against them they were liberated. The whole of the people then dispersed, and the town became as quiet as it is at this moment. Thus much for the truth of Captain Thornhill's boasting statement that ' the Frome squadron had completely dispersed the mob and restored peace and good order.' To the Cavalry every praise is due for their temper and moderation on this occasion. But by the judicious conduct of Mr Champness alone (whose names seems purposely kept out of sight) was the piece [i.e. peace – is the original wrong?] and tranquility of this town restored. I am, Sir, Your most Obedient Servant, John Allen.

P.S. This Captain and Adjutant did not arrive in town till *Sunday,* when all was peace and quietness.

*Al O'Kane, musician and 2016 Deputy Mayor*

# 5   CREATIVITY

*– artisans and artists –*
*– carnival spirit – the town with two theatres –*
*– performance, words, sounds, and visuals –*
*– punk heyday –*

*'In order to correctly define art, it is necessary, first of all, to cease to consider it as a means to pleasure and consider it as one of the conditions of human life. Reflecting on it in this way, we cannot fail to observe that art is one of the means of effective communication between people.'*

– Leo Tolstoy

*'Art washes from the soul the dust of everyday life.'*

– Pablo Picasso

FROME HAS MORE PEOPLE working in creative arts than any other small town in the country. It's true – it must be, I read it in a national newspaper. I also wrote it, the previous year in a promotion for the Frome Festival, without any research because my actual copy was 'Frome boasts...' since anyone can <u>boast</u> anything, but in repetition the fact had become absolute. And now it seems to be true.

Frome in the 21st century is certainly home to an extraordinary number of creatives.[1] Artistic skills span music, words, performance (live and recorded), visual arts and crafts, and every conceivable spin-off and combination, private and public, projected on buildings or shining from windows or enlivening open spaces. At the time that my first novel was published an interviewer asked me why so many

---

1   I intended in this section to include EVERYONE I know who is working creatively in Frome right now, but this quickly proved impossible: in one way or another that IS everyone I know, plus also everyone they know, so like the queen bee's egg habit, the outcome would be unmanageable. Instead I'll just remind you of some of the diversity that surrounds us.

artistic people live in Frome, and my top-of-the-head suggestion was a combination of leylines and poor transport. The first notion may be more than a bit whimsical, but the second is certainly a factor. With its charming architecture and – until recently – low house prices, if Frome had a more efficient train service and better road links, it would probably be a dormitory town for Bristol or London by now. As it is, current statistics show that many of Frome's recent population are self-employed in a creative field.

This is certainly nothing new. Arts and crafts have been made and traded in Frome since at least the early 1300s when one Thomas Jolf was recorded in 1325 as paying six shillings a year to dig clay for his pottery in Friggle Street. The first industry had a craft basis – wool, dyed by skilled craftspeople to specific shades. Frome's artistic heritage is visible everywhere: anglican churches used stained glass[2] made in Frome and streets are still adorned by Cocky's 'art nouveau' lamps. Creative contributions continued when the industry-base widened, as evidenced by the annual September carnivals when each group of workers put their float into the procession through town – a celebration dating back to 1270 which had virtually faded until 1927 when a group of workers at Butler & Tanner had the idea of reviving it.[3] What's pleasingly significant is that this initiative came from a group of night-shift workers on a fag-break – all local men. Frome's carnivals were never as big as Bridgwater, but they were homegrown, which made them unique on the Somerset circuit. Parade entries, contributed by nearly all the factories, initially featured elaborately-costumed tableaux and dance-dramas, but by the mid-nineties it became clear that carnival was another spin-off loss of industrial closures. Frome Carnival continues, much smaller now, but the community spirit survives and is supported by the *Home in Frome* group

---

2   Holy Trinity built from 1836 has a unique collection of nine windows designed by pre-Raphaelite artist Edward Burne-Jones and made by William Morris & Co. If you visit on a summer afternoon you may see their images projected by the sun on the stone flags of the church floor.

3   Butler & Tanner loaned their lorry for a hospital scene and there were many foot entries. A profit of £50 was divided equally between the Victoria Hospital and the Queen's Nurses. A second 'Rag Parade' was even more successful and the tradition grew until in 1948 it was formalised as the Frome Carnival Charities Association.

mentioned in the first section. They work with accessible local materials and use traditional skills, bringing people together through folk-art projects like withy lanterns, quilts and banners, to process experiences creatively.[4]

There's big emphasis on participation in much that goes on – seen not only in the 'open-mic' of many music and word events, but in community involvement in its widest sense. Our mid-winter spectacular, for example (still locally called the Extravaganza) has had various themes which have filled the streets with creative imagery and costume – including a wonderful Dickensian Christmas. And in frosty February this year, when Frome was invited to join the *Window Wanderland* weekend, hundreds of houses glowed with amazing window tableaux, from fairytales to fantasy and, for three nights, friends and families walked miles around the streets of town gazing in delight at this magical community response.

The creative spirit of the entire town is showcased in the Frome Festival, and this section will focus on some of the elements which contribute to these big celebrations – and sustain that ethos throughout the year. If you ask people what drew them to live in Frome, the most common answer is connected with its creativity. The two theatres are frequently cited, so let's start with them.

The Merlin Theatre was built in 1974 in the grounds of Frome College and when director Paula Hammond came in 2000 she worked closely with the college principals to ensure that the school, which was always desperate for additional classroom space, didn't encroach and swallow it like a python.[5] When Paula left, her successor Claudia

---

4 'When Singers' Knoll was demolished we created an illuminated paper-lantern procession about our houses, created by people who had lived there, so they could find ways to grieve and to celebrate the change.' These self-made-lantern processions proved popular with makers and audiences alike: when the council sponsored a similar one for the 2017 Christmas Light Switch-On ceremony, response was so enthusiastic that no fewer than 900 people went to the *Home in Frome* workshops where withies, tissue, glue, and patient expertise of two local artists were all provided. The subsequent event was magical.

5 Paula also came up with an idea for which I am endlessly grateful: because I had a habit of devising writer-events involving spoken word, she invited me to become Writer in Residence for the Merlin throughout

Pepler further enhanced the range of live drama and was able to add
film screenings of National Theatre productions. With community
productions by Frome Drama Club and Tri-art youth theatre too, Merlin
was doing really well at what a 240-seat-theatre does best – big shows
that come alive with a big audience – and counteracting the deterrent of
a longish distance from the town centre by offering pre- and post-show
supper options.[6] And then in 2010 disaster struck. Somerset axed all
Arts funding,[7] which as Arts Council grants all require matched funding,
annihilated all the Merlin's funding at a stroke, like a casually-amputated
leg taking with the same swipe the other other one with it. It felt like
that at the time, anyway. Incredibly and to her immense credit Claudia
managed to continue in role and the theatre still puts on a full and varied
programme of productions.

> It's a lot to do, but I've got a huge army of volunteers – about 80 or
> 90, who do all the jobs on a part-time basis instead of the people we
> had to make redundant,' she says: 'I just want Merlin to be known as
> a creative hub and a go-to place – for young people in particular. I see
> it as a grass-roots place, where we support and mentor them from
> first coming to watch a Christmas show, and then taking part, and
> then they often go off and make careers in the arts.

---

2003, to promote a diversity of projects around the town. I had a brilliant
year. Paula's support gave me not just funds but confidence to organise
and promote a whole raft of initiatives, culminating in *Urban Scrawl*, a
marvellous night of top-class performance poets in the theatre, putting
Frome briefly up there with Bristol. Once my year was up, I continued in a
more low-key way as a permanent member of the team of creative artists,
with no financial support but venue access for a continuing series of
various prose and poetry events.

6   My role as associate artist for spoken word continued with events moving
from the foyer to the stage itself in 'platter' nights where performers shared
their space with the audience in a kind of bistro atmosphere – an innovation
unique to Frome. Nathan Filer came back to one of these platter nights after
he won the Costa Book Award...

7   The Tory-controlled council voted to end £160,000 of direct grants to ten
organisations, including theatres and a film production company, as part of a
£43m programme of cuts across the services.

And then the phone rings and Claudia, who is covering box office today as someone is off sick, has to take the call. . . Claudia is too modest, and busy, to mention that she has won the prestigious Pat Hudson Trophy for her personal contribution to Youth Drama in her roles as Merlin director, co-director of Tri.art Theatre School, and drama workshop leader throughout both term-time and holidays. Her individual productions have won awards too, and Claudia has written and directed pantomimes, performs on stage herself, and even supports playwrights – we've had two International Short Play competitions, with staged productions for the winners.

The Merlin site also has an outside performing space – our unique amphitheatre ECOS: 'European Community of Stones', an amazing circle of monoliths around a tiered auditorium. Conceived by artist Barry Cooper, this is a part of Frome's history I actually witnessed. In 1992 I was working with a group of students right beside the site, and we daily recorded, in sketches, photographs and writing, the progress of the project from foundations to final placing of each of the twelve stones.[8] It was thrilling to see them arrive one by one, quarrying marks still fresh: giant stones from Spain, Germany, Luxembourg, Italy, France, Ireland, Denmark, Netherlands, Portugal, Belgium, Greece all brought to stand with the sturdy UK monolith and show we were now members of the European Union and could look forward to a less xenophobic, more egalitarian future...

The first event on the open-air stage was the rock-opera *Tommy*, directed by Martin Dimery who was also narrator, with George Williams (now acting professionally) as the deaf-dumb-and-blind kid – a thrilling production made unforgettable by a stunning *coup-de-theatre* when three troop-carriers coming back from Salisbury flew slowly and loudly over the stage during the scene when Tommy's father disappears, presumed dead. . . 'One of those magical moments,' Martin Dimery recalls.

---

8    This project was not without its detractors at the time. When the Somerset Standard published a total cost of £37,000, there were letters complaining that the money should have been better used, although in fact this was the estimated cost of quarrying and transporting eleven rocks across land and sea – costs all covered by their donors, who had been convinced of the merit of this project by Foster Yeoman project spokesman Peter Chapman. He should – along with Barry Cooper for having the original vision and Frank Turner who literally built it – take much credit.

Over on the other side of town, the town's other theatre 'The Mem', as the Memorial Hall is more usually known, is also steered by a Frome-bred director: Humphrey Barnes, chair of the trustees for more than thirty years, and also actively involved with the *Frome Musical Theatre Company*. Built in 1925 and used initially as a dance hall[9], the Mem was converted to a cinema in the 1930s and thrived for a while as 'The Grand' but in the 1980s when attendance dwindled the whole place was threatened with demolition. Humphrey was one of those who led the protest and the campaign to retain the hall as the memorial it was built to be, and as a place for live theatre, complementing the Merlin with a different style of programming.

Two theatres is pretty good for a town of Frome's size, but in fact there are drama performances in other places too, usually in pubs, although *Nevertheless Productions* – Somerset's first and only Pub Theatre company[10] – has taken promenade theatre into a graveyard, and Sioux How's *Little Victory Ball* , sharing less-known facts about WWI, can entertain just about anywhere from a tent. Frome has other small independent theatre companies too, including currently *Feet First*[11] creating family shows. Sadly, the excellent *Take Art!* programme of innovative small touring shows doesn't come near Frome now, as Mendip stopped providing support funding. We have our own street theatre though: the scurrilous and subversive duo *Rare Species*, and also the *SATCO* team offering spurious acts of mountaineering and synchronised swimming. We're also occasionally invaded by aliens when

---

9 'Regular live bands on Wednesday nights, we had Trogs, Tremeloes, Screaming Lord Sutch, Apple Jacks, Dave Dee and the Bostons – all the 60's bands,' I was told. This may have been in the cinema days, as 'all the seats were taken out for dancing'.

10 The inspiration of Rosie Finnegan, who I'm privileged to say asked me to co-found with her. For five years we put on mainly in-house productions, some of which toured to Bristol, to sell-out audiences. We mostly used The Cornerhouse but my favourite of all was the site-specific piece I wrote inspired by, and performed in, the Dissenters Cemetery.

11 This project developed from *First Cut*, already referenced, and instead of taking performances into classrooms, offers outdoor experiential activity: *Time Walk,* our current project tells the story of the earth in a thousand paces... children are awed at the end of their walk to realise they have less than one step left to cover the entire existence of homo sapiens...

the Frome Comic Con is on, but most frequently seen on the street are the immensely popular promenade performances from *Frome Street Bandits*.[12] Their founder Annabelle Macfadyen is also one of Frome's professional actors: after training in physical theatre in Paris, she joined Kneehigh Theatre and toured with them for some years, and now collaborates with other creatives to organise a whole range of community performances and shows.[13] Other actors live locally and contribute regularly to the creative scene, most notably Mark McGann, Stephanie Cole and James Laurenson.

Before we leave the stage, a word from an award-winning company based in Frome and performing on stage here as well as touring internationally: *Mark Bruce Company,* acknowledged as one of the most vibrant and innovative dance groups in the country, began in Frome in 1991 with no premises but now has its own space here: a custom-built home with sprung floor, for rehearsal and storage of their memorable sets, props and masks. Themes are massive and often monstrous – Dracula, the Odyssey, Macbeth – among others. Mark reckons Frome is his company's natural home.[14]

> Frome's done so much for the company. But that's Frome, isn't it. I never stop appreciating that, and hope that the work repays that. I don't know anywhere else I'd like to live right now. Frome is a special place – an extraordinary place – it's sort of magical, I think. It just seems to be. . . creatively out-of-control, there's so many things

---

12  Led by Annabelle Macfadyen, accordionist and performer-provocateur, in costumes of red, black, and gold, the Street Bandits flamboyantly feature their trademark gypsy-influenced medleys with choreographed displays of virtuosity – and their notorious duelling trombones – at many outdoor events around town and beyond.

13  Her projects have ranged from baroque extravaganzas like the *Cabaret Sans Frontiers* (with Howard Vause) to establishing a dramatic excavation in the street to raise awareness of fossil fuel exploitation, always with a fun side and community involvement.

14  Mark's father Chris Bruce was artistic director of Rambert for ten years, leaving in 2002 to come down to Frome full-time, and his mother Marian Bruce is an artist working mainly with installations and stage design – I was lucky enough to collaborate with her challenging and profound *Angels* project staged at the Merlin in the festivals of 2002-4.

happening – so much activity going on. It's almost like some sort of infection.

Infected by a creativity virus – that would explain a lot: a kind of creative synergy, an accumulation which enriches Frome's creativity exponentially, is something I heard expressed in different ways from many people I spoke to. Photographer James Bartholomew experiences it as a sense of 'one degree of separation' – a much closer mesh of connectivity than the commonly referenced six degrees. And it connects too, I would argue, with that dissenting trait that steeps the fabric of the town and colours its long history. 'True creativity comes from restriction and limitation' Paul Schrader famously said, and now that the national status-quo is reduced status (and funding) for art, our innately-dissident community floods the town with music, visuals, and words. 'Dissent' in church history didn't mean passive withdrawal but active re-envisaging and, like the al-fresco preachers of old, creatives of Frome throw out the rule book when they get together – or, at least, ignore the instruction leaflet. Phil Moakes who runs the widely-admired and uniquely-innovative Visual Radio Arts studio[15] agrees.

> There's a quality here that seems to allow people to do things, a 'can-do' spirit that doesn't exist elsewhere, because it's natural for people in Frome to become intrigued, interested, and invested, in things that are creative and interesting. My friends who don't live round here don't have the same experience but we take it for granted, and that in itself provides the confidence to have a go. It all comes back to that principle that underpins Frome – making things happen, and when some things happen, other things can happen.

Frome's current explosion of creativity is the consequence of both these factors: the 'just-do-it' approach of each new initiative, and the trail-blazing that preceded it. Phil identifies this from his own experience:

---

15 Described as 'The Old Grey Whistle Test for the 21st century', VRA provides an opportunity for bands to showcase their performances in a live video stream which is also archived, and a great chance for anyone listening/watching to hear new music live. I'm privileged that Phil also includes poetry sessions occasionally, in a slot called *Word Play*.

We wouldn't be doing what we're doing now in visual recording if
Frome FM hadn't existed, and Frome FM couldn't have happened
without the Cheese & Grain, where it first started. In 2004
broadcasting legislation changed to allow community radio, Mike
Adams[16] suggested that as Frome College had a specialism in media,
they might want to pursue the idea for the 2005 Festival. They
had teachers on board – Mike Walker, Lisa Millard (later Deputy
Principal), Martin Dimery, Howard Vause and Will Angeloro as
technician. Ofcom grant you a month of broadcasting, which means
an awful lot of work starting from scratch and one of the volunteers
was concerned it was all going to disappear and that would be a
crying shame, so he knocked on my door and said 'Do Something'.

I had no idea about radio. I listened to it, that's about the size
of it. But there was no-one else. . . so my involvement was never
intentional, it just happened. That's very Frome, isn't it. When you
get a nucleus of people who make some of those things happen,
then other things coalesce around it. The reason I came to Frome
is because one day in 1992 Martin Dimery asked me to do PA for
Tommy,[17] at the college. And I thought, 'These people have taken on
a complex musical project, in a college environment, outdoors – and
they're actually good!'

The fledgling radio station needed to move out of its college base
but Phil was chairman of the Cheese & Grain at the time, so it found a
new home there. He took on the slogan 'Don't do what's already there'
and encouraged volunteer presenters to make their shows accessible to
local listeners. Ofcom stringent regulations limited the listening range to
five miles ('-which is very very local, and we're living in a global community'),

---

16  Mike Adams, a Frome resident when in UK, was international coordinator of
First Response Radio (FRR), an emergency radio station to broadcast critical
humanitarian relief information to communities affected by disaster.

17  Tommy, the show that celebrated the completion of the ECOS project, is a
good example, since the amphitheatre itself only came about because artist
Barry Cooper virtually said to the college, 'could I have a bit of your car-park
because I want to ask twelve countries to quarry up a massive monolith
and transport it here, all at their own expense, to make a circle around a
performance space, because that would be nice, wouldn't it...' As Phil says,
Frome manifests through expectation.

so Phil turned to internet radio: the original Frome FM now flourishes in the Town Hall, while Visual Radio Arts attracts a wide range of bands from across the southwest and beyond for its regular shows, all streamed on Facebook both live and archived as *Sound Check*.

C O-OPERATION IS INTEGRAL to arts like theatre, radio, choirs and bands, but Frome has support groups for creative work often seen as essentially individual. Frome Writers Collective, founded in 2014 to encourage and support writers in every genre, now has over a hundred members and – uniquely in the entire country – its own book brand *'Silver Crow'*.[18] For the town's poets, there's the Poetry Cafe and occasional slam nights with the Hip Yak Poetry Shack.[19] Oral wordsmiths can enjoy Mr Rook's Speakeasy or Open Stories at the HUBnub.

Frome doesn't offer much historically in the way of well-known writers[20] but there are currently many 'names' living in Frome and supporting community writing events, often with readings and talks:

---

18  Silver Crow is not a publishing house but a support to the self-publisher, offering editorial guidance and operating as guarantee of quality. This very popular 'collective' had its own precedent in 'Words at the Frome Festival', the group of writers who came together annually to plan a programme of literary events and developed a continuing identity. Alison Clink, who started the internationally-renowned *Frome Festival Short Story Contest*, was also a leader in this group. Alison also initiated the 'Boot Camp' sessions for writers throughout the summer, moving support away from education into the community.

19  The vibrant poetry scene in Frome is another 'stepping-stone' example: 'Slam' poetry with its ethos of competition wasn't the right vibe for Frome at first: our initial steps into performance poetry were 'soap-box' poets in the festival initiated by Rosie Finnegan and a *Liquid Jam* night at Garden Cafe, which Will Angeloro generously supported with a CD. The Garden Cafe has hosted bi-monthly events ever since that first al fresco summer session, and it's still ticketless and inclusive, paving the way for the arrival of Slam at the Hip Yak Poetry Shack, brilliantly emceed by Liv Torc.

20  Elizabeth Singer Rowe already mentioned was widely read and admired in her time however. She spent her life in Frome, unlike Christina Rossetti who died around 150 years later and has oddly earned a plaque by staying here for a few months to help out in her mum's school. 'Christina did not look back with any pleasure to her sojourn at Frome' reports her biographer, Mackenzie Bell, an English writer and her contemporary.

among them Whitbread winner Lindsay Clarke, multi-awarded writer/ performer Pip Utton, prose writers Peter Clark, John Payne and David Lassman, and poets Liv Tork, Rose Flint, and Rosie Jackson, also known for her memoir work. There are more than a few writers of children's stories, and Palmer Street is the home of Chicken House publishing company, run by Barry Cunningham – the man who picked out J K Rowling's multi-rejected *Harry Potter* manuscript for his new children's list at Bloomsbury.

The story for visual arts is similar: a supportive cooperative hive, and many individual workers. *Frome Art Society* was founded in 1979 to encourage painting and drawing, and Black Swan Arts encourages a diversity of media in both its galleries and the makers' studios. Their exhibitions vary from internationally renowned artists to local groups – recently their *Young Open* featuring nearly 200 exhibits by artists aged eight to eighteen was superbly vibrant and impactful. Their mission statement sums up: 'As well as being able to bring national touring exhibitions to the town, Black Swan Arts is proud to showcase and celebrate the extraordinary creative energy of Frome. We believe that enjoying and participating in the arts makes life better for everyone.'

There are other display spaces too: notably the big hall in the Silk Mill and the balcony of the HUBnub, as well as small galleries in town, sometimes in cafes and pubs. OWL on Catherine Hill, where art and craft creatively merge, is co-run by eight impressively talented local artists including Steven Jenkins and Mel Day, the only person you'll ever meet who can create a recognisable portrait of Tony Benn out of fuse-wire. The best opportunity to see the full range of art, craft and photography in Frome is the *Open Studios* event – there were 74 individual artists in last year's town trail.[21] And Frome is long-time home to Christopher Bucklow whose work is in venues from London to New York, and to Leslie Glenn Damhus, her exquisite and mischievous allegorical paintings represented by Saatchi and also exhibited in a converted chapel in Frome. David Chandler leads *Frome Sketchers* around the streets, and in fact the entire old town is a kind of random art trail, where ancient, abandoned-looking objects mingle unexpectedly with commissioned art, open-air seating

---

21 Because of this admirable multiplicity I reluctantly decided not to highlight any names.

carved with words or woodland imagery, exhibitions in cafes and pubs, and of course the transient glories of graffiti.[22]

Many of Frome's visual artists work and exhibit widely, making connections mutually enriching for both locations. Barry Cooper has worked around the world, mainly with materials from the local environment,[23] using sculpture and painting to make profound political statements. And there are a huge number of traditional makers, representing the arts and crafts revival. Alan Campbell, video-maker and producer, has been show-casing scores of community projects since he arrived in 2000.

> There's an enormous number of artisans in Frome – people who make jewellery, and fantastic variety of crafts. For example, Chris Barlow who lives over the road makes pianos and he's making an upright harpsichord at the moment. And round the corner is Laurie Parnell who makes guitars – he's a wonderful musician, often to be seen playing in the Bishop's Palace garden in Wells at their special events.

From traditional crafts to projections and rave nights might seem a stretch, but not for Frome, where all these events can be seen in close proximity in the festival – and on other occasions. Andrew Shackleton came to Frome from London with a background of software development, and found

---

22 Mutartis, one of our most esoteric practitioners in this field, in an interviewed in 2009 for London Street-Art Design magazine spoke of this transience as part of the appeal – 'a channel of communication outside the control of the powers that be.. like lichen that just grows, layering up and constantly evolving.'

23 One of his recent projects was closer to home, when a 250-year-old, 60-foot oak tree was felled by a storm on the edge of Stourhead estate. When he realised this tree had featured in a 1798 painting by Turner, Barry conceived the *Last Tree Dreaming* project, and with a large team of young people from Frome plus eco-poet Helen Moore and sculptor Anthony Rogers, ran sessions creating carvings along the bark culminated in the final raising of the tree outside the college, providing 'a potent link with Frome's past within a forested landscape and its aspirations for a truly sustainable future'

a vibrant energy that makes you feel you can do something different.
Like Joseph Hyde (composer and sound&media artist)[24], Alex Relph
(metal sculptor), and Jack Vaughn Jublees (VJ), they put on *Sensonic*
at the Silk Mill for the festival each year – cutting-edge visuals, 3-D
holographic projections – it's extraordinary for a tiny town like
Frome. It's that open environment where people are up for doing
things – anybody can do what they want.[25]

Film-maker Howard Vause has been a major contributor to
Frome's creatives, in a role that started, as other initiatives had, when
funding from a Labour Government in 2002 allowed the Community
College to establish itself as a Media Arts centre. Mike Walker had the
responsibility for implementing this, and he established a media base in
the Old Coffee Block[26] run by Howard and Will Angeloro as technician.

I did it for ten years, loads of stuff,' Howard remembers: 'Barry
Bates the Principal had trusted Mike, and Mike trusted me to take
on whatever I chose, so I went for projects that seemed of most
benefit to the community, and the slightly evangelical nature of
creative technology. When I was growing up it had been difficult and
expensive, then digital stuff arrived and suddenly it was easy and
cheap!

---

24 If you want the technical description of this music and video combination,
   I refer you to Howard Vause, a fan: 'weird experimentally-flashing-blobbies-
   type technology.'
25 Andrew took advantage of this collaborative ethos to film the *Tales of
   the Tunnels* project already referred to, the site-specific collaborative
   performance under the river arches. Frome Scriptwriters – led by
   Nevertheless Productions – wrote scripts which were collated by David
   Lassman, Gladys Paulus created amazing headdresses, Aliss Vass provided
   costumes, and a powerful medieval-style pagan morality play emerged – but
   not without hope: as Andrew says, 'about humanity – how we got to this
   state, the sacrifices made for progress, and how it could finally come out
   better. People had to row themselves from everyday reality to the magical
   place we'd created There's a reason why the river's there, it's the possibility of
   transition.'
26 I remember those days: its awning advertising Nestlé sparked a protest from
   Tertiary students I'm glad to say.

I was one of the many creatives who benefited from Howard's esoteric imagination,[27] and even when funding ran out he continued to work with schools and on community projects as well as on his personal animated short films.

Other groups and individuals also fly the flag for independent film-making, notably *Bargus* Independent Film Company which in 2014 won the Salisbury Arts Festival 48-hour shoot-out competition with *Tenth Muse*. Nikki Lloyd who wrote the script for this also scripted their feature-length film *Metatron,* shown at the Westway.

Arts magazines have come and mostly gone, although *The List,* founded by Fay Goodridge eight years ago to summarise and celebrate all the creative ventures in town, still survives as hard copy in an online world, under the editorship of Rose Langley. We also had at one time *Furball,* tagline *It's a Frome Thing,* wittily edited by Will Angeloro and Barry MacDonald 'talking with confidence about things we don't understand.' More serious was the arts magazine *Encompass,* described by founder Charlie Jones-West and Tchad Findlay as

> a directory of cool creative independent DIY people, done in a way
> that people wanted to look at, so lots of photos, interesting articles,
> and links to what they did, so if you did want a connection you could
> reach out to them.

Another illustrated magazine, online this time, which appeared once only was *On the Door,* arriving in 2017 to celebrate Foo Fighters gig at the Cheese and Grain, Barry Cooper's *Last Tree Dreaming*, and one of festival highlights, the history of Frome as conceived by Edventure students' immersive production *Legends of Frome* in Sun Street Chapel.

---

27  Howard made a DVD of performance poetry for *Live & Lippy*, which was
    Hazel Stewart and me (there's a track here: https://www.youtube.com/
    watch?v=mrPu-9Xgwsg currently with 8,751 views), and among much
    else he has made a fantastic video for *Frome Street Bandits* (*The Wood, the
    Brass and the Funky*: https://vimeo.com/187438750) and the best (non)
    party political broadcast you'll ever see: viewable here: https://vimeo.
    com/124837931.

ABOVE ALL, AS ANYONE who has spent more than a few hours in this town will know, Frome loves music. From the accordionist on the bridge to the *Frome Symphony Orchestra*,[28] Frome virtually vibrates with live music. There are free sessions in pubs ranging from open-mic for folk, rock, and blues to popular bands like post-punk *Raggedy Men*, Bowie-inspired *Rebel Heroes*, and many others, with a performance somewhere most nights - often more than one - from the Grain bar by the river to the churches up the hill, from tiny bars to elegant halls, so anyone who enjoys live music has a full calendar. Morag McLaren at Cooper Hall has provided Frome with its very own Glyndebourne,[29] and there are bands in every style from the military Town Band to ukulele bands *Back of the Bus* and the *Frukes,* with choirs from *Jackdaws Songbirds* and the Community Choir (both no-experience-required groups) to the operatic society (now renamed *Frome Musical Theatre Company*) and music for the dance groups from Arabic to lindy-hop and swing.[30]

There's good retail support for fans too, from *Sounds of Frome* instruments and two highly-rated music shops: *Covers* on Catherine Hill and the legendary *Raves from the Grave* – more than a music shop: according to the Sabotage Times in 2014, 'a record shop To Visit Before You Die'. Richard Churchyard, himself a musician, opened this Aladdin's

---

28 Mark Gateshill is conductor and musical director of this self-confessedly 'ambitious amateur orchestra' with a mission to 'promote high-quality live classical music in the community, and to provide education and development opportunities for local musicians of all ages.' They also have a Youth String Orchestra for young players of violin, viola, cello and double bass. Their Orchestral Weekends in Frome bring performers from all over the country and take on complex works: last November it was Richard Strauss's huge tone poem, Eine Alpensinfonie which consists of twenty-two continuous sections of music depicting the experiences climbing an Alpine mountain. It requires over 100 musicians and the performance lasts around 50 minutes.

29 'I hope Cooper Hall will create a haven ... Artistic work and the creative process thrive in an environment where there is space, safety and peace to experiment, discover, take risks, make mistakes, play with new ideas – without harsh judgment.' says Morag, who established the foundation in 2012.

30 And this is just the public scene – the events and groups inviting audiences – there will be many more group and solo musicians practicing, writing, and composing in private, and performing to dedicated supporters, as there always have been.

cave of CDs, DVDs and vinyl in 1997: it's not only a great support for local bands but also a magnet to visiting musicians. 'We've had Tom Robinson,' Richard told me, trying to recall recent musicians who'd performed outside his crammed store on Cheap Street, 'we've had Billy Bragg, Cliff Difford from Squeeze fairly recently – Robert Plant came in last month when he was recording in Frome, he bought a few CDs. We've had Van Morrison in here, the whole of the Inspiral Carpets and two of the Yardbirds...' It's not all about names:[31] there's a prominent rack for local and unsigned bands: 'a lot of the artists just email us and we say, send it in the post, we'll put it in the rack.'

As with visual artists, and writers too, there are simply too many musicians and bands performing currently for me to include all the names that deserve appreciative mention, but I can't leave this section without sketching in some of Frome's current vibrant line-ups.

Frome Jazz Club has regular sessions which feature outstanding visiting musicians joining both Keith Harrison-Broninski and John Law, both acknowledged as leading jazz pianist/composers, who alternate as session leaders. The Cornerhouse is home to these and other sessions, and Three Swans hosts regular Trad Jazz. Cheese and Grain has excellent weekly 'Roots Sessions', started by Griff Daniels and now run by Domenic DeCicco and Colin Ashley, with both local and visiting guests. We have *Pete Gage Band* bringing classic blues to various venues, and some amazingly theatrical bands – more than a gig, you get a costume drama from a cast of nine from *Captain Cactus and the Screaming Harlots*. *Back Woods Redeemers* too create stories with their songs while scaring the ungodly with their chocolate Jesus. And there's a distinctively-Frome take on the tribute band: Martin Dimery whose fantastically successful *Sergeant Pepper's Only Dartboard Band* has finally hung up its Pop-Edwardian Peter-Blake-inspired costumes and moved to a muted palette as the *Unravelling Wilburys*.[32] Martin's talented family are still making

---

31  Though I did have a frisson hearing Russell Brand had been in buying DVDs -'twice actually, he buys stand-up comedy, he lay on the floor with his entourage browsing. We had quite a good laugh with him, we said 'We can never sell your stuff...'

32  For the disconcertingly large number of young who don't realise Bob Dylan joined with George Harrison, Roy Orbison, Tom Petty and Jeff Lynne in the late 80s to form a supergroup called the Travelling Wilburys.

Frome proud: daughter Olivia is drummer for '70s-hiphop influenced *Bad Sounds,* currently with over a million plays on Spotify.

Folk music locally is not as boisterous as those who at the mention of Somerset go 'ooh-arr ooh-arr' and chant about combine harvesters might think, but there was definitely a folk club in the Bennett Centre (previously known as St John's hall) in the '80s and Sue Clare, now with Gemma White and Lucy May in the amazing *Feral Beryl,* was playing even before then at a club in the Granary. Apparently there was also a regular folk session in the Blue Boar, where Ralph McTell used to play, but currently folk music tends to be diffused around different pubs. *Three Corners* founders Nick Waterhouse and Caroline Radcliffe in the early days of Cheese & Grain's revival ran *Acoustic Plus* sessions, their massively popular roughly-monthly music events involving up to three stages.[33]

As the west country is home to festivals throughout the summer, many of Frome's performers participate in these glorious outdoor events, from Glastonbury (the Avalon stage and the Poetry tent especially) to niche events like Flounder Murray's *Once Upon a Time in the West*, and *Field Trip* run by Jack Clink and Ryan Allcott.

Al O'Kane, superb guitarist and singer/songwriter, in his Town Councillor capacity supports creatives across the town, venue-providers as well as makers, with meetings to ensure every attendee has a voice. Al also this year organised a *Young Buskers* event around the town, and has brought Frome into the international *Sofar*[34] project which brings something of the 'happening' ethos of the '70s with music events in secret locations with a party atmosphere.

And as well as unforgettable Griff Daniels,[35] 'the man who made Frome the centre of the Rock & Roll universe' mentioned in the first

---

33 The total tally over twelve years was 100: their archive website is a time-travel tour through a pivotal era in the folk music scene: https://www.facebook.com/AcousticPlus/

34 Sofar Sounds actually started in UK but now has 408 cities around the world participating. Frome included, along with Barcelona, Kiev, and Ho Chi Minh City.

35 Griff not only supported performances and musicians, he also played in some amazing line-ups. *Havana Fireflies* was big when I arrived in the '80s, then later the wonderful *Critters*, also as a duo with Nicki Mascall, with the great Steve Loudoun and with so many others there's not space for me to give them more than silent appreciation.

section, Will Angeloro has been massively supportive of young bands and individuals. Nick Wilton who previously played in *The Operation* and now in the highly successful band *Ghost of the Avalanche* ("Genre: hard, loud, and fast") recalls Will's contribution to his musical development:

> Will had Handsome Llama studio but he didn't use it to make money, it was dirt cheap to rent a room so it was quite a communal place. He was running a Music Tech A level at Frome College – it wasn't on the curriculum, it was just his extra and I'd signed up. He invited me to audition as a bass player at what he said was "quite a good gig." I went along to his studio and Will started playing this hip-hoppy, trippy, kind of thing on his turntables – I think it was Timothy Leary samples – and I just started playing over it and he said, 'Right, cool. We've got a gig with Peewee Ellis in a month's time – you know, James Brown's saxophonist.' So I played two gigs with Peewee Ellis, when I was seventeen. It was just one of those things that happened because Frome does that.[36] Will just loves helping and inspiring people, and now I'm doing a punk thing and still using the skills he taught me.

Will no longer has the studio on Marston trading estate and regrets that he can no longer offer rehearsal space but he continues to support young bands:

> I still record demos and bits for students at the college I think are promising and will never be able to afford recording. Funding is depleted up there and we've got this tremendous well of talent right now – there always are talented students,but right now a huge amount – so I'm starting a little record label, a mix of recording up at the college and recording here – all students, all original music, printing up CDs and all the money going right back into the music department so next years' students can have that opportunity and hopefully it's something that'll roll.
>
> I mix here and I work in other different studios – I'll bring a band in to record from different places but I always end up in this

---

36 Pee Wee, saxophonist, composer and arranger who played with James Brown in the '60, now lives in Frome so we claim him as one of our own.

room to overdub and mix. It's more word-of-mouth now and a bit
more specialised – I do a lot of mastering for bands all around the
world because they're on the internet, you don't need to meet them
– could be music for video games, or a film, or straight to download
– for example I just finished the second album for 'Fearless Light' a
Frome-based band, and it's already out on iTunes and Spotify. 'Three
Corners' I'm finishing up right now, they'll do CDs, and I just finished
a folk album for a group called 'the 'Moonlit Poachers'. So I get a lot
of work out of here, but there's instruments lying around because I
do a lot of my own work as well.

THE FROME FESTIVAL brings most of these creative strands
together[37] – It really needs a book of its own, there have been so
many astoundingly great performers and events over the years. The mix
of professional visitors and locals is promoted with admirably equal
status in the brochure: this is a truly egalitarian celebration of fun as well
as culture. Rather than going for the traditional arts-heavy focus, partly
out of choice and partly down to virtually zero funding when it was
established, the Frome Festival has become renowned for its identity as a
festival accessible to local people.

And as will by now be apparent, Frome's creatives don't wait
for an organised opportunity when an idea that needs community
participation strikes them – they go ahead and make it happen.
Ceramicist Hans Borgonjon decided to make face masks and exhibit

---

37 Apart from street art. In my view we really need a Frome version of Bristol's
Upfest. Town Council is fairly broadminded, and the Environment Officer
told me 'The wall at Welshmill is painted regularly: we work closely with
a local artist and this is a colourful and interesting way to liven up these
spaces.' The artist is the wonderful Paris already mentioned, who has
enlivened various nooks in Frome with psychedelic imagery, but the overall
policy is aimed at acceptable decor: my own thoughts on these transient
public statements are more akin to Picasso's view: A painting should not
please, it should bristle with razor blades. Banksy put the same idea less
brutally with his suggestion that art should 'disturb the comfortable.'
Aesthetic judgment is mostly socialised preconception: Les Demoiselles
d'Avignon, 'arguably Picasso's greatest art piece and the introduction of
Cubism to the world', painted on a wall before 1907 would have been
scrubbed.

their moulds as inverse images, and a hundred people happily submitted to the process, contributing to a highly unusual exhibition at Silk Mill. Andrew Shackleton invited the community to offer their eyes for his ISIS-HORUS-OSIRIS project, converting 104 close-up photographs into 'large-scale printed composition and a triptych video installation invoking the ancient Egyptian Gods' also at the Silk Mill – a dazzling and fascinatingly unusual event supported by sound and visuals created live by artist/composer Andrew Heath.[38]

I F YOU, OR ANYONE YOU KNOW, are/is affected by creativity in Frome, you'll probably know stuff missing from this rough trawl across the sea of the townsfolk's achievements. I'm sorry-not-sorry about that, because others can take control now: there's so much more, and will continue to be – because people are still making music and movies and images and stories. As Tolstoy says,[39] 'Art is a means of union among mankind, joining them in the same feelings, and indispensable for the life and progress toward well-being of individuals and of humanity.'

What a dazzling tapestry the story of Frome's creativity presents, you may be thinking.[40] I hope you are. But there's still a big section

---

38  The eyes looked gorgeous, presented as if on butterfly wings: I am irrationally proud I was one of only two green ones submitted. There's a video of it all here: https://www.youtube.com/watch?v=1V6h7nFYY7k

39  Leo Tolstoy, in his essay 'What Is Art?': not the manifestation of some mysterious idea of beauty or God; not the expression of man's emotions by external signs; not the production of pleasing objects; and, above all, it is not pleasure; it is a means of union among men, joining them together in the same feelings, indispensable for life and progress toward well-being of individuals and humanity.

40  The story of Frome throughout the centuries, if you scratch through the patina of building and trading, is all about creating. And whether you call it self-obsession or civic pride, Frome's people have produced a plethora of studies of their town. The library has shelves of them, as does our wonderful independent bookshop *Hunting Raven Books*, which also promotes other books by the many local writers. *Frome Society for Local Study* is a prolific publisher and *Home in Frome* has collected local memories for a planned online archive. As well as personal histories in collections like *Working Memories* and *Frome Hundred*, there have been theatrical reenactments of Frome history, such as Peter Clark's narratives of Thomas Bunn and

missing, which I didn't know about when I started this book, when I
identified 'post-punk' as a vibrant element currently but leap-frogged
over what happened in Frome pre-post-punk – which is of course,
punk. Without a reference to the (dissenting) creative energy of those
embattled days, those demonised eighties and nineties, any history of
Frome would be incomplete. My thanks to those who talked to me and
shared their memories of this era, and revealed the vibrance of the local
punk scene right now, and an acknowledgement that others could be
named and much more could be said. But the great thing about punk is,
it doesn't care.

Paul Boswell was a teen in the early 80s, and remembers the vibrant
music scene in the pubs of the town.

> I don't like this papering over the past, as though we did nothing
> until the Cheese & Grain was taken over. We actually liberated that
> place – it was full of tyres and we got them out and started putting
> on gigs there – until the Lady Diana weekend that killed the One
> World Festival. I'm still involved in the punk music scene a bit now,
> but much more when we were younger and there was loads of bands
> – in fact there was more live music then than there is now. There was
> a punk thing going on here for years, and no-one knew about it.
>
> There were more venues, for a start. There was the Cellar Bar over
> where the kebab shop is, the Wheatsheaf had two bars so you could
> have a gig going on upstairs and another one down, and there was
> Capers Wine Bar even before the big 'London' scene, my friends would
> come down here from London and bring people who were a bit freaky.
> We used to put gigs on at the Ship, now the Artisan – there was a
> skittle alley out the back, we paid 100 quid and put gigs on – the crowd
> were in the run, like a kind of moshpit, and the band were in the pit,
> so we were under the crowd, looking up at them, it must have looked
> weird and it got very wild. I think we were particularly weird because
> we'd go all out to shock, androgynous and skinny, with white faces. We
> charged a couple of quid to get in and must have doubled our money.
> By the late 80s I was in this more gothic thing – Funeral Party.

recreation of Gladstone's visit, and David Lassman's Regency Detective
novels have inspired literary walks around Frome.

Punk has gone many ways. Here's some:

## PUNK / POST PUNK Case-studies (sort of):

**Beef Unit** are a post-punk five-piece, and very popular: they write all their own songs. I talked to Ant and Pete in their rehearsal cellar: Here's a taste:

**Me:** what's the difference between post-punk and punk?

**Punks:** I think it's something to do with the synthesiser. And it's reactionary – but I think we're more punk than post-punk.

**Me:** it sounds quite punky to me.

**Punks:** Thankyou. We've got anger issues – that helps! A lot of punk has irony in it, and humour, so it feels safe to call ourselves post punk because it's very amorphous. Punk ended probably by 1979. Post-punk as a genre is much more vague – individuals who have a distrust of authority – a disenfranchised part of society that no-one had listened to for a long long time and the only way they could break through was by making people angry.

Punk was a reaction against the massive superbands who would play big arenas, with a gap of twenty feet between the band and the fans. It was about trying to make that gap as small as possible- you're getting energy back from the audience, we jump into the audience, we run around a bit. I do want to sing about the things that people don't sing about, and some of that is more awkward territory. I wouldn't want anyone to feel excluded. Which again is a punk thing, isn't it. And the thing about punk and post-punk is, there was a disenfranchised part of society that no-one had listened to for a long long time, and they had something to say, and the only way they could break through was by making people angry. And we've all got stuff we want to say – whether people want to hear it or not remains to be seen. But if we were just a punk band we wouldn't play any more than three chords, we wouldn't have a synthesiser, we would probably spit at the audience, well we might do that, yeah but it would be limiting, and it's fun to play the keyboard and wear dresses, which hard core punk would not do.

It's the demographic of Frome too, it's not a university town and you don't have to stop going out when you're twenty-five which maybe in some other towns you do. There are a number of venues: Toby at

Number 23 was very helpful when we started, he said we could come in and practice. There's a broad base of audience. And also Frome as a town is quite creative.

## Terraplanes

Ralph Mitchard doesn't live in Frome any more: he came over on the bus to talk to me about the scene in his day, which was the late 1970s, so definitely can claim to be the real thing. He remembered *The Three Swans*, where we met, from those days.

**Ralph**: This is the pub we used to go, and people would come from Trowbridge and Radstock & Midsomer Norton to hangout here and put records like The Clash and The Damned on the juke box.

**Me:** So Frome was a big punk centre?

'It was: '76, '77, '78, we were such a commercial force they actually put on punk nights at the Hexagon Suite – it's called the Assembly rooms now – on a Tuesday night. They were great. People would come in from out of town and have a great time. It was a hub for villages all round the area. I started playing with Henry Hutton – he's now known as the man of the *Bad Detectives* – in about 1976 and we went under various different names and played pretty much every venue in Frome. We used to do punk-rock covers – we'd buy dog-collars, and homemade tee shirts -it was very DIY, mostly we used to go to the Oxfam shop and get gaberdine macs – things like that. It was quite fun. Getting your hair cut was a big leap in those days. When I first got my hair cut everyone thought I'd joined the army, that's the only time anyone would, normally. No – become a punk!

'It was a bit violent though. Not everyone was thinking these punks are great! It could be quite scary. In those days there was a lot more violence, casual fights.. We used to get squaddies from Warminster going to the Hexagon Suite, and if they didn't pull a girl, they'd want a fight instead. So it was quite rough. I was glad when I got out of it, really, because it used to be quite hairy sometimes.

*Bad Detectives* are still popular though no longer punk: at that time they were doing only covers and Ralph, wanting to write his own songs, left to start his own band, initially anarcho-punk *Animals and Men* and (after bass player Nigel House left) as *Terraplanes*.[41]

---

41  https://www.hyped2death.com/animaliner.html for the full story

'We got played on John Peel[42] – he offered us a session but unfortunately we'd broken up, and we became friends with Adam Ant who was our mentor for a while – that was more the beginnings of Goth really, when people started wearing make-up. That was quite fun. We still get played on the radio on specialist shows – Mickey Bradley who's bass player of *The Undertones* has a show on radio Ulster and he likes us and says things like, *'They must be the only group to come out of Frome Somerset!'* but there's Frome groups more famous than us. Well, there's *Frenzy* – that's a rockabilly group, all from Frome, and *Ozric Tentacles*, hippy type band.

'About seven years ago we got discovered again by a label over in America and they released a compilation of our old stuff that did really well, so we did a tour in America in 2011 – San Francisco, Seattle, all those kind of places.[43] So we've got quite a lot of contacts in America, there's a radio station called WFMU which specialises in outsider music, they play us quite a lot.

'Our biggest gig we ever did was at the Bath Pavilion with Toyah. She was really horrible. We've played in Paris a few times, clubs, we got quite a few fans there. *Bad Detectives* still play a lot round Frome, they're very entrenched in the community now. Which in the early days we weren't – we were the *enfants terribles*, we weren't at all popular. They write a lot of songs about the west country experience now – *'Sheppards Barton Secret Agent'* – they're very geared towards Frome.'

Ralph has recently reformed the Terraplanes, and is recording under that name: it's mostly for social purposes' he says, but not many local bands have a letter that reads *'enjoyed your tape — any chance that you might bring your own record out? I think you should.. Anyway, keep in touch. John Peel.'*

**SickOnes** are a three-piece 'groove driven, frantic, hardcore punk' band claiming a healthy respect for '80s punk pioneers and identify as

---

42 You can hear the broadcast track here: http://peel.wikia.com/wiki/ Animals_%26_Men?file=Animals_and_Men_-_Terraplane_Fixation

43 Paul Boswell, who played in *Animals and Men*, describes the band as Stonehenge-anarchist-travelling-punk, influenced by Subhumans. 'They became very hip in America thirty years later – the tracks were all re-issued and there are bands in California who say that band was their biggest influence, which is crazy because they're five thousand miles away.'

'frantic old school sound blended with modern fury'. Ben, Andy, and Charlie were over in the States while I was writing this, touring the East Coast with an Ohio band called *DiveBomb*[44] but Andy and Charlie talked to me just before they flew off on what turned into a highly successful trip. We began by talking about *Encompass*, an alternative arts magazine Charlie had been involved with before the band took off and took over from his other DIY arts enterprises. 'There was a lot of stepping stones,' they agreed, 'Encompass running parallel to Andy joining Frome FM, started it, then a chance reading by Huey Morgan introduced him to Andy's radio show and helped us as a band, then this band we've discovered on the other side of the world reach out to us and we build a friendship.' That friendship took *SickOnes* along the East coast of America, from New York down to Miami, and inland to Louisville: they've returned to a string of bookings from support spots in London to festivals and more EU dates.

It sounded like Frome's environment had contributed to their development as a self-confident young band, I suggested, and they agreed. 'Frome is the perfect place to start,' **Charlie said** '- it's musically involved, people are receptive to new ideas and, although it's in the countryside and not a massive population hub, it isn't a million miles away from other places where you can expand your ideas.' 'Frome is like a micro-version of the music scene in America – it's ridiculous to think a place like Frome could have a really alternative music scene, but it actually happened. Ten years ago there were young people, doing things. And at that time, it was almost unheard of. When we were in our early teens there was definitely a (quote/unquote) 'young music scene'. Cheese and Grain used to host a lot of young bands, and they got a great turnout. There are venues in Frome where young people can play now, but it was quite a different world back then.'

Andy concurs, citing Will Angeloro as crucial to his own development: 'Frome's been up and down with its music scene. The Football

---

44 Andy also has two music show on Frome FM, one of which is *Velocity Rock*, so had asked the band to send their tracks: their response was enthusiastic, sending over also teeshirts and other merchandise, which led to the plan to do a 'split release' – a cd with three songs by each band to effectively double the fan-base for sales. 'And then six months later' says Charlie, 'they message us to say, we're planning a tour!'

Club, which you wouldn't necessarily think of as a music venue now, used to be one of the hubs. Ten years ago, it was every weekend, You'd have *The Operation* headlining the Cheese and Grain, with their stadium anthemic rock, then a week later hard-core punk pioneers *More Than Life*, who're from Frome – they had a major influence on hard-core punk in a way – and they would have been playing. You'd have a lot of young punk, and ska kids gathering, nearly every weekend.'

The popularity of punk, whether continuing or revived, is another one of those stepping-stones identified in one way or another by everyone I talked to. Andy and Charlie attribute some of their inspiration to Nick Wilton, the bass-player for *The Operation* who got his start with Will Angeloro, who brought a New York vibe to a town with an insatiable thirst for creative dissonance. Nick now also plays in a punk duo (genre: noise-punk):

## Ghost Of The Avalanche

Growing up in Frome, already deep into music from when he was at Selwood Middle School, Nick Wilton was playing in bands from the age of fifteen. He reckons himself lucky to have had support from Frome College colleagues and their musical parents and always wanted to make his own music rather than play covers.

Nick: There was a lot of people interested in music at that time, through bands on the radio like Greenday and Blink 182 – it was just enthusiasm for electric guitars and drums, everybody was into playing music. When I was fifteen, sixteen, it was all very punk orientated, it was like riding a wave of revived pop punk in the 90s. That was the kind of counter-culture in my teenage years, if you were alternative you were into that side of it. So we wanted to replicate it in bands sounding like that.

Nick heard that *The Operation* wanted a bass player and he got the audition.

'We started recording demos and we were really fortunate because Greg's dad John Freeman was my media teacher, we'd record demos in John's studio and we got a good reputation for being a young band who could play really well because we'd honed our craft. We started setting up our own gigs and did a lot of shows in pubs like the Griffin, and the Cheese & Grain and the Football Club. We'd hire the club for about 50 quid and get all the local kids from the college and middle schools and a bunch of adults too – there was no other band at that time doing classic rock with a punk rock, DIY set up. We were very much a punk band in our approach to music, everything was DIY, we recorded our own stuff, put on our own shows and printed our own t-shirts. We'd hire the Cheese & Grain ourselves, the door staff, sound engineer, everything, and we'd get get 3-400 people through the door. We used to wallpaper-paste our posters around the town, and the council wanted to charge us £800 so we said sorry but since all our posters are available to download on our website and we have an avid fan base, we have no idea who did it. . .

'The band got more and more successful, and we uploaded a couple of singles on a Bristol music site, and next thing we know we got an email from a guy called Joe in California. He said, I think you've really got something here, and I could push it to some record labels, and a couple of months later we heard something like ten record labels were prepared to pay for us to fly out and audition.'

Nick was not yet 19 and in the middle of working for A levels, but the band took the chance to respond and had what sounds like a dizzying time in Los Angeles, playing to all the major labels as well as gigs on Sunset Strip. While a great experience for the band this was a bad time for the recording industry, and although they were signed up by Sony provisionally, no further promotion followed.

'It was really frustrating – we were playing the top of our game and getting better, but it was a product of the time so we went back to DIY punk mentality.

'A lot of it comes down to that being able to see people doing it at a young age, and in Frome, you've got the creativity. Maybe if I was in another town I wouldn't have had that spark that ignited me. People say how great Frome is now but I think actually, when I was 13,14, which for a lot of kids is a very difficult age, I was very lucky that creative things were supported. I could phone The Griffin and book a gig, they'd take a chance you'd bring people and they'd sell drinks, so that's what we'd do until we were too big and the pub was rammed, you couldn't get in. It was exciting, when you're 18 and you can book the Cheese & Grain and you can headline a show that brings in a few hundred people, that's a testament to the town.

I don't know why the myth has grown up that there was nothing happening in Frome – I've seen photos of punk bands in the early '80s at Westway cinema, so it's always been happening here. Maybe it was rough but there was still that creativity. Frome has always been a leader in alternative culture and trying to make something of a small market town.

We're still that community, same people, we're now all older and we got kids but we still do it – and we still organise our own gigs and do our own teeshirts, we still play in bands.

"Very Frome?" I suggest and he says. "Yeah it is. Very Frome – whatever that is."

# Threads: A Digression

> *'Dress is at all times a frivolous distinction, and excessive solicitude about it often destroys its own aim. It would be mortifying to the feelings of many ladies, could they be made to understand how little the heart of man is affected by what is costly or new in their attire. No man will admire her the more, no woman will like her the better for it. Neatness and fashion are enough for the former, and a something of shabbiness or impropriety will be most endearing to the latter.'*

So wrote Jane Austen, unimpressed by the fashion trends of nearby Bath.[45] Frome was not similarly famed for fashion in earlier eras, though this view, like every other aspect of the town, has recently undergone an upwards reappraisal. Designers like Hayley Trezise of *Raggedy* and Marie-Louise of *M-L Hats* who both have studios in the Silk Mill, describe their work not as mere adornment but as self-expression – the Raggedy tagline is 'dress like nobody's judging'. Hayley's work featured in the Alternative Fashion Week in 2009 and now she has a wide client base for these unique and splendid garments, designed intuitively,sculpted asymmetrically and 'scribble-stitched'.

Ethical fabrics feature in Cheap Street styles and Catherine Street's tiny shops are a magnet for anyone hunting vintage. *Poot Emporium* is a creative collective which came about by what owner Ciara Nolan terms a 'happy accident' though twelve years ago it seemed devastating. Ciara was a key figure in the music industry in London until she came to Frome and

> basically all our clothes got thrown out when we moved in. It was really bizarre and ridiculous but on Catherine Hill people put their rubbish in bags on the street because bins get rolled down the hill, and all of our clothes were in bin-bags. The bin men picked them up and off they went.

---

45 Fortunately, there's no record that her landau or barouche ever trundled Frome's streets although a short film imagining the authoress sauntering through modern Bath was created by a Frome firm, and Frome historian David Lassman has organised the live-streamed novel-readings for Jane's birthday for some years.

I'd had all these incredible clothes that I'd collected over the years on shoots I'd been on with music stars – Shirley Bassey gifted me things – all gone. Beautiful old kimonos. Just, gone. Compressed, compacted, destroyed.

At that point it seemed to Ciara she had lost not just her career but her identity:

Vintage is a massive thing in Dublin, it's in my DNA really. I cried so much I lost my voice for a few days, it was devastating. But when things like that happen I'm very good at just going, OK, right. Start again. How do we do this? What are we going to do next? And because I had to go to Trowbridge to buy clothes for all of us, I realised there was a gap in the market for interesting clothing, so that was it, that was how Poot was born!

For modern retro, there's Hollywood glamour at *Deadly is the Female,* specialising in silver-screen-style '40s & '50s fashion. Claudia Adrianna, who dreamed up the 'million-dollar-look' concept, believes dressing up should be about fun and femininity and celebrating curves. Deadly frocks are sensationally sassy and, like the bespoke outfits of Raggedy and the previously-loved pieces in Frome's other clothes shops, are about expressing personal style and so never go out of fashion...

Extreme attire often features too in the special events at the Cheese and Grain: the Frome Steampunk Extravaganza can kit you out like a post-apocalyptic Victorian from boots to top hat and goggles. For an outfit with dramatic impact on a one-off event, Frome has two notable hire shops: *Absolutely Fabulous* on Bath Street and *Bath Theatrical Costume* Hire, established 1969 and with more than 25,000 costumes.

To complete your alternative look, there are (currently) four tattoo parlours – *Punctured Skin, Sirens, Black Moon,* and *Black Inc* – and an annual tattoo convention at the Cheese & Grain. Nancy Norte who organises the Lady Inc contest says 'Frome has more of an artistic edge than other towns I know and is more open and accepting of expression in many forms. In all aspects of life, we live in a very diverse town.'

# Vittles and Drink – another digression

It's fair to say that through the ages Frome did not have a high reputation with epicures. This is from a letter Jane Carlyle wrote to her husband Thomas dated Thursday 5 August 1852:

> 'I saw several Inns, and chose The George, for its name's sake – I walked in and asked to have some cold meat and a pint bottle of Guiness's porter! They shewed me to an ill-aired parlour and brought me some cold Lamb that the flies had been buzzing around for a week – I ate the bread however, and drank all the porter! and 'The ch-arge' for that feeble refection was – 2/6! The Inn and Town were 'so disagreeable' that I went back presently to the station preferring to wait there.'

Things have improved, of course, though we still lack Michelin Stars, and Trip Advisor can be cruel. Obviously chefs come-and-go and eateries change hands, but I thought it would be interesting to freeze-frame the foodie scene right now, the way those old postcards of Frome show a street with styles of another era, so here's a quick thumb-flick through some current names.

New girls on the block *Fat Radish* and *Lottes Bistro* are hugely popular and there's cachet if you get in at weekend-only *High Pavement* which features 'slow food', but in a good way. *Archangel* has a good menu and marvellous frescos in the loos, *Sam's Kitchen* has waiting-for-the-plasterer decor, *Castello* is a wallet-friendly Italian, and other national dishes are provided by from *From Peru to You, Thai Kitchen* and various takeways. *Lungi Baba* is especially interesting, with a daytime outlet in the ex-toilet venue *Loop de Loop*[46] – Mahesh Kommu also runs a monthly supper club at the Grain Bar, and his talis are popular at evening events.

By day, cafe culture rules. Trendy *River House* is always rammed, *Rye Bakery* combines organic produce and children playground more

---

46 https://loodeloo.wordpress.com/cafe/ – current occupier Mahesh offers vegetarian food using whole spices and exploring the six tastes of nature: sweet, sour, salty, bitter, pungent, and astringent. Mahesh also offers cookery workshops, special event catering, pop-up kitchens combining 'food, fun and folklore'.

elegantly than you can easily imagine.[47] Cheap Street positively dribbles with day-time options: *La Strada* has amazing ice-cream and excellent lunches, *Settle* has mob-caps and bobbins, and *Sagebury Cheese* has demon deli produce. Down by the river *Black Swan Arts* has its own cafe too, with patio seating, and there's a garden as well as great vegan & vegetarian food in Stony Street's *Garden Cafe:* there's an outdoor cafe in Victoria Park and an indoor one in *Forward Space* behind the Wesley Chapel, and by the time you read this book there will almost certainly be others (and I will probably have remembered more) – basically, all have something to offer so take your pick.

The Wholefood shop in Cheap Street is one of the independent shops that bring people to Frome. (Music, books, cheese and eco clothing are the principal others.) Jon Evans, now owner of the *Garden Cafe*, first introduced the concept and products to Frome back last century when he ran a shop in Phoenix Terrace at the top of Catherine Hill. He recalls the days when

> nobody knew about things like brown rice, or muesli, and tamari. It was exciting going off to London in the van each week and bringing back sacks of all these unknown foods. Then I moved to Cork Street, where the Bottle Bar is now, and started selling biodegradable eco stuff nobody had even heard of: soya milks, organic jams, biodegradable cleaners - people would come from Trowbridge and Shepton and miles away. It wasn't busy, but it was educating people. When I opened the Cheap Street shop and started doing organic products, other traders told me it would never catch on.

Defying that prediction, the shop became enduringly popular, while Jon now sells organic wholefood in the shop next door to his cafe, helpfully called *Next Door.*

Organic produce is a feature at *Rye Bakery* in the old Whittox Lane Chapel, another recent entrepreneurial venture, this one run by Amy Macfadyen with her partner Owen Postgate who have created a uniquely child-friendly space with a gated garden. 'People were whispering "Frome

---

47 see HUBnub in section 4 for details of this deconsecrated-chapel complete with withy play areas, baker-chef and its own organic garden.

doesn't need another cafe!" when we opened,' Amy said, 'but we're packed every day. We're providing a service that's really different to anywhere else in Frome, so we get a lot of young families, and also people working on their laptops.'[48]

At the top of Cheap Street, the Italian-street-style cafe *La Strada* in the 'pepper-pot house'[49] is run by Jude Kelly, who had an impressive role model in her mother – also a feisty woman well able to prove herself in business.[50] Margaret Vaughn, the farmer's wife who became a television personality with her own cookery show, ran *The Settle* and devised the famous Frome speciality still on sale there. 'The bath bun is the most boring thing,' she told Miles Kington when he came to Frome for the BBC's *Down Your Way* in 1991, 'and I thought it would be fun to be the Sally Lunn of Frome, so I used apricots you find in the gardens here, and soaked them in scrumpy cider and made a roulade – and as Frome used to be a weaving town I took the name bobbin.' Margaret went on to run the Lacock tea-rooms and to represent English culture in a book for Russian students, and in person for the British Council in Osaka in 2005 baking scones to lure Japanese visitors to the UK.

Also blazing a trail for Frome beyond the shores, Sarah Hillman's *African Safari Kitchen* was successful enough for her in 2004 to establish Mama Upendo children's home in Kenya, receiving the *Remember Africa* Award in 2008. Sarah also competed in TV's *Come Dine With Me* – and of course won.[51] And you might not expect a care home to provide gourmet food, but Gracewell, beside the river at Welshmill, has been doing just that: Head chef Simon Lewis has a passion for foraging and local seasonal foods, and makes a point of evoking memories in his multi-sensory meals – he's won the Southwest

---

48 Rye bakery, perhaps most self-consciously hipster cafe in town, serving coffee in bowls and fibrous savouries on flattish slabs of pottery, is a good example of the employment opportunities these successful new niche businesses provide: the largely-young staff are gaining experience as well as a wage so they don't have to leave town.

49 Looking mock-tudor but actually the oldest house in town – there's more about this in section 3

50 Notice a recurring thread? check section 1 if not, there's a positive murmuration of entrepreneurial women there.

51 In another TV appearance, Old Bath Arms successfully competed in C4's *Three in a Bed* in 2015, with some jocularity reported over the poached eggs.

Regional Final of the National Care Catering Chef contest for the last two years.

Frome Festival each year features a Food Feast in the market yard, with a score or more stalls providing cuisine from around the world, and the range of food stalls in the monthly Market made this awarded 'best food event' in 2017 *Crumb Magazine* awards. Also bringing punters in their hundreds to Frome are the occasional food festivals in the Cheese & Grain organised by Jo Harrington: Her annual *Chocolate Festival* attracts chocolatiers from across the country, and in 2018 the inaugural *Vegan Fair* had over two thousand visitors.

M OVING ON, AS YOU DO, from food to drink, it's the sheer number of pubs that visitors to Frome tend to comment on. Even when I came to Frome there were still pubs next door to pubs – you could be barred from *The George* and simply stagger next door to *The Crown*.[52] The national shift in consumption habits from pub to home, or street, drinking is part of the cause and consequence of closures, but we now have two bottle-shops and a micro-pub[53], as well as licensed cafes.

The surviving pubs all have their own distinctive ambience: many support the free music scene – and hence enhance the safety of our town's streets at night. The very popular *Three Swans,* meeting point for the Writers' Collective, dates from 17th century and was once two buildings – there's still an exterior passage between them – and has the most eclectic decor in town. Local businessman Chris Moss bought it because he wanted 'somewhere to go for a decent pint', and filled it with an assortment of furniture and wall displays which must be uniquely bizarre. Impromptu play-alongs occur randomly downstairs in the front bar, with trad jazz upstairs on Wednesday nights. The *Cornerhouse* is currently home for any other kind of jazz, the *Grain Bar* has a weekly music night usually with a folk-bluesy vibe, the *Lamb and Fountain* for traditional folk, punk in the *Griffin* and rock in the *Artisan*... in fact when you include open mic sessions and fund-raising gigs, there's music in

---

52 Now a *Fat-Face.*

53 Whether these are part of the blight of 'gentrification' or an interesting return to 18th and 19th century small alehouses is discussed in the final section.

just about every pub – and *23 Bath Street* now has a dedicated stage.[54]
For more specific detail, go to CAMRA[55] (Campaign for Real Ales) online
*What Pub* guide: they list all of Frome's fifteen remaining town pubs with
attentive detail to brews, decor, and even dogs.

At one time all the pubs had their own breweries:[56] The *Griffin,* on
the same site for 300 years,[57] still has a direct connection with its original
brewery, now the mega-award-winning Milk Street Brewery, reopened by
Nick Bramwell and Rik Lyall when they took over the business in 1999.
Nick now runs the brewery and Rik[58] has taken on the pub, which has a
loyal fan base and in 2010 was CAMRA's 'Pub of the Year' for this area.
When Rik and Nick took over, they found the pub was being used for
late-night blue movies. 'Some old boys asked me when the film show was
starting,' Rik has recalled – 'they said "You know – the mucky 'uns!" '

I was going to give a selection of funny and weird anecdotes about
our pubs but they would fill a book, and there is one, so I refer you to the
hugely entertaining ale-centric social history chronicles in *The Historic
Inns of Frome* and suggest you open a can of Milk Street's *Same Again* or
*Usual* and enjoy a fascinating read . .

---

54  Bands move about a bit too! – see the section on creativity for more –
    although inevitably still incomplete, information.
55  https://whatpub.com/ – search 'Frome'
56  Frome historically is notorious for its strong ale, but wine is also known to
    have been made in this area from the 10th Century from local vineyards as
    climate improvement during growing led to an improved grape, and home-
    produced wine probably suffered less than imported wines from oxidation.
57  Constable Gregory in 1818 was riled to find a customer there drinking on the
    Sabbath, but on that occasion the culprit was penitent enough to be spared
    the stocks.
58  Ripples of alarm ran round town last year when Rik considered a sale, but at
    time of writing he has relented and decided to continue as landlord.

# THE WAR TO END ALL WARS . . . AND THE ONES AFTER

*'Owing to the summary rejection by the German Government of the request made by His Majesty's Government for assurances that the neutrality of Belgium would be respected, His Majesty's Ambassador in Berlin has received his passport, and His Majesty's Government has declared to the German Government that a state of war exists between Great Britain and Germany as from 11pm on August 4th.'*

Too long for a tweet by 249 characters but long enough to kill ten million soldiers, and leave over 40 million casualties, changing Europe forever, thus did Mr Asquith announce in 1914 that the Great War had begun.

With Frome's historical habit of resisting imposed authority you might expect some dissent but this was a distant enemy, and neither Anglicans nor Methodists shared the moral imperative of the Quakers. 'War, in our view,' their 1916 statement explained[59] 'involves the surrender of the Christian ideal and the denial of human brotherhood. … We regard the central conception of the [Military Service] Act as imperilling the liberty of the individual conscience which is the main hope of human progress'

Interestingly, nearby Street had a strong Quaker tradition and employers like Clarks were practising Quakers: Hilda Clark herself had trained as a doctor before the war and went to France to help set up the *Friends War Victims Relief Committee* which supported refugees and civilians caught up in the war. But Frome was predominantly Congregational and Anglican at that time, and neither side of the high-low divide endorsed pacifism.

Frome historian David Lassman in his scrupulously researched study *Frome in the Great War* found only a few of those deemed eligible to refuse to join up actually took that option. A number of 'essential trades' were permitted exception, mainly those actively supporting the war effort (though curiously exemption was allowed the caretaker of the public baths), but most of those resisting the call to arms were COs – Conscientious Objectors – claiming exemption to conscription because

---

59 London Yearly Meeting, Quaker faith & practice minute 23.92

their conscience didn't allow them to kill. The options were to be either an 'Alternative' – i.e. prepared to join the forces in a noncombatant role – or an 'Absolutist'.

It must have taken some courage to face the tribunal with the claim of conscience. Questioning was hostile and challenging, and answers received either with disbelieving jeering or disgusted anger. A mood of moral outrage seems to have swept the country, and Frome COs presumably had to suffer the same taunts and white feathers as other places – with 'conchie' a term of abuse, along with slacker and shirker.[60]

My personal view is best expressed by Harry Patch, the last surviving soldier of this conflict – and a Somerset man – who famously wrote before his death age 111 in 2007, 'I felt then, as I feel now, that the politicians who took us to war should have been given the guns and told to settle their differences themselves, instead of organising nothing better than legalised mass murder.'

Harry went home after that war, but according to friend and biographer Max Arthur for the rest of his life suffered with post-traumatic stress from the experience of Passchendaele. Another soldier who remembered that battle was Siegfried Sassoon, also buried in Somerset: he lies just a few miles from Frome in Mells. His poem *Memorial Tablet* is a lament for all the young men who were 'nagged and bullied' by the local Squire to sign up and then died in hell – They called it Passchendaele...

Sassoon, while not as well-known as Wilfred Owen for poetry mourning the horrors and wastage in this 'war to end all wars', was equally strong on blaming the hawkish culture of their social superiors which turned young men into cannon fodder. He wrote in another poem

> You smug-faced crowds with kindling eye
> Who cheer when soldier lads march by,
> Sneak home and pray you'll never know
> The hell where youth and laughter go.

By the end of the war, the Somerset Light Infantry had nearly 5,000 casualties. Nearly 600 war memorials were erected across the county's

---

60 According to Quaker research, there were around 2300 COs in WW1, a quarter of whom were imprisoned with many others detained in punitive conditions.

towns and villages, with only seven communities excluded. These were the so-called 'Thankful Villages', where every soldier had come back home, a poignant term coined by Arthur Mee in his 1936 book *Enchanted Land*. Of the 16,000 villages in England at that time he could find only twenty-four who lost no-one. Chantry is the nearest to Frome. Somerset is lucky with its seven ~ most had none or only one, though England fared better than France, where Thierville in Upper Normandy was the only village in the entire land by 1918 with no fatal casualties.

When the slaughter was over, Frome like the rest of the country was determined to honour its lost warriors, and one ambitious plan involved a full-size statue of a soldier in full kit using as model a young man who had been a worker at Singers foundry before the war. Charlie Robbins had enlisted, survived, and returned to Singers to be re-employed: the factory had been requisitioned during the war for munitions and now needed experienced workers to meet the demand for memorials. Charlie modelled for a sculpture but for some reason, probably financial, this wasn't erected publicly until the 1970s and then only within Singers' premises, moving with them to Marston Trading Estate when the firm changed hands. It was a hundred years, nearly to the day, after the start of the war that Charlie Robbins took his more appropriate stance in front of the Memorial Theatre built in 1924 in memory those who fell in that war.

These memorials are particularly valued by the 'sad shires' who had lost so many, as the thousands killed in France were never brought home. Those who are buried in England, perhaps dying from wounds when shipped home, are honoured by the Commonwealth War Graves Commission with white headstones – there are several of these in the Dissenters Cemetery which dates from 1851 and still accepts burials from all denominations.[61]

---

61 I discovered this tradition while researching for a site-specific performance for Frome Festival in 2015. *Midsummer Dusk* was a Nevertheless Theatre production to reimagine some of the lives buried here, and my chosen soldier was Norman Case who served in the doomed battalion referenced by Robert Graves in *Goodbye to All That*. I used this data, and the moving exhibition at Frome Museum of stilted letters home by soldiers banned from leaking information and reluctant to distress, to give a voice to this young man who never returned from the Somme so only his name on the family grave

At the end of the war, small towns like Frome had been gutted of many contributors to their community – the makers, menders, and distributors of all the basic goods. As historian David Lassman writes:

> before that fateful day in August 1914 they had been the milkmen, postmen, grocers, butchers, fishmongers, bakers, printers, electricians, plumbers, draughtsmen, fitters, solicitors, teachers, drivers, painters, architects, coachmen, gardeners, draymen, labourers, clergymen, miners, florists, booksellers, porters, wheelwrights, colliers, saddlers, drapers, and all the other occupations at the heart of any town.

And beyond that measurable loss, there is the grief of families and the mourning that poet Wilfred Owen, Sassoon's friend, foresaw before his own death a week before the end of the war: 'The pallor of girls' brows shall be their pall;

> Their flowers the tenderness of patient minds,
> And each slow dusk a drawing-down of blinds.'

Sioux How in her research on the impact of this war on society, particularly for women, has developed *Little Victory Ball* as a historical story-telling performance and a 'peephole into the past, a kind of non-material war museum, where instead of gaping at a uniform in a glass case, we can see a vision of ourselves as we were.' She acknowledges that many women relished their new roles as workers, finding them life-changing, but the distress of the bereaved was a problem for the Government. The Grave of the Unknown Warrior was intended to solve this, by representing every woman's lost husband, son, or sweetheart.[62]

---

commemorates him. Oliver Wright, the actor who took the role found an authentic uniform and gave a performance so moving that the local reporter published his image as the defining image of the festival. Another Frome lad brought home.

62 The dead were civilians as they had been called up, and for their families to be told they would not be brought back created a deep sense of loss for people left with no body or burial place to mourn. An army chaplain named David Railton came up with the suggestion, based on a shamanic concept,

The Cenotaph was never intended to be more than a temporary installation but people continued to visit it with flowers and Lloyd George saw the propaganda value of allowing this outlet of mourning to continue. The after-shock of this particular conflict is still felt today, as the children and grandchildren of those who fought in France are making pilgrimages to their graves and writing their biographies – as two of Frome's writers, Mike Grenville and Ed Green, have recently done.

WORLD WAR II had a different impact on Frome as it affected the entire community more directly, and continues to be in living memory for older townsfolk. I heard tales of German prisoners of war held in the Keyford sawmill and in Nissen huts by the Mendip Lodge, with American soldiers billeted around Marston (often seen in the Gaumont cinema with the local girls, according to nostalgic letters in the *Looking Back* section of the Somerset Standard), and evacuees filling the school rooms to spilling point. Hilary Daniels has a vivid recollection of the East End children in his family house.

> It wasn't really a requisition, it was more like, "Would you mind...?"[63] and my grandparents had just died so we moved into their house, and actually my mother was quite pleased otherwise we'd be involved with six evacuees from the roughest part of London. The billeting officer said nobody else had wanted to take them. It was incredible how deprived they were, some had never eaten at a table before, just sat on the doorstep eating fish and chips, never seen a fork.

---

of ceremonially bringing just one back for all. The Grave of the Unknown Warrior drew thousands of weeping survivors -people travelled for miles and queued for hours, bringing white flowers for remembrance (scarlet poppies were imported later from a French tradition) and buying souvenir cenotaphs – in fact the deluge of grief that greeted Diana's death was not, as often reported, a shift in the culture of 'Englishness' but a very similar outpouring of shared grief.

63 I've left this bit of the story in because it sounds so like Sergeant Wilson out of Dad's Army, and in a rather gaunt section it's nice to have a reminder that as Shaw says, life doesn't stop being funny when people die any more than it stops being serious too when they laugh.

Other inner-city children probably experienced similar culture shock but a *Home in Frome* event in 2014 recalling the evacuees' arrival attracted several returners with happy memories of 'green fields – going cycling and fishing and growing vegetables.' A stone seat in St John's churchyard, donated in 1999, recalls with gratitude that Frome people 'generously opened their homes' to the children of Coopers' Company School. The arrival of so many had a big impact: all schools were closed for two weeks in the autumn of 1939 for a major reorganisation of rooms and staff, with up to three classes sharing a room. Batches of children were arriving in numbers of up to 100, often with clothing and boots reported as 'deplorable'. Air raid warnings, gas masks and shelter practices would all have made the war very real for children, but there seems to have been a kind of optimistic innocence that would be unlikely today: Hilary Daniels remembers games involving devious ways to check the soles of grown-ups' shoes to see if they were German spies, and that

> For a kid, war was wonderful – it was so exciting, even when they were bombing Bath we were never frightened. And we never, never thought we were going to lose the war. We all listened word-for-word to Churchill's broadcasts, though post-war he didn't catch on to the new feeling. He wanted to put the old Britain back, and the people felt, we've lost so much we might as well start afresh.' Labour did look very exciting then.[64]

For adults the 'War Effort' dominated life, ripping railings from the walls and disrupting daily routines yet, as already mentioned, there were only a couple of minor raids and two casualties. Not everyone shared the exuberance of young plane-spotters and spy-trackers. The Frome Standard *'Looking Back'* section in August 2004 reprinted a letter from a Mr Lamb to highlight 'the Absurdity of War':

---

64 Hilary identified another positive outcome: 'All my younger life Frome wasn't very enterprising, and it's since the war that Frome got self-conscious and started going places. What really stirred us up was that during the war almost everyone I know had lodgers of various kinds – we had some kindertransport boys too – so that widened a lot of our horizons.'

Not only did the truce result in fraternisation in no-man's land, football matches, carol-singing, practical jokes, the sharing of food and even visiting each other's trenches, it also showed the absurdity of war when enmity could not be sustained among the troops who had to fight it.

The letter continues with a castigation of British military high command for treating shell-shock as tantamount to mutiny, and for their draconian executions in the field.

F ROME HAD AT ONE TIME a complete record of its losses in all three 20th century wars, on eight bronze plaques which are still identified by the Imperial War Museum[65] as located in Victoria Park, in the rather nondescript corner now occupied by an acknowledgement of Frome's twinning in 2011 with Rabka-Zdrój in Poland. There are 224 names listed for the First World War (Served and returned: 0), 70 for the Second World War (Served and returned: 0), and one for the Falklands Conflict in 1982 (Served and returned: 0). There was also a tank there, donated by the Government on request after the war apparently as a souvenir and somehow driven up Park Road and parked within the park. This memento has also disappeared.

England's involvement in international aggression continues, and so also do local protests, with large contingents from Frome participating in the major anti-war events like the Iraq protest in 2003; *Frome Stop War* actively protests at conflicts over Iraq and Syria and *Frome Friends of Palestine* is constantly active to raise awareness of the situation there.

As a literal footnote to this brief look at international conflict: the 2001 'shoe bomber' came from London but his mother lived at the time in Frome, giving every one of us a remote tangential connection with those miles of queues across the globe as billions of travellers take off their shoes to pad through the check-in after chucking their water bottles in the bin to join the debris of the ocean.

---

65 https://www.iwm.org.uk/memorials/item/memorial/1369

*Catherine Street wall*

# 6   DISSENT FOREVER!

*let's all move to Frome! – no let's not – old sores, new wounds
– will neoliberalism eat my town? – blow-ins: the new schism
– the sourdough backlash – why we came –
– what next for Frome? Frexit!*

*'Frome is the hub of cool culture'*

– Guardian

*'As a long-time resident I'm totally fed up with the gentrification of
Frome'*

– facebook comment.

S OCIALLY UPWARDLY-MOBILE, and with a recent economy that
could be summarised as Being Frome, what is happening now? You
would expect a town that threw out the book of common prayer and
rebelled against the monarchy, stopped industrial development in its
tracks, and elected the first fully independent town council, to have
strong feelings about the trend to homogeneous 'gentrification'[1] and
indeed, dissent is still a dominant trait in Frome's psyche.

The gush of enthusiastic journalese in recent years has been
greeted with responses ranging from exasperated to antagonised,
which brings me back to the start of this unzipping. Gentrification in
terms of coffeehouses, bottle shops and vintage shopping outlets is
paradoxically also one of the new industries of Frome, with roots in the

---

1   The term was coined in 1964 by sociologist Ruth Glass to describe the 'urban
renewal' of lower-class neighbourhoods after an influx of artists, attracted
by cheap rents, bring the neighbourhood a more bohemian air. This attracts
yuppies who cause rising rents and drive out lower-income residents – and
artists – thus changing the neighbourhood and causing 'yuppification' of
local businesses, so shops catering to yuppie tastes replace local outlets
displaced by higher rents. A perfect storm of urban affliction, you could say.

town's pragmatic tradition of grabbing recovery wherever it can find it. In fact the new bottle shops, and the micro pub on Stony Street which claims to be the first in Somerset, actually represent a return to one of the oldest trades of Frome or any town: the ale house. Smaller than inns and without their resources for travellers, ale-houses thrived in Frome for centuries. Ale houses usually comprised of just one room, directly off the street, and were often run by women who brewed the beer in their kitchens.[2] they became noted as places of sedition because it was easy to meet likeminded others and share opinions.

True, a 'London style' men's shop set up just below Catherine Hill, but so did local-owned Kushi. There are indeed tribute bands in *Cheese and Grain,* but there's plenty of original music in pubs like *The Griffin* and *The Castle* and just about anything in *23 Bath Street.* Both our theatres still provide a stage for local talent and a town-crafted carnival still brightens the autumn night. Frome has a new, local-inspired, approach to steering the town's council, a strong commitment to helping those needing support whether physical or financial, the biggest street market in the country, and a community expressing its creativity in myriad ways. And everyone is communicating – in live meetings and online – about their town, its past, and its future.

Yet the divide between those who are thriving and those who are not is growing. Bob Ashford, talking of his arrival thirty years ago, recalls

> a strong sense of community then, and I think it's really important in terms of the town that there is a strong fabric and people all have a sense of belonging. I think there is a real danger now that that cohesion has been lost. It's not the 'gentrification' itself that's the problem, it's that there has to be a strong ethos of working together. If you don't get that, you don't have respect for the people who live here, and then there's antagonism – people being alienated and getting angry.

---

2   The ale was stirred with a stick which was hung outside on days when it was fit for drinking. This custom goes back to Roman days apparently and is the origin of our dangling pub signs. 'The Crooked Billet', a fairly popular pub name, is thought to refer to the wooden stick originally hung above the entrance.

I moved here the same year as Bob, and Frome to me seemed an oasis of calm after London. Even the street litter seemed benign – the crisp packets weren't sticky with glue from night-sniffers, no dumped syringes in the gutters. To me it had a gentle, hippyish, vibe, not the heavy flower-power thing of Glastonbury or seriously worthy like Totnes, just an unpretentiously alternative town doing its own thing. We had our own currency back then – a variant of LETS which was negotiated at point of use, with a base rate roughly equivalent to five pounds.[3] I was enchanted to find myself living in a community ready to try out new ideas, and with so many friendly people. I met absolutely no prejudice against incomers from those who had lived here from childhood – in fact they were the least defensive about their indigenous status I'd ever known: unlike Devon where newcomers are called grockles or Cornwall where we're emmets, there wasn't even a short-hand vocabulary to distinguish us.

Non-Frome-born town residents are now called blow-ins, and there's a consciousness of their difference among original residents that borders on resentment – and in some cases, vigorous annoyance. In 1987 my new neighbours became immediate friends, and when I talked with them about this emerging divisive rift, they agreed there's been a seismic shift in attitude to incomers.

> A lot of people are really anti the blow-ins – especially on those
> Sundays when it's like 'spot the Frome person'. I meet people playing
> golf at Orchardleigh who typically have sold a million quid's worth of
> house – that could be a terrace in Peckham, but they can come down
> here and spend 400,000 on a house and they've got still got 600
> grand to live on, and they haven't even got to work! We've got this

---

3   Local Exchange Trading System, first devised in 1983 in British Columbia. Unlike barter, it gives credit which can be used with anyone else in the group. Ours worked well for time-based activities: an hour of legal advice or construction cost the same as an hour or ironing or baby-sitting which meant big financial savings for those not cash-rich, but was less useful if you offered anything involving personal outlay. I took quite a lot of photographs for people on LETS and, since those were the days of buying films and paying for processing, I never recouped anything like my costs. But the point is, Frome was special even then.

influx of people but what do they actually bring to the town? More expensive restaurants! They don't support Frome -football, cricket, rugby, angling clubs are all run by people that have been around for donkey's years – we never see blow-ins at matches.

The town has grown out of proportion – there's no industry any more – all the sites have been built on with housing and it's not even affordable to local families. People are moving out of town when their families start growing because they can't afford to stay.

Merlin Theatre manager Claudia Pepler, who identifies herself as 'old school', confirmed my sense of a change in attitudes.

There's definitely an old Frome and a new Frome now, very much so. I would say that started around the creation of Babington House, and the Steiner school has brought new people in. Some of their attitudes upset the 'old Frome', because there must have been something here already that attracted them and made them want to come! I've got a foot in both camps, as I work with a lot of artists who have moved to the area recently, so it's quite funny hearing old Frome and new Frome witter on about each other.

This book started, in a way, after the Foo Fighters gig when yet another rapturous accolade for Frome published in a glossy supplement appeared on Facebook and was greeted by the usual chorus of annoyance. One of the exasperated comments pointed out that Frome had a creative scene before 1998 (the opening a few miles away of that slightly-dilapidated magnet for the affluent and/or aspirational) 'and in many ways it was a lot better then.' I wanted to know more, and started asking people about their experience of living in Frome. The book you're holding is the result of talking to nearly a hundred of them. It seems the dissenting energy in Frome is thriving, and with the disappearance of the traditional divide between anglican and non-conformist, Frome has found another outlet. Let's all talk about gentrification. Here's Jake, Frome-born rapper and poet.

It's a funny one: on the one hand you've got benefits for Frome's independent economy and the Market, which has given opportunity to artists and lets independent small businesses expand, which is great. I do think however there's been a certain negative impact, in that some new establishments don't fit well with the character of Frome and there is a change in the atmosphere that I would call a little bit supercilious. I do definitely feel that influence coming in from London, and for me the Steiner school is not a 100% good vibe. Because although the ethos for the kids might be empowering and creative, you get the feeling that parents are not actually immersing themselves in the culture or the community. But again, on the flip side, I've definitely noticed more diversity in ethnicity, which is important because it brings everyone a wider perspective. There was definitely a more racist culture in Frome fifteen years ago.

Frome was certainly more violent in previous eras. It's already been noted that one spin-off of full employment had been to make Frome notorious for Saturday night arrests. Ralph Mitchard recalled the response to squatters during the Trinity debacle:

It was scary – a time of real hostility.[4] Naish's Street was squatted by hippies in about '78 and a lot of Frome youths didn't like them being there. They used to go down the street kicking down doors, and we saw a breeze block thrown through a car windscreen. We lived on the corner and we used to watch out the window and think, thank god it's not us. There was a travelling community living in one of the quarries by Vallis Vale and some of the Frome youths went out there to throw boulders, and there was a lot of tension when they came in to shop.

Clearly much has improved. The sense of common purpose and a creative, exciting atmosphere George Monbiot detected, mentioned

---

4   Ralph also suggested a possible reason why Frome was historically an unusually violent town might be identified in the after-effect from their support of Monmouth, 'because after that the Royal army stayed in Frome. Having a hostile army quartered in your town is tantamount to being raped and pillaged – they weren't nice people, the armies of those days, and it was probably pretty horrible and your property was ruined by the horses and oxcarts too. I think it might have made Frome more brutal as a town.'

in the first section, has brought the town initiatives not only compassionate but outstandingly innovative, and many of those who have moved here recently are actively supportive: they chose Frome not to abuse the opportunity of still-comparatively-low house prices, but because of the values they perceive here, perhaps as a chance to fulfil long-held ideals like buying property to offer as affordable lets, or land for community ventures. The self-employed and the retired have been able to move to this job-thin town, and had time to find a niche where they could contribute.

What causes the resentment that some see as a major rift, however, is the assumption embodied in the second half of Monbiot's appraisal referenced above: 'and quite different from the buttoned-down, dreary place I found when I first visited, 30 years ago.'

Frome journalist James Wood had already picked up on the growing exasperation at this attitude a year previously, in an interview with locals on their views after 'In only a matter of months Frome has featured on two listicles in The Times, labelled one of the coolest places in Britain and the best place to live in the South West.' He found one resident insistent that the town was better off in 1959. Aside from the missing industries, Janet Turner pointed out,

> We had a working police station, with cells, magistrates' court and police houses. There was a tax office, social services department, two local authorities – Frome Urban and Rural District Councils – who provided much needed housing, to rent, for local people. We had two cinemas, a really useful art and technology college in Park Road and a grammar school. There was also the wonderful Victoria Hospital which was all things to all people and where new mums were allowed to stay in for a few days to rest and recuperate. Drinkers were spoilt for choice in the number of watering holes dotted around the town – not serving posh food, providing locally brewed ale and a good atmosphere.

There are some fair points in this list, although sadly the authority responsible for the hospital (it's Somerset Partnership Foundation Trust now) can do little about the dismantling of the NHS by the Tory government. But while inclusive education up school-leaving age is

generally agreed best practice, the loss of post-16 training in town was
certainly careless[5]. Pubs without posh-nosh do still thrive, and though
there are fewer snooker tables and skittles alleys – Ring O'Bells had a
popular one – Frome still has its own skittles league. But the article
caught the zeitgeist. Frome was grumbling[6] and the sourdough backlash[7]
had begun.

'Gentrification' is the presenting problem, but the resentment of
the indigenous (and long-established) people in Frome is not so much
about our newly-flourishing culture as its misappropriation. The Market,
for example. Fay Goodridge, who watched from her home on the hill
as well as contributing to the revival of artisan trading in the town,
remembers clearly:

> It was Lyn Waller and her friend Hilary who started it all when
> they got the medieval fair going again – that's a lot of work which is
> forgotten now. It's not just this 'new wave' coming in – the foundation

---

5   I was working at the college when FE was finally axed: my 16-18 Life Skills
    social training course was the last to go. There are currently calls for re-
    investment in a technical college for Frome to give training in carpentry and
    brickwork & electrical skills to replace the one in Park Road, closed 1980 and
    demolished. Currently training is delivered in other towns, mainly out-of-
    county.

6   Frome grumbles are clearly put and vigorous. When the *Guardian* rashly
    ended a piece on the town in September 2017 with an appeal for 'pet hates'
    Facebook took up the option and in three days had collected a deluge. Early
    on the thread came
    • bastarding supplement sections and their lazy, pointless dribble
    • twatty national newspapers bigging up the town and having nobby
      Londoners move here pushing up the house prices

7   The people of Bedminster in 2017 had anger issues when their local bakery
    was replaced by a bespoke Sourdough emporium: *Bristol Post* summarised:
    "Denny's was one of North Street's traditional stalwarts. A cheap and
    cheerful bakers where for £2 you could still get a proper cheese and ham roll
    – a gurt big one at that – and still have change" folded, and nearby another
    bakery opened: "Hobbs House, run by two TV-famous brothers, think
    absolutely nothing of not only selling yeast and dairy free sourdough bread,
    but of charging £10 for a loaf of it." Sourdough bread came to represent
    the clash of cultures in a long-languishing area of the city which locals were
    finding, reluctantly, was becoming newly fashionable…

was laid down twenty odd years ago plus. Creatives were naturally drawn here because it was affordable and then because they want a nice environment, a coffee shop and good entertainment, it has a ripple effect. Artists turn places around – look at St Ives – it's the creative energy that does it! Without the first influx, our wave and then the next, this town would look like any other crappy town – all out-of-town shopping – it would be dire. Gavin Eddy has been instrumental in a huge way because he had the money to put behind the ideas. But it still would have happened, probably in a more slow organic way.

Lyn too admitted it was difficult to hear radio broadcasts where

things have been forgotten and virtually all credit given to people far more recent who quite honestly wouldn't have wanted a shop up here twenty years ago because the banks considered Catherine Hill unviable for trading – it took a long struggle for me to get a mortgage.

As Fay observed, Frome is tribal, and integration isn't really in the nature of tribal communities. Like football and 'social class', people take their energy and support from a defined identity, and some people enjoyed the vibe of the old days without wanting it too much to change. Mutartis Boswell, musician and artist, agrees:

Yes Frome was pretty raw, but we don't want to be cleaned up too much. The Carnival is still very working class – my kids love it, it's fun but trash fun, a little bit crap as well. I do get quite defensive over articles making out the town was quite bereft. Yes it was run-down, but that's when you make your own excitement – it encourages creativity, finding places and making things happen.

Frome's kind of a funny place really, it reminds me a little bit of a Breughel painting, the different types of people, you could almost make a mural of it in a kind of medieval style... that's something I'd like to do, or like Hogarth... there's so much going on.

Frome-born Chris Bailey's work as a local photographer gives him a double perspective view.

I've seen a lot of change. I chose to stay because there's a great community, but I do feel sorry for the generations who have lived all their life and now they're forced to leave. Obviously there's this whole divide of angry Frome people thinking the whole town is being taken over by Londoners, that local shops are going and it's all high-end boutique and unaffordable. There was that smart menswear shop featuring pictures of Big Ben in the front window and it almost felt like it was rubbing salt in the wound to see it on Palmer Street – I thought, that's going upset a lot of people!

Everyone I spoke to, original resident or incomer, agreed that the recent divide isn't mere churlish prejudice. Fear that 'gentrification' will penalise, and perhaps even ultimately expel, the town's indigenous population is at the heart of the rift, and the focus on London for resentment is both symbolic and specific. London has always represented wealth and power to country areas – it was to London that people marched in protest when costly wars were stripping them of their means of survival, and nowadays the capital is seen as assuming priority in cultural importance and taking a lion's share of funding for development.[8] The significance of 'London types' goes beyond the city itself, it's the notion of a 'type' too: people who have chosen an 'ilk' persona, a group-member

---

8  The 2014 project *Instructions for an Ordinary Utopia* provides a good illustration of the incipient divide when Foreground organised (and more to the point for many, acquired arts funding for) a project to 'make an ordinary town a little less ordinary' – not an ambitious aim as Frome had recently been named for 'creative energy' one of the UK's best places to live. Artist Peter Liversidge devised a book of whimsical *'Proposals for Frome'* and chose to do the one about slinging £100 in pennies around the town, which according to organisers was 'more special than standing around looking at paintings.' Ruth Proctor had been commissioned to devise a motto for Frome and *'Something Wonderful Will Happen'* was consequently trailed behind a plane above the town, adding environmental pollution to the list of reasons why many were exasperated by the entire project. There were of course some supporters, but Facebook seethed with comments expressing angry alienation. Ironically, Frome already had a motto widely used in shops and offices with framed versions available on sale, designed by Sean McDonnell of the George Hotel in 1998: *'Frome – It's a Wonderful Place.'*

rather than a distinctive individual. Most of the older residents I spoke to had fond memories of idiosyncratic individuals they saw around the town. Hilary Daniels summed up this feeling:

'People in Frome were never afraid of being characters. Everyone is expected to conform these days. I remember a lot of eccentrics, colourful characters people it was lovely to have around.' The much-missed Looking Back section in the *Standard* had provided a rich trove of social history in letters from older members of the community. Trevor Biggs wrote of life on Horton Street, remembering (with surprising affection) Moppy Coombs, who used to cross the children over to Trinity School in a brown mac and trilby with long white hair. 'He would see you across the road whether you wanted to go or not.' If children teased him 'he would rush into his house to fetch his old blunderbuss and chase us along Vallis Road.'

Individual anecdotes may suggest that routes of social support have improved, but collectively these are memories of a community that found strength in its diversity, and to the people of Frome who experienced this, city-style 'gentrification'[9] diminishes the character of the town. To the outside world, Frome's identity seems to have acquired almost mythic status: the town which hosts legendary post-grunge Foo Fighters yet still has a Town Crier to call *Oyez* wearing sky-blue velvet livery and a tricorn hat. Magazine editors are feverishly flicking through thesaurus sites to find superlatives to extol the voguishness of this quaintly on-trend town, yet in part as consequence of their hyperbole Frome is facing a huge, possibly fatal, wobble in its onward trajectory. Defining Frome as a good place to pop down to from the capital for cheap bargains – not only retro-chic collectables, but houses too – is blamed for the price-rise spiral in accommodation costs, supercharged by the national press with their passion for bite-size tips for the canny investor.

Very little has happened in Frome without complaint. Cobbling Catherine Hill met complaint. Skateboarding stirred up complaint.

---

9   Some also appreciate the satirical opportunities: a promotion for a music night at the Griffin read: 'KING SPORKS – Frome's newest band brings you: Hand crafted artisanal funk, seditious jazz and ungentrified reggae in an outrageous night of original live music.' Comments required reassurance, quickly given: 'This IS tongue in cheek.' 'As we are awash with gong baths and assorted artisan/vintage tomfoolery' was the reply, 'it's always best to check these days.'

Woolworths closing aroused complaint, although no-one in Frome could be held responsible for the credit crisis that caused that retail chain to topple. There are constant complaints about late music (from people who buy a flat next to a music pub!), graffiti,[10] anything the council does that costs, litter and dog poo (although I do agree with the last two)[11]. For everyone who takes a bag and gloves on a walk to pick up litter as they pass, there will be someone who prefers to write to the paper or post a complaint online.

Anyone who puts their head over the metaphorical parapet can become a target. Back in the early days of regeneration, there were abusive letters in the local press about Lyn Waller's work to reverse the decline of Catherine Hill. The eclectic collection of retro furnishings and collectables in Robin Cowley's shop *De Hepe* on Bath Street annoyed one anonymous passer-by so much he trolled the entire display in a startling piece of hate mail, which Robin featured in the window for the entertainment of passers-by. But this is more serious than the

---

10  I'm not talking just unanatomical scribbles or tags: there was a complaint on facebook when the obliterated Buckminster Fuller quotation reappeared recently to bring a meditative moment to a back wall decorated otherwise only by drainpipes. Admittedly less neatly inscribed than the original, but this had already inspired Frome poet Rebecca Brewin, who gave me permission to quote her short Ode to a Drainage Hole:
>    That little mouth in the wall,
>    It may be shy, masking a stutter,
>    Scrambling its unformed letters
>    From behind a tentative hand,
>    But these illuminous words
>    Keep boldly reappearing, spewing
>    Like an insuppressible spring
>    Their flurry of unrehearsed texts...
>    The lid is off, utterly ungentrified
>    Spirit of Frome has risen again

11  There is actually a *Frome Dog Poo* campaign, with a two-page policy statement containing with four key messages, six key activities, thirteen key people plus local volunteers to 'spread the word' and six necessary resources. One of the activities is getting children to design anti-poo posters. I saw some of these on the railings of Milk Street: they were delightful and would melt the heart of all but the most recidivist poo-bag refuser.

usual small-town squabbles. Robin previously owned 'the Wedge'[12] on Catherine Hill and remembers the 1980s when three-quarters of the hill was boarded up or empty. He summarises the concern of many in Frome now.

> Frome was always in the backwater – this has been its saving grace. Frome was downtrodden so it was cheap, so individuals could come along and say, 'I've got an idea' about a shop – and that was the rebirth. But the whole point about this is, because of that dire depression rents were very low, which opened the door to the rebirth of Frome – the small independents. One of the things that's always been outstanding around Frome is its independence. It's why people come now, and the reason it has survived: strong-willed people and a strong artistic community and creative community.
>
> So now that Frome has become desperately popular, I am fearful that the greed of landlords is going to price out the independents. The very people who made this happen are the ones who will struggle the most. Of course there's no reason landlords shouldn't benefit, but there's an ethic of responsibility here – to the community, to the town, and to the individuals. When Frome was on its uppers, it was those individuals who provided the seed and now that that's come to fruition, others are taking advantage – and thereby penalising the very people who did the planting in the first place.[13]

---

12 Robin had a bookshop there which developed from his mobile bookshop – an old library van which he drove around Somerset. Lyn Young, wife of publisher Graeme, ran this for him and when the business folded they filled the gap in the market by starting Hunting Raven. When Lyn died and Graeme left Frome, John and Caroline Birkett-Smith took over and enhanced the bookshop's reputation further, adding a large children's section and introducing author evenings. Another of those creative evolutions...

13 In a sad and painfully relevant footnote, when I contacted Robin to confirm his quote (as I did everyone) he wrote back: 'I am now a victim of my own prophecy and have to leave Bath Street next March due to a rent increase I can't afford from my new landlord. From my perspective as a trader I have seen the change in Frome's clientele and status with mixed feelings, many of the new occupants are wonderful new additions to the Frome family but many others are of such a different mindset that I fear for the Independents and Independence of our unique town.' Robin spoke further

Rising rents for shop-owners will destabilise the economic infrastructure, and rising house prices will affect the character of the town profoundly too. Prices that buyers from the south-east might find appealing are out of reach to local people on lower wages, for whom 'affordable housing' is a misnomer. The hundreds of new houses already built are merely spies to the battalions encroaching on every side, and a feeling of beleaguerment was evident in the concerns of many people I interviewed.[14] The real issue with the 'gentrification' claim isn't whether ex-Londoners have a right to sell Independent State of Frome T-shirts in the market, but the cost in upwardly-mobile property leases and prices. And this really is serious. It's not changes in culture, its the change in ability of locals to live and work there that is the real problem for Frome.

House prices rising means young people who planned to stay near their family home – perhaps to carry on an independent business or continue their creative path in a supportive environment – can't afford to do so. Rentals rising means the end of all those the quirky 'arty' shops which currently make enough, but only enough, money for their enthusiastic owners to continue trading. Which is most of them. Frome has still not recovered completely from the closure of the small industries which had supported the social centre of the town by their clubs and societies, and though there's a fantastic support network in Frome, as the demographic subtly shifts that new slogan *MAKE FROME*

---

when we met, acknowledging his landlord's right to use the property himself and emphasising that most of his customers are pleasant, interesting, and appreciative, he noted in general a distinct difference in ethos and social concern between old Frome and new Frome: 'At the time we all pitched up in Frome, we might have been hippies but we were full of ideals - we had consciences, and what we wanted was fulfilment, not money. I've been here six years now and an increasing number of people who come in are just here because it's "the best place" - they're very disdainful, they regard me as just a shopkeeper. So much of Frome is changing - yes, let's make it shit again, at least it had integrity.'

14  Many follow *Keep Frome Local* on facebook: 'a pro-town centre group, part of a growing UK-wide Town Centre Movement… We essentially exist to try and uphold existing council planning policy.' The current topic is Selwood Garden Village, or as anxious residents on the south side of town call it, Little Keyford Greenwash Suburb. It would – or will – obliterate the medieval fields and ancient lanes and public plans exist at present only as an outline comprising a mass of housing with no apparent infrastructure.

*SHIT AGAIN* should surprise no-one.

Already a number of those praiseworthy initiatives referenced in the first section are stretched to respond to a disturbing level of need in the most basic requirements of any community – food and shelter. As well as the invaluable *Food Bank*, the *Food Fridge* finds takers for around 4000 donations a month, and there is also an initiative working on providing affordable flatpack semi-independent living space. Neither of these are longterm solutions and both underline this in their promotion, and the council's attention is rightly on increasing need in these areas. *Fair Frome* has a vital role to play, as Bob Ashford found when he took on the role of chairperson:

> We went out and asked people, what do you need? and the answer came back loud and clear. Food. Every one of the people who come along has a story that's a bloody tragedy. They're not feckless or work-shy – these are people who may have young kids, sometimes juggling two or three part-time jobs, zero-hours contract – if something goes wrong and they haven't got the hours one week, they're stuffed! They really are. There's no safety net – only the food bank.[15]

> On the surface Frome looks like this marvellous town where everyone wants to live so house prices have gone through the roof – and at the same time there's a freeze on welfare benefits, introduction of universal credit, zero hours contracts, and a low level of employment and wages. Even if you can find somewhere to live, if you're on a low income you can't afford it because the cap on housing benefits doesn't reach the local market rent, so you can't afford the rent unless you can supplement from the rest of your income, which has been frozen or reduced, so you just can't afford to live here any more. Children who grew up here can't afford to stay – and if you're homeless in Frome, they will advise you to seek private accommodation in Shepton Mallet or Westbury. Forget Frome – that's what the homeless officer has told me. Because there's nowhere in Frome now that's affordable for families.

---

15  The original food bank was run from Warminster under the Trussell Trust, a religious organisation with strict guidelines: Frome Food Bank has its own rules, aimed at being maximally responsive to its users.

I'm not against people moving here – I did – but there was a strong sense of community then, it wasn't anything like the divide we've got now, people struggling to make ends meet with their noses pressed against the success of others. 'Gentrification' can be ok, if there is respect, and a working together, between people who move here and those who actually live here. Without that respect for the people who live here, there's antagonism, people feeling alienated and getting angry. And that's what I see happening here.

Many incomers have arrived with money from other house sales and time to play golf after retiring with good pensions, it's true. Many of these are keen to use that time to volunteer and to offer that money to support valuable initiatives in the town. The bigger problem lies in the hands of the property-owners, not always individuals but companies with other agendas than Frome's unique and precarious culture. Hiking up the rents of niche traders will have the same effect on thriving trade as trashing the newly-invented spindles did, effectively destroying Frome as a cloth town. Even worse, increasing house prices will drive out the next generation of Frome – the young people who reflect everything that Frome does best – everything everyone has told me they value most: the creative spirit and the confidence to make things happen.

The issue of Frome's changing face is complexified by the accelerated speed of change in social habits, meaning many locals still have vivid memories of earlier days as times of knowing every neighbour and chatting in the streets outside shops selling affordable produce – you only have to look at the memories of Keyford to see why the rows of houses sadden those who recall the banter, conviviality, and comradeship of days when everyone knew everyone in the queue for 'the best ice-cream in the world'… That reality, of course, has disappeared everywhere, kicked into the long grass of L.P.Hartley's sonorous truism 'the past is a foreign country; they do things differently there' by supermarkets, cars, recessions and neoliberal policies, but the Futureshock speed of change within a lifetime means you don't have to be metathesiophobic to see why residents respond scathingly to incomers' blithe talk of regeneration and renaissance.

The need now is for a 'regeneration' not just for entrepreneurs and niche traders but for the wider community too. History suggests that the urban cohesion recalled by some as lost perhaps never existed, as there were always haves and have-nots, and newcomers and residents too: the problem now seems to be that both these polarised categories have overlapped – with 'blow-ins' seen as not only having it all but rearranging it all to suit themselves. There are so many genuinely good initiatives, and there's already a developing trading ethos of cafes and bars, but Frome needs more autonomy to deal with this one – and, at the bottom of a three-tier system of administration, as Martin Dimery said right at the start of this unzipping, 'You have to beat at the door every time.'

Martin in his role as Green District Councillor for Frome East also told me then:

> What worries me is that our services are so depleted, and if it goes on for another couple of years like this, they will be too depleted to recover and it will need an enormous injection just to restart them. Everything has been cut to the bone. Mendip has let us down badly over the years, partly because we've got this radical, independent-thinking, quite left-wing, local representation. The fact that there are two of us representing the Green party is really quite remarkable – we're the first and only Green party representatives ever to be on the Somerset County Council, a council in which 35 of the 55 seats are Tory. And our own elective community area is dragged along in this enormously long, blue area and we have no relationship to it whatsoever – this side of the Mendips we look to Bath and Bristol, and always have done. Frome would be better served as a single unitary authority – for the town and surrounding areas: a small single-unitary authority, with devolved powers from county.

In the short time since we spoke that day, after another outrageous decision by Mendip (to jeopardise Frome's vitally important Sunday trading revenue by charging £2 parking fees, which would slash attendances) Martin decided enough was enough and has called for **Frexit.**

Likening Mendip District Council to 'an absentee landlord who takes the rent, but never repairs the house', he references the parking issue as an example of the fact that Frome entrepreneurs and businesses have taken it upon themselves to develop a flourishing range of crowd-drawing activities in the town on Sundays is of no consequence to the pariah-like, revenue greedy district council, who want to raise charges or build on car parks, whilst having inspired absolutely no regeneration initiative in Frome for at least 10 years.

Frome's politically Independent council has had the vision to support regeneration and Frome is now regularly hailed as one of the most pleasant and impressive places to live in the country. Frome Town Council could seize the initiative offered by the suggestion of re-organising local government to reinstate the former Frome Urban District Council as a unitary body. Also, town management of Frome's own car parks would ensure a system uncompromised by a district-wide policy and see the revenue spent in Frome on our own targeted needs.

It is clear to me as a county councillor, Frome has been short-changed by Somerset in the past, and as the biggest town in Mendip, we are providing a large share of the revenue to be spent by councillors who are not elected by the people of Frome. The startling fact is that Frome elects a total of 17 town councillors, 11 district councillors and 3 county councillors, of whom only 4 out of the 31 total, are Conservatives, and yet we are governed by a huge Tory majority in both Mendip and Somerset.

It's early days – in fact, it's not even a week, at time of writing, but the initial response I've seen is, *Well said that man*. This is a precarious time for Frome, although the glazed and envious eyes of media can't yet see it. Already as I was finishing this section, *Harpers Bazaar* announced 'the small town of Frome, near Bath, has been named the UK's most stylish town', in the same breath explaining 'The home of celebrity favourite Babington House, along with 50 independent boutiques and an award-winning street market – sees Frome top the list, compiled by trouva.com.' Another hike in the house prices. . . another frustration for the town. . . just another exasperating day in Frome. It's true that some new arrivals do boast they've made it to the pinnacle of cool, but most of those I talked to gave reassuring reasons for choosing to move here:

\*  It looked like any other grey town, but there was a busker!

\*  **I really liked the ambience and the people**

\*  it kind-of felt like this could be the community – and also what's happening with the Council

\*  the people are polite and easy-going. And there were not very many coloured people here, and I felt that the world needs to mix up a bit, hahaha!

\*  I came here from a hippie commune 40 years ago and bought a shop, it was cheap because it was derelict when I took it on and restored it. I suppose because Frome was so down-trodden it attracted more individual people

☆  *Frome is my spiritual home really, I've known people here for years and spent a lot of time here*

\*  from the moment I arrived I just felt really really at home here. And – this is going to sound quite hippy, I'm not really, but this is true – people tend to come to Frome to get healed.

\*  We had friends in Frome and loved it when we came to see them

\*  there's a vibrant energy that makes you feel you can do different things – an open environment where anybody can do what they want.

\*  water is very important to me, and I found a lot of like-minded people were here. I heard that Frome was like a mature Glastonbury, lots of alternative opportunities

\*  It's a real melting pot here, so many different people, people who've always lived here, new people who've moved in, you just feel instantly it's really friendly and welcoming and kind here -and people when they land here seem to quickly get involved in the community, which is quite something because I don't think a lot of towns are like that.

\*  I wanted to open a shop somewhere in the southwest and my friends said, anywhere but Frome, so of course I came straight here.

\*  It was the 'buzz of sociability, a sense of common purpose and a creative, exciting atmosphere' that persuaded me, back in 1987. That's what has always attracted people who do things like this, which is why they happen, which attracts more like-minded people.

* There's a lot of creative people, and it wasn't Warminster which I'd had enough of. And I like the transformation, even since I've been here, eleven years – it's changed again. There was always a scene, it wouldn't have been everyone's scene, it's quite an elevated middle-class scene now, which is fine, it's up to people what they're into, but there was always a rave scene. Frome is a nice place to come back to.

* a lucky accident really. The first time I set foot in the town I thought, it's so beautiful, there's something really special about it here, and a lady who had bright blue hair stopped me in the street and told me all about the town's history and how she had been colouring her hair with woad. And I just thought, I've never been anywhere in my life before where you're stopped in the street to talk to somebody you've never met who is whacky and crazy and inspirational, and I felt there's a creative energy here, I can feel it in the street. Yeah Catherine Hill. Oh is there a leyline there? Well that's doesn't surprise me at all. It's really special.

GOLDEN ERAS ARE A FANTASY, and probably there never was one: the oft-quoted perception of William Cobbett that Frome in 1830 was like 'a little Manchester' was not intended favourably, as he goes on to say 'There are here all the usual signs of false paper stuff, called money: new houses.. new gingerbread 'places of worship', as they are called; great swaggering inns. . .' Perhaps the kaleidoscope is just shifting again, to a pattern similar but different, and will continue to turn. Meanwhile we continue to make music, create art, share words, perform shows, and argue for equity.

Throughout all my research for this book the two strands that recurred were creativity and dissent – in the sense of doing things differently. It seemed to me that beyond the formal history of Frome there was always, like those Francis Bacon merging portraits, another energy, more elusive and more subversive. . . the One World festival-before-the-festival, with its aim to create connections 'identifying and appreciating each others' ideas and perceptions'. . . the young Abnormalists manifesto 'let's come together to praise those who are moving with us'. . . the self-resurrecting cosmic principle of metaphysical gravity. . . the secret gallery of Saxonvale 'blatant vandalism, blatant creativity, free'. . . the ghosts of punk rock still streaming live. . . all reviving a centripetal energy as invulnerable and unstoppable as the water flowing unseen beneath the town. . . Alternative Frome.

> *It's something unpredictable, but in the end it's right*
> *I hope you had the time of your life*
>
> *– Green Day*

# ALPHABET BOX-SET OF DID-YOU-KNOW?

**A is for ACHILLES** – an English shaft-drive voiturette manufactured in Frome by B Thompson & Co. between 1903 and 1908. At least 5 different models were produced including the 8 hp, 9 hp and 12 hp, according to a car journal of 1902 and in 2008 a 1903 Achilles BE 54 completed the London to Brighton veteran car run.

Frome's own car is now chiefly notable for featuring in French comic book created in 1963 by Michel Regnier (Greg): Walter Melon, originally titled Achille Talon, is a sputtering old jalopy based on the 1903 Achilles.

**B – BIKES...** Two-wheels is big in Frome despite the hills: the legendary Cobble Wobble, an individually-timed sprint up cobbled Catherine Hill, began in 2009 to celebrate the *Tour de France* Stage 5 leaving from Frome, and was a popular event for four years. This 179 yard dash with an average gradient of 15% attracted scores of competitors, some in fancy dress but win-times were serious, all under 24 seconds, with Chris Akrigg, mountain-bike trials rider, clocking a staggering 21.51 seconds. It's hoped there may be a revival...

For even faster biking, Frome was also the home Difazio Motorcycles, where T E Lawrence bought spares for his Brough. The business was inherited from his father by Jack Difazio, successful grasstrack racer and pioneer of the hub-centre-steered motorcycles, who was born in Catherine Street in 1914 and lived to be 97.

**C for carol:** 'Follow the Light' words by Roger McGough but musical setting created by Frome's Ann Burgess, who won the 2015 BBC Radio 3 contest by national vote. 'Sing out...' the poet wrote, 'For those with faith and those without, For those who hope and those who doubt'. Ann's carol was played on the R3 Breakfast show on 25 December, sung by the BBC Singers conducted by David Hill. You can still hear it online.

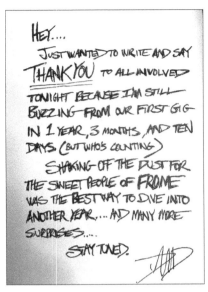

**Dave Grohl** left a love letter to Frome at the Cheese and Grain after Foo Fighters played there in February 2017 – a free event, secret until the day, at which they confirmed the less-secret rumour that they were headlining Glastonbury: HEY... JUST WANTED TO WRITE AND SAY <u>THANK YOU</u> TO ALL INVOLVED TONIGHT BECAUSE I'M STILL BUZZING (FROM OUR FIRST GIG IN 1 YEAR, 3 MONTHS, AND TEN DAYS (BUT WHO'S COUNTING)) – SHAKING OFF THE DUST FOR THE SWEET PEOPLE OF FROME WAS THE BEST WAY TO DIVE INTO ANOTHER YEAR... STAY TUNED

**Electron Microscope technology** was born here! Well, the developer of its use for commercial scanning was... well, he initiated research at Cambridge, anyway. Charles Oatley, acknowledged pioneer of scanning electron microscopy, was born at 5 Badcox in 1904. Knighted in 1974, he lived to be 92.

**Frome town logo** was designed by Luke Manning at his workshop Pencil Studio, above the Old Fire Station. The brief for the branding carried its own solution, he says, as 'they said the Independent Council were we're all very different characters and they wanted something that reflected that. So we used 5 very different font characters, when normally 3 would be the maximum, because Frome town council isn't corporate in their way of looking at things, they're not governed by rules. And we wanted to show their quirkiness in the branding.'

**German bomb alert…** In 2013, Milk Street resident Terry Pinto was informed by a policeman at his door that there was a WWII unexploded bomb in his garden. The previous owner had been overheard chatting about it with his daughter over sherry in his Care Home, and within 24 hours Terry's terrain was shuddering to the vibrations of a Magnetron brought in to find it. A hundred houses and two schools were evacuated while a team called up from Kent removed the device, and the story was headline news on BBC Points West. The old man later popped round to explain to Terry he'd found the unexploded shell when a boy and taken it home because 'If you found live ordinance, you buried it six feet under and notified the authorities – that was the procedure. And it wasn't German, it was bloody British.' Frome's genuine German bomb was dropped late in the war on Nunney Road which is why the architectural style changes briefly half-way up, on both sides.

**H is for the Hoard,** a collection of 52,503 Roman coins found in a massive pot by metal-detector-wielding Dave Crisp near the town. They include 760 coins from the reign of Carausius, who ruled Britain and Gaul from AD286 to AD293, including rare examples of silver denarii in mint condition. It's all been valued at over £300,000 but you have to go to Taunton to see it: Dave wanted it to stay near its home but short of a force field around Frome's elderly little museum there was no way this could be a secure option. At least it stayed in Somerset. See also Mysteries…

**I for incredible innings:** Somerset cricketer Harold Gimblett had his career highlight in Frome, in May 1935. Turned down for the Somerset team, Harold was called in suddenly to fill in for a missing man in a match against Essex on Frome's ground. He missed the bus from Bicknoller and hitched a lift, borrowed a bat, and strode onto the pitch to achieve the fastest debut hundred in cricketing history. John Arlott, BBC cricket commentator, composed a 13-verse poem about the feat, and journalist David Foot in his biography of Gimblett wrote: 'The century belongs to fiction. It came from the genre of sporting stories of excessive heroism on the field, written by Victorian and Edwardian clergy, warmed by their imagination as they sat in draughty rectories. Young readers enjoyed but did not need to believe. It was all part of the romance of cricket. Yet it did happen, at Frome.' For cricket fans, Somerset won the match by 49 runs with an innings to spare.

**JAM, as in Bike Jam** – there was one at the opening of Welshmill Pump Track in 2013 for riders aged from 4 to 18, with the fastest lap time registered at 13.9 seconds. That's less than fourteen seconds round a double loop track with no pedalling allowed... Think about it, and be massively impressed!

**Karting champion 1991-97**, Frome schoolboy Jenson Button continued his winning streak when he entered the world of Formula 3 and then Formula One, becoming World Champion in 2009. A crowd of thousands plus TV cameras greeted him when he returned to 'switch on the lights' in the Frome Extravaganza four years later. Our local hero sped up and down the (specially prepared) main road demonstrating donuts in his Formula One racing car, then cruised the same route waving from the team car, stopping several times to hug old friends and sign autographs for young fans. There's a video of the drive still online – Google his name plus 'Frome 2013' – or for cuteness-overload google 'Bath in Time' for archive images of Jenson as a kid in a kart.

*LOVE is metaphysical gravity* on the wall at the bottom of Catherine Hill has been there as long as I can remember. Never overscrawled, never removed, this Buckminster Fuller quote stays through all seasons. (It was scrubbed shortly after I wrote that, but we who saw it will never forget.)(It came back as this went to press, misspelled but emphatic anarchy in GR⒜VITY.)

**Mahābhāratam (महाभारतम्)** a major Sanskrit epic of ancient India, was published in English in 1785 as Bhagavad-gita, translated by a printer from Frome. Charles Wilkins, known as *the Caxton of India*, worked for the East India Company in Calcutta and became renowned for his many oriental translations, also publishing dictionaries and designing type-faces for Asian languages.

**N is for Nigella's red 'wiggle' dress.** When the media's favourite cook Nigella Lawson went on American TV in 2013 in a dress from Deadly is the Female on Catherine Hill, the *Daily Mail* reported that 'the small burlesque-inspired boutique in Somerset which supplied the dress was overwhelmed with orders after Nigella tweeted the shop's name to her 300,000 Twitter followers.' The 'teasingly named' vintage store sold out of the dress known as 'The Billion Dollar Babe' within hours, to the delight of founder Claudia Kapp. Nigella may have made introduced the dress to ABC viewers, but Frome poet Rosie Jackson was wearing That Dress in Frome two years earlier...

**O – the missing one in Froome...** It is apparently a myth that a careless craftsman in the early days of map-making omitted the second O, thus condemning every visitor to confusion, but two maps of Somersetshire, dated 1575 and 1612 respectively, identify the town as Froume. St John's eccentric Vicar Bennet, relocated to the parish in 1850 for causing pandemonium in Pimlico, always used the spelling Froome.

**P – PANNICIA'S ice-cream** is literally legendary. A family business started in 1926, their ice-cream was made and sold in Naish's Street, and also from distinctive green-and-red vans (American Rios, converted by Osborne in Brislington, for vehicle enthusiasts) – eventually requiring five to cover their 30-mile catchment as fame spread. When Tony Pannicia retired in 2015 after a long working life rising at 4am, his many fans mourned him like a rock star. *'Best in the world'*, *'Nothing will ever replace it'* & *'gutted I'll never taste it again'* were repeated themes on facebook, with some comforting each other *'We were the lucky ones to have been around'*. The 365 memories are aptly summarised by this from Derek

Chapman: '*Frome has never been the same since Paniccia's closed – It was the best ice cream there ever was !!!!!*'

QUESTION TIME – the long-running BBC current events debate programme – at the end of the penultimate decade of the 20th Century was broadcast from Frome Community College and featured Fay Weldon, Michael Heseltine, Enoch Powell and Tony Benn. The Frome Labour Party put on an alternative unofficial post-show party in one of the demountable huts on the campus, and spirited Tony Benn away for a private soiree with masses of tea – his favourite bevvy – and adulation. It wasn't public knowledge but I know, because I organised it.

**Roundabout of Love:** not the official name, but the Keyford junction of Christchurch Streets and Keyford was the impulse location for passionate naked copulation one Wednesday afternoon in 1991. I was one of the lucky ones driving past, alerted to drive with care and attention by the gleeful toots of traffic ahead of me. Someone with no joy in their hearts called the police, and the couple had to face the magistrates court and the Evening Chronicle headline tag 'Naked Romp Couple.' Still, at least it's a tick off their bucket list.

**S is for our shield.** Flanked by two Wessex Dragons and topped by a sheep, this is the shield of the Worshipful Company of Clothworkers as re-imagined by Dyke's bazaar on Catherine Hill. The chevron comes from the Leversedge family arms, the two sallow trees represent Selwood and teazles were used in the wool trade by raising the nap of cloth. The original somewhat ominous legend TIME TRIETH TROTH is replaced simply by FROME. You can still find ornaments featuring it on eBay, and the Frome museum has a small collection.

**Town Twins** not only are there reciprocal visits regularly with Château-Gontier in France (since 1975), Murrhardt in Germany and Rabka-Zdrój in Poland, we also have toilet twins within Uganda, Cambodia and Ghana. Frome was officially twinned with *The One Show* in 2009 after winning a competition to find the quirkiest town in the country. Mandy Stone, who at the time ran *LoveArts* on Catherine Hill, nominated Frome and presenters Christine Bleakley and Adrian Chiles dropped into town from a helicopter to congratulate the Mayor and meet the evidence. The recommendation of Sean McDonnell, manager of *The George*, to twin with Drogheda, was not followed up despite reports in the Drogheda Independent in July 2001 of 'an immense amount of eagerness and enthusiasm'. Sean was apparently struck by the resemblance to Frome of this fortified Irish town with its Norman castle and strong Sinn Fein presence, but for some reason the plan did not progress.

**U for Unicorn** – there's one in The Three Swans. Also the Unconformity, out at Vallis, but that's rather too big to fit here.

**V is the Valentine Lamp** on Catherine Hill, a working gas lamp cast locally and restored in 1992 by craftsman and showman Reg Ling. It is he who choreographs, and has ensured the continuation of, a lamp-lighting ceremony using an original Victorian lamp-lighters' pole on February 14th each year. It's quite a party, starting with the town crier and a firework and finishing with mulled wine. Proper Trumpton.

**Whhee – Wheel of Four Tunes** was the inspired brainwave of Frome's Lark Porter who needed to fill that tricky 2-till-3-Saturday-night spot on her stage at Glastonbury and devised a karaoke with two men in Power-Rangers costume spinning a large wheel to generate random choices. Four and a half thousand people thought it was a great idea and a legend was born. 'One act that epitomises the Glasto spirit

– an incendiary mix of an anarchic gameshow and a hedonistic, genre-hopping, wedding disco on acid', reported one music blog, and it's still listed in NME's Ten Weirdest Things to do at Glastonbury, with the added advice 'For maximum headfuckery, go as a Teenage Mutant Ninja Turtle.'

**Xmas: in 2017** the first class stamp for Christmas postage was designed by Frome's Ted Lewis-Clark, age 10, in a national competition. Eschewing angels, Ted chose the traditional scarlet-clad gift-giver steering his vehicle through a night sky that would have delighted Van Gogh. The stamp and its young designer were featured on BBC's *The One Show*, Ted's name was included in the December franking, and Frome's central postbox was painted sky-blue in his honour. With stars.

Ted Lewis-Clark, age 10

**You'll never walk alone…** Yes, the Anfield anthem was literally forged in Frome, by Ken Hall the blacksmith who designed and built the Shankly Gates in 1982. It took him, he recalls, ten frantic weeks that summer to create the design that enchanted Mrs Shankly and the selection committee. 'We were shattered at the end' Ken admitted, when tracked down in 2013 by *The Liverpolitan* – luckily though he was always a huge Liverpool Football Club fan.

**Zanzibar** was where Clara Grant, born 1867 and educated in a Seminary for Young Ladies in Frome, intended to join her fiancé but when he died she went instead to London's East End to become known as 'The Farthing Bundle Lady' for children of deprived families with toys. Initially, they had to walk through a low archway inscribed *'Enter all ye children small, None can come who are too tall'* but later a 'Penny Shop' was introduced for older children. Clara wrote that she was thankful to have been born in Frome, a place which 'counted so much in establishing impressions, habits, standards and relationships.'

# EPILOGUE

F OUR MONTHS to research and write was the plan. You may think, as
I came to realise, that is no way long enough to do any kind of justice
to a town as complex as Frome – and realistically no time would be long
enough as the layers are deep and the strands unending. Everyone has a
story to tell: the people who grew up in Frome grounded in the traditions
of the town, the incomers bringing comparisons from other places,
the old who remember, the young who explore, the preservers and the
changers, the fans and the trolls – as with every other place on earth.
But this is not any other place. It is Frome. Unzip it how you will, there's
something about this place.

While I was working on this book literally every day I discovered
a new item or person or place which really should be included.... and,
frustratingly, this won't stop. That's what life in this town is like –
intriguing, inspirational, and extraordinary. Frome has been developing
and changing for thousands of years so inevitably there are masses of
pieces omitted from this mosaic account. Keep sharing the ones you
know – online, or in tales and talks. That's how history stays vivid,
through apocrypha and sharing.

The big issue at the time I started writing was a proposal to install
twenty shipping containers in the market yard to provide office space.
This is not the kind of yard that invites such installation: it's the final
stretch of the river walk and regularly used by the canoe club as well as
providing band access to the Cheese & Grain. A furious town meeting
made these points, and the planned placement shifted to an 'alternative
site' – on the other side of the market yard, just outside the art gallery
and ancient Round Tower. The leader of MDC concluded his statement
with slightly staggering optimism 'I hope the local community will be
supportive of our new plans.' By now you will probably know whether
these 'hideous things that will make Frome look like a rubbish tip or a
dockyard' will end up squatting beside the river, overshadowing the art
gallery, or straddling some other space in Frome.

Then the furore moved quick as a fox, as furores do, to the costly
redevelopment around Boyles Cross, with confrontations about the
Saxonvale site already oiling up for the next bout of conflict and those
implausibly massive housing estates waiting in the wings. . . but life in

Frome will go on: contentious, creative, perverse and paradoxical. Frome is a cacophony of voices, and while preoccupations change there's a common thread. Frome relishes friction. It is instinctively stroppy and sublimely contra-suggestible.

You can't kill the spirit.

*Gentle Street post*

# FURTHER READING

## BOOKS
(FSLS = Frome Society for Local Study)

Colin Amery and Dan Cruickshank, *The Rape of Britain* (Elek, 1975)

Peter Belham, *The Making of Frome* (FSLS, 1973)

Roger Bland, Anna Booth, Sam Moorhead, *The Frome Hoard* (British Museum Press, 2010)

Janet and Colin Bord, *Mysterious Britain* (Garnstone Press, 1972)

Alain de Botton, *The Architecture of Happiness* (Penguin, 2006)

Leslie Brooke, *Some West Country Lockups* (Fox Publications, 1985)

Annette Burkitt, *Flesh and Bones of Frome Selwood and Wessex* (Hobnob Press, 2017)

Sue Clifford & Angela King, *England In Particular* (Hodder & Stoughton, for Common Ground, 2006)

Mick Davis and David Lassman, *The Awful Killing of Sarah Watts* (Pen & Sword, 2018)

Mick Davis and Valerie Pitt, *The Historic Inns of Frome* (Akeman Press, 2015)

*Essential Guide to Frome* (pamphlet, Frome Library)

Roger Evans, *Somerset: a Chilling History of Crime and Punishment* Countryside Books, 2009)

Adam Fox, *Oral and Literate Culture In England, 1500-1700* (Oxford Studies In Social History, 2002)

Andrew Foyle and Nikolaus Pevsner, *Somerset North and Bristol* (Yale University Press, Buildings of England, 2011)

*Frome Hundred: a Collection* (Round Tower, 2004)

Frome Rotary Club, *Frome: a Special Town* (Butler & Tanner, 1995)

Derek J Gill, *The Sheppards and 18th-century Frome* (FSLS, 1982)

Derek Gill, *Frome* (Britain in Old Photographs, 1995)

Rodney D Goodall, *The Buildings of Frome* (Frome 1300 Publications, 1985)

Hilary Green, *Around Frome* (Francis Frith, Photographic Memories, 2001)

Carolyn Griffiths, *Woad to This* (FSLS, 2017)

François Hartog, *Regimes of Historicity: Presentism and Experiences of Time* (Columbia University Press, 2017)

David Lassman, *Frome in the Great War* (Pen & Sword, 2016)

Roger Leech, *Early Industrial Housing: the Trinity Area of Frome* (HMSO, 1981)

Jean Lowe, *A Survivor's Practical Travel Guide to Parish Councils* (Earthscape, 2015)

Robert Macfarlane, *Landmarks* (Penguin, 2015)

Michael McGarvie, *Frome Through the Ages* (FSLS, 1982)

Michael McGarvie (ed.), *Crime and Punishment in Regency Frome: the Journals of Isaac Gregory* (FSLS, 1984)

Michael McGarvie, *Frome in Old Picture Postcards* (European Library, 1989)
Michael McGarvie, *Marston House history and guide* (Foster Yeoman, 1997)
Michael McGarvie, *Around Frome (images)* (1998)
Michael McGarvie *The Book of Frome* (Barracuda Books, 1980; updated 2001)
Jonathan Meade, *Museum without Walls* (Unbound, 2013)
Mendip District Council, *The Trinity Area of Frome* (1984)
Ralph Mitchard, *The Days of King Monmouth* (Radstock Books, 2005)
Eunice Overend, *The Geology of the Frome Area* (FSLS, 1985)
John Payne, *The West Country: a Cultural History* (Signal Books, 2009)
John Payne (ed), *Working Memories: Frome workers tell their stories* (Home in
        Frome, 2012)
John Payne (ed), *Fifty Frome Banners* (Home in Frome, 2015)
Susan M Pearce, *The Kingdom of Dumnonia, AD350-1150* (Lodenek Press, 1978)
W.P. Penny, *History and Description of the Public Charities in the Town of Frome*
        (1833)
David Pierce, *Conservation in Britain since 1975* (Routledge, 1989)
Adrian Randall, *Riotous Assemblies: Popular Protest in Hanoverian England*
        (Oxford Univ. Press, 2007)
Alan G Sandall, *Going Going Gone* (March Press, 1991)
Stephen Tuck, *Wesleyan Methodism in Frome* (1837)

**PDF DOCUMENTS** available to download
A Portrait of Frome 2008
Frome Conservation Area Appraisal and Management Proposals 2008
English Heritage Extensive Urban Survey An archaeological assessment of
Frome

**ONLINE**
**Current information:**
Town Council information site: http://www.discoverfrome.co.uk/frome/
Frome Times: www.frometimes.co.uk
Childrens activities: http://www.fromeactive.org.uk/
Retirement activités: http://www.fromethirdage.org.uk/

**History of Frome:**
Benjamin Baker:
        http://www.benjaminbaker.org.uk/life-and-times-of-benjamin-baker.html
Brief outline:
        http://www.localhistories.org/frome.html
Buildings:
        http://www.thebluehousefrome.co.uk/about-us/history-of-the-blue-house
Butler & Tanner:
        http://spitalfieldslife.com/2014/05/14/so-long-butler-tanner/

Canal:

    http://www.bradfordonavonmuseum.co.uk/archives/822

Carnivals:

    www.frome-pastcarnivals.co.uk/egallery1.htm

Crimes of the past:

    https://www.facebook.com/FoulFrome/

Discover Frome:

    http://www.discoverfrome.co.uk/category/history-blogs/

ECOS stones:

    http://www.boxrockcircus.org.uk/ECOS/

Frome Society for Local Studies Handbooks on CD:

    https://fromesociety.wordpress.com/bookshop/frome-society-yearbooks/

Frome Street Names:

    http://www.gomezsmart.myzen.co.uk/places/frome/frsts.htm

Frome Teeth:

    http://www.british-history.ac.uk/vch/som/vol1/pp35-39

Geology:

    https://www.bgs.ac.uk/mendips/geology/geological_structure.htm

    http://www.earthsciencecentre.org.uk/mendip-geology

General:

    https://www.chris-hardy.com/stories-of-frome

    https://fromefables.wordpress.com

    http://homeinfrome.org.uk/shop-talk/4589241394

    http://doorsoftime.wikidot.com/gallery

    http://fromediary.com/frome-story/

Holy well:

    http://people.bath.ac.uk/liskmj/living-spring/sourcearchive/ns1/ns1jr1.htm

Regeneration award:

    https://www.academyofurbanism.org.uk/frome/

Selwood Forest: (David Craig's historical site):

    https://www.strum.co.uk/twilight/selwood.htm

Thankful villages:

    http://www.historic-uk.com/HistoryUK/HistoryofBritain/Thankful-Villages/

Tunnels:

    http://askwhy.co.uk/frome/12frometunnels.php#mystery

    https://www.facebook.com/FromeTunnels/

Valentine lamp:

    https://www.valentinegaslamp.com/.

Wool trade (mill workers):

    http://www.gomezsmart.myzen.co.uk/fabric/millers.htm

**Images**:
General:
   https://www.facebook.com/pg/ImagesofFrome/posts/
Listed buildings:
   https://www.britishlistedbuildings.co.uk/england/frome-mendip-somerset#.WbqkmxNSxAY
Walking Tour of Frome Old Town:
   http://askwhy.co.uk/frome/07frometour.php
Past and Present images and memories:
   https://www.facebook.com/FromePP/
   https://www.facebook.com/fromepostcards/
   https://www.instagram.com/fromepostcards/
   https://www.francisfrith.com/uk/frome -
Restoration:
   http://non-modern-world.blogspot.co.uk/2016/01/frome-stonemasons.html
   http://www.minervaconservation.com/blog
Buildings saved:
   http://m.mendip.gov.uk/CHttpHandler.ashx?id=3466&p=0
Urban award summary 2015:
   https://www.academyofurbanism.org.uk/frome/

**Groups**
Carnival: http://www.frome-pastcarnivals.co.uk/history.htm
Family History Group: http://www.fromefamilyhistorygroup.co.uk/reports.htm
Home in Frome: http://homeinfrome.org.uk/
Friends of the River Frome: http://www.fromeriverfriends.org.uk/
Frome Recreation Ground supporters: http://www.fromefrogs.org.uk/
Key Centre on the Mount: http://www.mcafrome.org.uk/
Museum: https://fromemuseum.wordpress.com/
Nature Reserve: https://www.roddennaturereserve.org.uk/
Save Our Spaces: http://www.spanglefish.com/sosfrome/
Town Council: http://www.frometowncouncil.gov.uk/
SUSTRANS cyclepath: https://fromesmissinglinks.org.uk/

Lightning Source UK Ltd.
Milton Keynes UK
UKHW021006101019
351302UK00003B/13/P